C. L. R.
JAMES

SUNY Series, INTERRUPTIONS: Border
Testimony(ies) and Critical Discourse/s

Henry A.Giroux, editor

C. L. R. JAMES

■

A POLITICAL BIOGRAPHY

Kent Worcester

State University of
New York Press

■

Published by
State University of New York Press, Albany

For information, address State University of New York Press,
State University Plaza, Albany, NY 12246

Production by Christine Lynch
Marketing by Theresa Abad Swierzowski

Library of Congress Cataloging-in-Publication Data

Worcester, Kent, 1959–
    C. L. R. James : a political biography / Kent Worcester.
        p.   cm. — (SUNY series, Interruptions — Border
    testimony(ies) and Critical Discourse/s)
      Includes bibliographical references (p.   ) and index.
      ISBN 0–7914–2752–8 (pbk. : acid-free). — ISBN 0–7914–2751–X (acid
    -free)
      1. James, C. L. R. (Cyril Lionel Robert). 1901–   —Political and
    social views. 2. Politics and literature—West Indies—
    History—20th century. 3. Authors, Trinidadian—20th century—
    Biography. 4. Revolutionaries—Trinidad—Biography.
    5. Politicians—Trinidad—Biography. 6. Historians—Trinidad—
    Biography. I. Title. II. Series.
    PR9272.9.J35Z93   1996
    818—dc20   95-6899
      [B]   CIP

10 9 8 7 6 5 4 3 2

CONTENTS

ACKNOWLEDGMENTS

My aim in writing this book is to have produced an accessible, empirically grounded account of C. L. R. James's remarkable life, one that affirms his relevance for the contemporary world and contemporary politics. In attempting to carry out this relatively broad agenda, I have been fortunate to be able to count on the assistance of a wide array of institutions and individuals.

First of all, for their assistance with this project, I would like to thank the librarians at the Archives of Labor History and Urban Affairs at the Walter Reuther Library at Wayne State University; Butler Library and the Rare Books Collection at Columbia University; the C. L. R. James Institute in New York; the Houghton and Widener Libraries at Harvard University; the New York Public Library; the Newspaper Library of the British Library, Colindale; the Prometheus Research Library in New York; the Schomburg Center for Research in Black Culture in New York; the Tamiment Institute Library in New York; the Trinidad and Tobago National Archive; the Trinidad Public Library; the University of Massachusetts at Boston; and the University of the West Indies (St. Augustine). I would also like to extend my thanks to the administrative and library staff at Queen's Royal College in Port of Spain, as well as to Jorge Heine and the Centro de Investigaciones del Caribe y America Latina at the Universidad Interamericana de Puerto Rico.

A number of helpful individuals assisted me in locating interviews, manuscripts, photographs, old buildings, and other documentary materials relevant to this project. In this context I would especially like to thank William Carr, Dianne Feeley, Martin Glaberman, Louis Homer, Phyllis Jacobson, Alan MacKenzie, E. Ethelbert Miller, Mackey and Dexter, Hugh Morrison, Courtenay Quintyne, Jean Tussey, Alan Wald, and James D. Young. Special mention must go to Bill

French, whose University Place Book Shop houses a remarkable collection of first-edition and other valuable books on the African diaspora. I have also benefitted from conversations and correspondence with individuals working in related fields of inquiry, especially John Agnew, Stanley Aronowitz, Tony Bogues, Bridget Brereton, David Ames Curtis, Selwyn Cudjoe, Ralph Dumain, Anna Grimshaw, Steven Hastings-King, Paul Le Blanc, Jack Spence, Kenneth Surin, Roderick Thurton, and Richard Williams. Other individuals who offered advice and encouragement along the way include Doug Barnes, Buddy Bradley, Monica Crowley, Bob Guldin, Nancy Gutman, Peter Kraus, Joanne Landy, Guy Lawley, Barbara Lipski, Peter Lowber, Helen Roberts, William Shea, and Chris Toulouse.

Over a period of many years, Paul Buhle has showered me with a stream of letters that are full of insight and kindly advice. His approach has always been extremely encouraging, and I wish to thank him for it. Through lengthy, stimulating phone conversations I have learned a great deal from Scott McLemee. He has conducted extensive research in the relevant archives and has come up with some magnificent sources, both primary and secondary, that I draw upon freely in this study. I await his thematic study of James with eager anticipation.

Cary Fraser offered characteristically astute comments on chapter 6. Glenn Perusek helped me to think through some of the more difficult issues raised by the question of James's stance vis-a-vis the Western canon. Heather Cateau, of the Department of History at the University of the West Indies (St. Augustine), and Lisa Lindsay, of CUNY Graduate Center, both provided useful research assistance in an efficient and timely manner. And Jim Murray, Director of the C. L. R. James Institute in New York City, has provided active and ever-helpful assistance in matters both editorial and archival.

In this book I draw on conversations I was fortunate to have with C. L. R. James (1981), Lloyd Best (1992), Robin Blackburn (1992), Martin Glaberman (1980), Phyllis and Julius Jacobson (1992), George Rawick (1980 and 1987), B. J. Widick (1993), Steve Zeluck (1984), as well as a correspondence with Hal Draper (1980–1982). On my behalf Heather Cateau conducted an informative interview with Cyril Austin, a cousin and childhood friend of C. L. R. James, and also consulted the archives at the Oil Workers Trade Union in San Fernando. At different stages in the development of this manuscript, I benefitted enormously from the editorial guidance of Lisa

Haugaard, A. P. Simonds, and David Terrien. Joann Ransdell did a superlative job as an indexer. Finally, there is one person, Jennifer Scarlott, who not only offered incisive comments on the manuscript but lived through its lengthy gestation period. The book is dedicated to her.

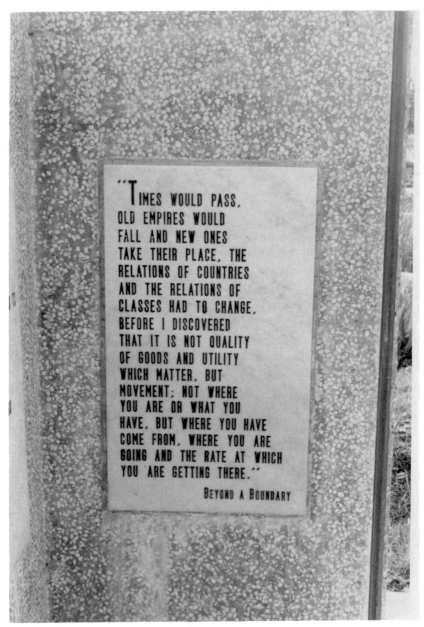

Gravesite
Tunapuna, Trinidad
Photo: Kent Worcester 1992

INTRODUCTION

By any measure, Cyril Lionel Robert James enjoyed an extraordinary career as a writer, theorist, polemicist, and revolutionary activist. A major, but neglected intellectual figure of the twentieth century, C. L. R. James has been described as "the sharpest and most interesting mind that the British Caribbean has produced in three centuries of learning."[1] A product of the schools, playing fields, and literary sub-culture of colonial Trinidad, James went on to become an influential strategist of Pan-African politics and a sophisticated proponent of a heterodox and critical Marxism. By the 1960s, he was an elder radical statesperson on several continents, famous for his writing and historical impact. Yet for many years he worked in obscurity, adopting pseudonyms and struggling (almost always with the help of others) to pay the rent. Fame was never his goal, nor money or a nice house; his interests were intellectual and political, and also historical, in that he sought to understand, and to have an impact on, the underlying forces shaping modern society.

There are many dimensions to James's life. Born at the turn of the century in a small town in Trinidad, James spent many years residing in New York, London, and other First World cities. Having imbibed a first-rate classical education, he defended B-movies, comic strips, and radio plays, and wrote lengthy documents pertaining to issues of revolutionary strategy and engagement. As a Marxist, he had one foot in the Old Left and one foot in the New, advancing the political autonomy of women, blacks, and young people at the same time that he insisted on the centrality of the industrial working class in the transition to socialism. A self-described Pan-Africanist, he maintained a cool distance from nationalist and communalist doctrines and defended Western literary and philosophical canons. While he practically embodied the idea of the "man of letters," he often scorned the work of his peers and openly rejected the category of "intellectual." Furthermore, while generally disdainful of electoral politics, he helped formulate the political program of the People's National Movement in the late 1950s, and later created a Trinidadian electoral vehicle, the Workers and Farmers Party, in the mid-1960s. His mature political vision, which evolved through a sustained encounter with the ideas of Hegel, Marx, and Lenin, exhibited considerable continuity with his youthful sensibility, which was modern, artistic, and democratic in character.

Perhaps the most impressive aspect of James's life was his purposeful creativity as an essayist, historian, literary critic, and pamphleteer. Major works include: *Minty Alley*, a novel; *The Black Jacobins: Toussaint L'Ouverture and the San Domingo Revolution*, a justly famous historical study; "The Revolutionary Answer to the Negro Problem in the USA," a subtle Marxist polemic; *American Civilization*, an investigation of the connection between popular culture and democratic politics in American history; *Mariners, Renegades and Castaways*, a work of literary criticism; and *Beyond a Boundary*, an evocative study of the impact of cricket on Caribbean society. Diverse in subject matter and tone, these books and essays share in common a beautiful appreciation of the English language as well as a learned and articulate populism.

These writings also constitute only a small portion of a largely unexplored canvas. James wrote on dialectics, modern art, the slave trade, the city-state, the rise and fall of the Communist International, Shakespeare's stagecraft, Aristotle's poetics, existentialism and alienation, contemporary African politics, the Rastafari, the West Indian nation, the history of Pan-Africanism, the future of the novel, and a host of other topics. As this list makes clear, James was a prolific, eclectic writer whose work was driven by an innate curiosity and a rare sense of political determination. His entire corpus betrays the mark of a singular intellect, one that was concerned above all with the power of reason and especially with the inventive potential of the masses engaged in social movement.

Moreover, and in large measure through his writings as well as through speeches and other activities, James made a special contribution to the construction of a postcolonial West Indian identity. An early critic of colonialism, James argued strenuously in favor of a political and economic federation of the West Indies, and also actively promoted indigenous cultural forms—such as calypso and other types of popular music—as expressions of a West Indian nation in the process of formation. His forays into fiction, which largely date from the 1920s and which were produced in the context of a flourishing, politically engaged literary subculture, mark him as a major figure in the development of Caribbean literature and letters.

Thus, while only a handful of organizations or publications in the region can meaningfully claim to be "Jamesian" in inspiration, his broad legacy continues to shape the work of intellectuals, writers, and others in the Anglophone Caribbean. By combining a concern for the autonomy of culture with an active pursuit of the social revolution, James helped carve out a bold identity for Caribbean artists and intellectuals, one that draws on European ideals even as it condemns the imperial project. His legacy also signals a willingness to move beyond conventional conceptions of liberal democracy and to try and open up the political process in countries like Trinidad and Tobago to new kinds of institutions and new forms of civic participation.

James was able to play an important role in the deepening of the anticolonial project not only in the Caribbean but across the entire African diaspora. This can be seen in his work with the International African Service Bureau, a London-based organization formed in the mid-1930s that agitated on behalf of African national independence and exerted a tremendous influence on postwar movements for decolonialization. His dispensation was also manifest in his work in the 1940s in rethinking the political significance of African-American struggles for social equality. During what might be termed the "third wave" of black-diasporic mobilization, in the 1960s and early 1970s, James defined himself primarily as a teacher. His calls for new forms of pan-regionalism and participatory socialism in the Third World went largely unheeded, however. Yet through his friendships with such notable figures as George Padmore, Kwame Nkrumah, Jomo Kenyatta, Richard Wright, and others, James was able to forge a space for his idiosyncratic brand of radical and democratic politics within the context of Pan-African and black nationalist movements.

James's politics were forged in the crucible of classical Marxism, and in many respects his life and work can only be understood with reference to his lifelong attachment to Marxist principles. Raised in a disorderly political culture that seemingly attached equal value to the incompatible ideals of late Victorian romanticism, Marcus Garvey, and trade union activism, James underwent an ideological conversion in the early 1930s, when he embraced Trotsky's Left Opposition and declared himself an anti-Stalinist and a revolutionary socialist. It was as a Trotskyist that he penned some of his best-known writings, addressing fundamental questions facing the international revolutionary movement. These included the nature of revolutionary leadership, the degeneration of the Russian Revolution, and the linkage between movements in the Third World in general, and the African diaspora in particular, to struggles in the advanced industrial world. And it was as a disaffected post-Trotskyist that he began working with a small circle of friends and comrades to develop an alternative Marxism suited to the postwar era.

The characteristic approach of this circle was to stress the independent capacity of subaltern groups to defend their collective interests and move society in a more cooperative direction. This circle, the so-called Johnson-Forest tendency, rejected the notion of building a revolutionary vanguard party and concentrated instead on publishing newspapers and pamphlets that celebrated the political and social creativity of the masses. It was as a leader of the Johnson-Forest tendency and its successor organizations that James came to terms with the theoretical underpinnings of Marxism and carved out a political niche for himself. While the tendency's polemics reached only a relatively small number of individuals, their antibureaucratic and "pro-autonomy" thematic helped demarcate the distinctive vision of the early New Left.

In many respects, however, James went further than his North American collaborators, weaving their unique problematic into a spirited analysis of literary and popular culture. His overarching thesis concerned the centrality of the mass audience in the construction of both classical drama and contemporary popular culture. In the 1950s he started work on a book on Shakespeare's tragedies that was intended to highlight the special role of the audience, and the entire theatrical performance, in nourishing the Bard's craft. In this period he also explored the foundations of literary criticism and closely studied ancient Greek civilization, and wrote occasional pieces on various aspects of modernism and the arts. Much of this work emphasized the historical significance of culture as an independent force in society. While many of his insights foreshadowed themes popularized by the new field of cultural studies, James was equally at home with the reproachful teachings of William Thackeray and Matthew Arnold as with his beloved gangster and detective movies. As the brilliant 1954 essay "Popular Art and the Cultural Tradition" demonstrated, few critics were better placed to simultaneously defend Western canons and champion postwar popular culture.

Throughout his life, this "indigent and itinerant West Indian Black Marxist historian"[2] struck up friendships with artists, athletes, journalists, musicians, scholars, and political activists. In combination with his distinctive persona—at once decorous, reserved, amiable, and ironic—his wide range of personal relationships and experiences helped to further distinguish him from his comrades in the socialist movement. In Trinidad in the 1920s he fraternized with writers and sportsmen such as Learie Constantine, Albert Gomes, and Eric Williams. As a resident Briton, he consorted with an eclectic mix of activists, from Amy Ashwood Garvey (Marcus Garvey's first wife) and actor-singer Paul Robeson, to European social theorists like Daniel Guerin, Karl Korsch, and Boris Souvarine.

It was also in this period that he renewed his connection with the great Pan-African organizer (and his childhood friend) George Padmore. In 1939 he conducted a perceptive series of conversations with the banished Leon Trotsky in Mexico. Shortly thereafter, in the United States, he argued politics with James Baldwin, James Cannon, Ralph Ellison, Irving Howe, Max Shachtman, Meyer Schapiro, and other celebrated New York intellectuals. As leader of the Johnson-Forest tendency, he was immersed in a tiny political subculture—but the group functioned more like a pressure cooker than a fraternal order, and the unstable mixture tended to blow up from time to time. Relations proved less fraught with younger West Indian writers like Wilson Harris, George Lamming, and Andrew Salkey, as well as with the singer Mighty Sparrow. By the late 1960s, James's list of correspondents read like a veritable Who's Who of the international left. Toward the end of his life, he came to know a number of younger writers, such as Ntozake Shange, Maya Angelou, and Alice Walker, as well as the tennis star Arthur Ashe, who interviewed James at length for his celebrated book on blacks and sport.

These associations highlight the diversity of the communities through which James moved. They underscore the fact that there is no single political or social culture that can meaningfully claim James's undivided loyalty. No one problematic—Marxism, black nationalism, West Indian history and culture, and so on—can be used by itself to explain the totality of his life and work. His personal development and intellectual contributions are complex and multifaceted, and I have endeavored throughout this book to accentuate, rather than occlude, their complexity.

A number of recent initiatives have made it easier for the general reader to gain access to a broad swath of James's writings on Pan-Africanism, Marxism, the Caribbean, and culture. It is hoped that in tandem with these initiatives this study (and others) will encourage readers to explore James's writings for themselves. In the interest of imparting a sense of James's own inimitable writing style and personality, I have quoted liberally from a wide array of published and unpublished sources. If these quotations, and the study as a whole, help to suggest the power and imagination of its subject's labors, then the effort has been worthwhile.

The organization of the book is as follows. The first chapter examines James's childhood and young adult life in Trinidad, with special reference to his intellectual, political, and literary development. The second chapter concerns his activities in England in the 1930s, paying particular attention to his transformation from humanist and novelist to socialist and revolutionary activist. The third and fourth chapters explore his American sojourn and his emergence as an original Marxian thinker; the third chapter focuses in particular on the issue of African-American politics. Chapter 5 covers the period from 1953–1958, when James was living in London; chapter 6 reviews James's participation in Trinidad's movement toward independence. The final chapter examines the years subsequent to 1962, when the *eminence grise* of Caribbean letters attained some measure of literary and academic respectability. Three appendixes offer a list of abbreviations used throughout the book, short biographies of over forty of James's associates, and a guide to the secondary literature.

PART ONE

A man with a reflective turn of mind, walking through
an exhibition of this sort, will not be oppressed, I take
it, by his own or other people's hilarity. An episode of
humour or kindness touches and amuses him here and
there . . . when you come home you sit down, in a sober,
contemplative, not uncharitable frame of mind, and
apply yourself to your books or your business.

—William Thackeray, *Vanity Fair: A Novel Without A Hero* (1848)

Beyond a Boundary

CYRIL LIONEL ROBERT JAMES was born in the village of Caroni, Trinidad, on January 4, 1901. He was the eldest of three children. His parents, Robert Alexander and Ida Elizabeth (Bessie) James, were hard working, respectable members of the community who expected that their three children, C. L. R., Olive, and Eric, would concentrate on their studies and one day make a contribution to the wider society.

The James family had solid working-class and West Indian roots. Both of C. L. R.'s grandfathers were skilled craftsmen who had immigrated to Trinidad from Barbados during the second half of the nineteenth century, and Bessie Rudder, James's mother, was herself born on Barbados. In Trinidad, James's paternal grandfather found employment as a "pan boiler on a sugar estate . . . a post in those days usually held by white men."[1] His maternal grandfather, Josh Rudder, held the post of engine driver on the Trinidad Government Railway and was responsible for the run between San Fernando and Princes Town, while one of his cousins, Cudjoe, worked as a blacksmith. Sheltered from the harsher aspects of the colonial economy, James's immediate family aspired to a stable, middle-class status. Robert Alexander worked as a school teacher and principal, while Bessie performed various duties around the home and the community. In the eyes of both parents, and of the many neighbors and assorted family members who lived in sometimes remarkably close proximity to the family, it was up to the next generation to ensure that the Jameses cemented their middle-class station in West Indian society.

This supportive, close-knit, and propriety-conscious home environment left an indelible impression on C. L. R. and his younger siblings. But it was by no means the only influence at work in James's childhood and adolescence. The family was itself part of a dense network of overlapping groups—from teachers and clergy, to shopkeepers and school children—who helped constitute the broader milieu within which family members operated. Not surprisingly, school was a particularly important influence, providing a powerful source of friendships, ideas, and aspirations. For C. L. R., school initially meant his father's classroom, where he studied as a little boy, and later Queen's Royal College, the most prestigious school on the island. Another key influence was games and sport, especially cricket, which his family and teachers mostly encouraged and which James readily embraced from an early age. Finally, books, newspapers, and magazines formed a ubiquitous element in James's daily life. While family, friends, and school authorities recognized his talents, this exposure to the world of books and print—literature, biography, history, journalism—helped turn him into an intellectual and placed him on the path of a writing career.

Long after he had graduated from school, history and literature remained two of the central pursuits of his peripatetic life. One author who made a particularly powerful impression was William Thackeray. In the autobiographical *Beyond a Boundary*, published in 1963, we learn that he read Thackeray's *Vanity Fair* several times a year, on average, throughout his adolescence. Thackeray's satirical dissection of English middle- and upper-class manners during the early part of the nineteenth century must have held a great fascination for the precocious son of Bessie and Robert Alexander. From a very early age C. L. R. James seems to have been conscious of the role of conventions and rituals in society, the overdetermined interaction of the individual personality and the wider social environment. It is almost as if by nature he was a literary anthropologist, one who readily responded to Thackeray's wicked characterizations and brilliant vignettes.

◆◆◆

Although his father later moved up to positions of authority within the school system, the early years were no bed of roses. For nearly a decade, the family divided its time between Caroni's larger neighbor, Tunapuna, and the village of North Trace, where Robert Alexander found employment as a schoolmaster. The schoolhouse in North Trace was tiny, and yet James's father was entrusted with the education of over one hundred children of various ages who walked—barefoot—into town from neighboring villages. The family home in Tunapuna was also cramped. In a letter written to his close confidant, Constance Webb, C. L. R. described the house as initially having "two rooms, one divided by a paper blind." Added together, both rooms were only "about 12 feet by 18 feet." The house was so old that "there were holes in the floor . . . It had a thatched roof, and the rain came in." He went on to report that the entire extended family—two parents, three children, two aunts (Judith and Eva), and his maternal grandmother—crowded into these two rooms. "My aunts were in their early twenties. My grandmother was about sixty-five. They washed clothes for a living and my aunts also were seamstresses."[2]

Despite these claustrophobic conditions, Tunapuna, North Trace, and indeed Trinidad itself offered a marvelous setting for the development of a young man's empathic gifts. At the turn of the century, Tunapuna, located approximately nine miles from the capital in a prosperous agricultural belt, was little more than a provincial village. Slavery, outlawed in 1834, was still a living memory for a handful of the town's residents. Nearby Port of Spain was a small but bustling city, a "microcosm of the world's peoples."[3] North Trace, by way of comparison, was a tiny settlement lodged deep in the country's south-central interior. As someone fortunate enough to call all three places "home" at one time or another, James exhibited a real knack for moving around, making new friends, and talking to people from all kinds of backgrounds. The experience of migration, which is central to the notion of the Caribbean as a place of recent settlement, was deeply etched into the pattern of James's childhood.

Through all the commuting and relocations, Robert Alexander and Bessie sought to provide their three children with a secure environment and a stable set of values. As family patriarch, Robert Alexander was austere, detached, and analytical in nature, and he demanded a great deal from his students and his children. He worked as a teacher and school principal for his entire adult life, not only within the public school system but as a private tutor on weekends. His main subjects were composition and grammer, but he also taught musical theory, and his nephew Cyril Austin recalls that he had mastered the Pittman method of short hand.[4] After his retirement—at the age of sixty, several years after his son had left Trinidad to pursue a literary career in the metropolis—Robert Alexander continued to tutor individual students and worked as a correspondent for the *Port of Spain Gazette*. Within the school system he was known as a first-rate teacher, teacher trainer, and administrator, and he received a number of promotions.

As headmaster, one of Robert Alexander's primary tasks was ensuring that his students passed the annual scholastic examination. But it was apparent early on that his eldest son had a special gift for scholarly pursuits, particularly reading and composition. When C. L. R. was eight years old, his father began tutoring him for a special island-wide scholarship competition, which enabled families of modest means to send their brightest sons to Queen's Royal College (QRC). By 1910 this promising pupil was one of four entrants to obtain a scholarship, or "exhibition," to what has long been regarded as Trinidad's finest secondary school. No one had ever won an exhibition at such an early age. James later boasted that as a child he was "bright as a new shilling and everybody said I would be sure to be something one day."[5] It seems likely that his special status as the eldest son and prize student of the area's schoolmaster would have ensured that he was detached in some sense from his immediate peer group. But he had a friendly manner and got along well with everyone. The transition from the schoolhouse in North Trace to Queen's Royal College was certainly eventful, even momentous, but it was shrouded in an air of inevitability.

As a staunch believer in personal discipline and corporal punishment, Robert Alexander was especially strict with his eldest son, who nevertheless rebelled at school and spent more time playing sports and reading novels than reciting Latin. While he was proud of his son's scholarship, he disapproved of his decision to pursue a full-time literary career. C. L. R. later said that his father "didn't like the writing business too much, but if I was going to write, I should write something that the newspapers would accept." He derided his father as a "philistine of note," and claimed that he had wanted him to pursue a career in the public sector, which offered the prospect of a decent pension.[6] While C. L. R. may have admired and consciously emulated his father's code of propriety and civility, his unconventional career aspirations and radical politics were something else again. In this sense, C. L. R. fulfilled the mandate of the fourteenth-century Arab proverb, which holds that "men resemble their time more than their fathers."[7]

Although both parents shared the same religious affiliation. Bessie James was the family's devout Anglican. To neighbors and friends she was known as "Aunt Bessie," and she left a deep and lasting impression on family and friends. James later described her as "a very tall woman, my colour, with a superb carriage and so handsome that everybody always asked who she was." He remarked that she "dressed in the latest fashion—she had a passion for dress and was herself a finished seamstress." But his most important recollection was that his mother "read everything that came her way." He later wrote: "I can see her now, sitting very straight with the book held high, her pince-nez on her Caucasian nose, reading till long after midnight. If I got up there she was, reading, the book still held high. As she read a book and put it down I picked it up."[8]

As a result of his mother's varied reading habits, James was exposed to a raft of highbrow authors, including not only Thackeray but also Jane Austen, Arnold Bennett, the Bronte sisters, Thomas Hardy, Rudyard Kipling, William Shakespeare, and Anthony Trollope, as well as popular writers such as P. G. Wodehouse. Charles Dickens was a particular favorite, but Matthew Arnold's *Culture and Anarchy* also made a lasting impression.[9]

The works of these authors were supplemented by a daily diet of newspapers and magazines. While his mother approved of James's preoccupation with words, she may not have fully appreciated the nature of his literary gifts. He later remembered one incident in particular:

When I was about seven I sat up late one night and wrote a poem. About eight verses of four lines each in imitation of a poem in my reading-book. Why I felt to write I do not know. No one wrote that I know. No one had ever said that people wrote. Another day my mother put down *The Last of the Mohicans*. I picked it up and read it. I read as she did—straight through except [when] I saw a chance of playing cricket or shooting with an air-gun. When I finished *The Last of the Mohicans* I got a copy-book and began to write a story of my own. But after two chapters my mother read it and said it was exactly like *The Last of the Mohicans* and I stopped. I know now that this was the worse thing she could have done.[10]

Despite this tactical error, Bessie was supportive of her son's enthusiasms and tolerant of his individuality. Perhaps what he valued most in their relationship was the emotional space she allowed him to establish between himself and the rest of the family. James would later spend far more time reminiscing about his mother than his father, siblings, or relatives. In this context, it seems hardly accidental that his only novel, *Minty Alley*, is dedicated "To My Mother," not both parents. Yet before he left Trinidad he was extremely close to both siblings, who admired and looked up to their elder brother. Eric and Olive knew their brother as "Nello," which was the family nickname, and which became the name that James was known throughout the West Indies. In later years, both siblings took pride in their brother's achievements, although there was a certain amount of tension over the fact that he spent so much time abroad, even during the long years of his mother's illness, in the 1930s and 1940s.

As far as the father-son relationship is concerned, it was difficult and at times stressful. Robert Alexander gave the impression that he was never quite satisfied with his son's efforts. He regularly voiced doubts about whether C. L. R. would be able to earn a living and provide for a family. Their relationship was at its most strained during James's adolescence, where their arguments centered around his extracurricular activities and his performance at school. In an essay written in the 1970s, C. L. R. described a recurrent nightmare where he would bring home an inadequate report card and face his father's wrath. The nightmare went away only after he had become a successful author.[11]

Under the tutelage of their parents, all three children became "very well trained" in the area of manners and good grace. "My mother saw to that," C. L. R. later wrote, "respect for elders, good manners at table, modesty and self-respect." This cultivation of proper behavior took place in a climate of economic uncertainty. "My father made about forty or fifty dollars a month and was always desperately in debt. But he always dressed my mother well and we never needed anything. My mother kept us scrupulously clean and kept the house the same as did my aunts." Despite their financial anxieties, the family occupied a privileged niche in the local community. "I was somehow aware," he confessed, "that we were not common people or laborers."[12]

At the same time that Bessie and Robert Alexander were working to instill a sense of moral values in their children, they were also committed to maintaining certain social conventions. For this reason, his mother and aunts made it clear that C. L. R. was not to socialize with neighborhood ruffians like Matthew Bondman. Bondman was "an awful character" who "would not work," but he was a graceful batsman. He would "often without shame walk up the main street barefooted, 'with his planks on the ground,' as my grandmother would report. He did it often and my grandmother must have seen it hundreds of times, but she never failed to report it, as if she had suddenly seen the parson walking down the street barefooted."[13] As this anecdote suggests, C. L. R. James grew up in a socially self-conscious environment. Although he had access to the works of many different authors, the household's general atmosphere was one of moralism, status consciousness, and religious piety. As the emblem of the family's hope for the future, C. L. R. was burdened with an extraordinary set of pressures and expectations. But at the same time he was cushioned and protected, and at least on his mother's side there was no doubt that he was also loved.

His family, and later his schoolmasters, were largely successful in their attempts to raise this prodigal son in accordance to the public school code of Victorian England. One writer has summarized this code as a matter of upholding "the standards of fair play": "do not play for personal ambitions but for the team's; keep your head when the fortunes of a game have swung against your team, do not criticize teammates for failures, and do not withhold praise from opponents who are succeeding . . ."[14] Or as James later remembered: "I never cheated. I never appealed for a decision unless I thought the batsman was out. I never argued with the umpire. I never jeered at a defeated opponent. I never gave to a friend a vote or a place which by any stretch of the imagination could be seen as belonging to an enemy or to a stranger . . ." This moral code became "the framework of my existence. It has never left me."[15]

The public school code was a central component of the education provided to successive generations of students at the august Queen's Royal College (QRC). Opened in 1870, and moved to its present location in 1904, the main College building is one of seven formidable structures situated on the northwestern side of the two-hundred-acre Queen's Park Savannah, straddling the northern edges of Port of Spain. The College's expatriated "masters," educated at Oxford and Cambridge, instructed students in such subjects as Latin, Greek, French, geography, ancient history, mathematics, and literature.

James was one of thirty-nine pupils to enter QRC in January, 1911 (the school year ran from January to December), and he graduated with a "school certificate" in 1918.[16]

At first, his "marks" or grades placed him at the very top of the class, but they slowly deteriorated as sports and reading took precedence over his studies.[17] The school records indicate that his French was better than his Latin, and that he showed promise in the field of mathematics.[18] Despite his disappointing academic performance—he later insisted that his "scholastic career was one long nightmare to me, my teachers and my family"[19]—James secured teaching positions at a succession of secondary schools, including QRC, upon graduation.[20] "I was teaching practically after I left college," he later remembered, "I found it rather exhausting. But I couldn't leave it alone . . . After a time, they paid me well."[21] During the 1920s he also taught students on an individual basis. One of his pupils was Eric Williams, who became the first prime minister of Trinidad and Tobago. Williams prepared for his Oxbridge entrance exams under James's tutelage.[22]

The public school code was also internalized through the norms of cricket and the refined sensibility imbricated in the French and English novels that he read as a child. *Beyond a Boundary* opens with a "small boy of six" standing on a bedroom chair to observe the cricket matches on the pitch below. From this chair the child was able to "stretch a groping hand for the books on the top of the wardrobe." As James has it, "thus the pattern of my life was set."[23] Apart from family and school, cricket and books were key formative influences at work on the aspiring intellectual. His enthusiasm for Thackeray was matched only by his ardor for the delicate rhythms of the cricket pitch. It would seem as if all aspects of his educational, family, and social background was aimed at imparting gentlemanly and scholarly values.

Cricket played a Janus-faced role in James's moral development. The colonial authorities had introduced organized games in an effort to instill a temperate style of sportsmanship in a potentially disrespectful population. With its elaborate rules, distinctive costume, and parlor room etiquette, cricket seemed particularly well suited to the task of "civilizing" the restless and the discontented. In the hands of West Indians, however, cricket effectively became "an opportunity for the West Indian to beat the master at his own, beautiful game."[24] By organizing teams and leagues that brought players from different islands into close contact, West Indians acquired skills that would later prove useful in the political realm. Inadvertently, then, cricket became an occasion for regional self-expression and self-organization. William Carr tells us: "Cricket is not a game in the West Indies—or not merely a game. It is the means whereby the colonial showed his human equivalence to the coloniser."[25] The eminent novelist V. S. Naipaul (who attended Queen's Royal College many years after James), provocatively suggests that cricket filled a major void in the West Indian experience. "In islands that had known only brutality and greed," he writes, "cricket and its code provided an area of rest, a release for much that was denied by the society: skill, courage, style: the graces, the very things that in a changed world are making the game archaic."[26]

On the pitch James came into contact with men such as Matthew Bondman, learned to play cricket by watching them, and became familiar with their plebeian habits. He later remarked that he had played cricket "uninterruptedly" from the age of four to the age of thirty-one.[27] Exposure to the practices of cricket expanded his social horizons and provided him with material for his lively anthropological curiosity. Literature also played a steady and complex role in his personal development. Reading and efforts at journalism offered tools for autonomous intellectual achievement. In his early twenties he began to nurture a pronounced dissatisfaction with the restrictions placed on an educated black man in colonial society. This discontent was to gestate slowly, but the roots of James's anticolonialism and radicalism are to be found in his formative personal experiences on the playing fields and as a reader of literature, history, and biography.

As a student James was placed in a contradictory social position. The public school code, his parent's moral teachings, and his scholastic training were valorized in the midst of a colonial setting. The code stressed fair play and yet British rule was manifestly unjust. His family wanted their eldest son to establish himself within the preexisting political and judicial institutions, and yet a range of dissenting beliefs were discussed at home. Queen's Royal College taught the history and culture of societies many thousands of miles away. These contradictions helped to foster a certain kind of rebelliousness and self-consciousness in the mind of an observant and confident Trinidadian youth. An expression of these contradictions was the fact that as a young man James read the *Times Literary Supplement*, the *Spectator,* and other high-brow weeklies, but also purchased *Negro World*, the

newspaper of the Jamaican-born black nationalist leader Marcus
Garvey "every Saturday morning down St. Vincent Street in Port of
Spain."[28] Garvey, the founder of the Universal Negro Improvement
Association (UNIA) who championed the cause of Pan-African pride,
attracted thousands of followers across the globe, calling for a mass
exodus "back to Africa."

The multiple tensions driven by the conflict between the mores
of the public school code, and daily life under colonial rule, gave
James an ambiguous perspective on relations of race and class.
Although his parents disapproved of calypso music, their eldest son
was "fascinated by the calypso singers and the sometimes ribald dit-
ties they sang in their tents during carnival time."[29] One gains the
impression that he watched everyday life from a distance. His growing awareness of social issues seems not to have been matched by any
specifically racial consciousness. "In our little Eden," he wrote of
QRC, racial discrimination "never troubled us."[30] In unfinished
notes for his autobiography, James goes so far as to say that "for
many years the race question did not seem to exist in the college at
all." He describes studying and joking with two boys in particular:
Ulrich and Hahn, both scions of prominent white families. The
friends spent considerable time marking out their own private space.
"We were concerned," he writes, "that we would be able to read privately while the master was holding forth on French composition or
algebraic equations . . . The three of us happened to like each other
and particularly the books we used to read and most enjoyably during class hours."[31]

Although the environment of Queens Royal College allowed for
various kinds of social interaction, black students were nevertheless
subject to official forms of discrimination. In *Beyond a Boundary*,
James discusses being denied admission on racial grounds into the
local English regiment near the end of World War I. Yet he insists that
this incident left no scars on his psyche. The historian John La Guerre
pointedly suggests that James's isolation from more virulent strains of
racial prejudice "gave rise to a 'detachment' on racial questions that
was rare for a negro intellectual of his time . . ." La Guerre goes on to
suggest that this sense of detachment was "destined to be one of the
outstanding characteristics of his entire career as a political
thinker."[32]

The "real world," however, did touch James's life beyond modest
interactions on the cricket pitch and snatched portions of calypso

Queen's Royal College, Port of Spain, Trinidad
Photo: Kent Worcester 1992

songs. In the winter of 1919–1920, a strike by dock workers in Port of Spain turned into "a series of violent challenges against British colonialism."[33] Other unionists joined the dock workers and disrupted urban life with mass pickets and stormy public meetings. Returning veterans proved especially eager to join labor organizations and participate in strike activity. Within a couple of weeks, strikers in several industries were granted 25 percent across-the-board wage increases. The authorities blamed the Garveyites and their *Negro World* for the unrest, but the "major cause for this wave of strikes was undoubtedly rampant inflation and worsening economic conditions," with "racial feeling playing an important role in heightening tensions . . ."[34] Through a fellow cricketer, James "knew some of the men who were leading it and I am positive that they were Garveyites . . . All I did was to go and watch what was happening without taking any part."[35]

Despite these dramatic episodes of labor unrest, James remained more interested in athletics than political ideology.[36] Margaret Busby reports that he held Trinidad's high jump record (5'9") from 1918 to 1922.[37] At QRC his best jump had been 5'5", which earned him a place in the school's record books. He also played cricket for QRC, and was listed as one of the school's best bowlers for 1917 and 1918.[38] Throughout the 1920s, James batted and bowled for the Maple team, a club based in Port of Spain. A passage in *Beyond a Boundary* describes how the cricket clubs symbolically represented different social groups on the island. The Queen's Park Club was for the white and the well-to-do. At the other end of the scale was Stingo, the club for black laborers and the long-term unemployed. James faced something of an identity crisis when he had to choose between Maple, which was for brown-skinned players of the middle strata, and Shannon, for lower-middle-class blacks. "Faced with the fundamental divisions in the island, I had gone to the right and, by cutting myself off from the popular side, delaying my political development for years."[39]

Apart from athletics, literature was his other main concern after graduation. Alfred Mendes, a leading participant in Trinidadian literary circles, and a wealthy confederate of James's, later identified World War I and the Russian Revolution as major factors motivating West Indian intellectuals and writers of the 1920s and 1930s (although both events are given short shrift in *Beyond a Boundary*). An expanding black middle class and increased social and commer-

cial contact with the world beyond the Caribbean led to the formation of literary circles and the publication of West Indian journals of
commentary and review. In addition to his obligations in the spheres
of teaching and cricket, James belonged to a literary club, the Maverick, and participated in amateur dramatics.[40] In the late 1920s
Mendes and James produced two issues of *Trinidad*, and both men
contributed essays and short fiction to *The Beacon*, published
between 1931 and 1933, which was edited by a seditious-minded
Portuguese Creole, Albert Gomes. (Later, in the 1940s and 1950s, a
right-leaning Gomes helped negotiate the terms of political self-rep-
resentation prior to the period of independence.)

James's first literary success came in 1927 with the publication of
"La Divina Pastora" in *The Saturday Evening Review*.[41] By the middle
1920s writing had become the central focus of his activities. Teaching
and tutoring were enjoyable day jobs, nothing more and nothing less;
and while he was a competent bowler, he was unlikely to become a
top-rank, professional cricketer like his friend Learie Constantine. By
way of contrast, writing brought him virtually instant acclaim. It was
the natural accompaniment to his favorite pastime, reading, and it
held out the promise of freedom and independence. He became used
to writing in his apartment for long periods of the day, mostly in long-
hand on legal-sized pads. (His script was firm but often jerky, as if he
were in a rush.) Later on, he suffered painful cramps in his hands and
stomach and had to carefully husband his energies. But his commitment to the discipline of writing on a daily basis, on a range of topics,
remained unflagging.

"La Divina Pastora" tells the story of Anita, a woman (from North
Trace) who picks cocoa from 7 A.M. to 5 P.M. for thirty cents a day.
Hard-working Anita quietly prays for marriage to a gentlemanly
farmer of her acquaintance. She visits Siparia, the south Trinidad pil-
grim site of La Divina Pastora to enlist the help of the saint, leaving a
gold chain around the neck of the statue. Lo and behold, the pilgrim-
age is successful, and the farmer asks Anita to a local dance. Following the dance, Anita returns home, happily singing to herself. When
she arrives she faints after finding the gold chain back in its cigarette
tin. The story itself is unremarkable, except that it conveys a sympathetic interest in belief structures and religious practices of the working poor. Its unadorned prose tells us about a humble woman without
resorting to sentimental flourishes or condescending asides.

James's fiction for *Trinidad* is of the same type. "Triumph" focuses more directly on the infamous Trinidadian "barrack-yards" or slums. In this story, the same elements of poverty, just rewards, and the plight of ordinary women are present. A depressed Mamitz works overtime trying to secure steady lovers who will pay her rent and her bills. She is not amoral, but nevertheless "saw to it when she moved that you missed none of her charms."[42] She is popular with all of her neighbors except Irene, a religious woman who disapproves of Mamitz's amorous relations. Irene tries to set Mamitz up for a fall, but revenge is pure and sweet for Mamitz, who triumphs in the end. To a greater extent than either "La Divina Pastora" or the story "Turners' Prosperity," which also ran in *Trinidad*, "Triumph" relies on sexual and violent situations to provide sociological insights into barrack-yard behavior. Women are routinely beaten, sex is traded for cash, and only a thin veneer of humor lightens scenes that are fraught with physical conflict. At one point a wronged lover, Nicholas, wearing his "bloody butcher's apron," holds Mamitz tightly by the throat:

> "I will stick my knife into you as I will stick it in a cow. You had Popo des Vignes in that room for the whole day. Speak the truth, you dog."
> "You' mother, you' sister, you' aunt, you' wife was the dog" shrieked Mamitz, quoting one of Celestine's most brilliant pieces of repartee.[43]

The Beacon—which improbably billed itself as "A Guiding Light For All Who Are in Intellectual Darkness and Who Seek Great Things"—expressed a more openly political tone than *Trinidad*. Albert Gomes in particular was highly critical of the colonial regime. As founder, publisher, and editor of *The Beacon*, Gomes called on the masses to rise up in revolt: "Black man, bearded old son of a slave, your children are being slain by the dozens in America, in Africa, in the Indies . . . Bare your fangs as the white man does. Cast off your docility. You have to be a savage like a white man to escape the white man's. But the white man won't spare your neck."[44] Compared to that, James's comments in *The Beacon*'s following issue should have reassured at least a few readers:

> I am not touchous [sic] on the race question. If at times I feel some bitterness at the disabilities and disadvantages to which my being a

negro has subjected me it is soon washed away by remembering that the few things in my life of which I am proud, I owe, apart from my family, chiefly to white men, almost all Englishmen and Americans, men some of them of international reputation, who have shown me kindness, appreciation, and in more than one case, spontaneous and genuine friendship.[45]

Indeed, virtually all of James's essays for *The Beacon* were characterized by their moderate tone. One piece, which ran under the heading "Books and Writers," commended the work of Victorian author Arnold Bennett, while another addressed "The Problem of Knowledge" and warmly spoke of Trinidad's "bookshops, music-stores, newspapers, and conversations . . ."[46] At the same time, he initiated a fierce debate over the comparative intelligence of the races in an article on "The Intelligence of the Negro: A Few Words with Dr. Harland," which generated a number of responses throughout the second half of 1931, and in addition traced the intellectual roots of black nationalism in an informative piece on the nineteenth-century lawyer and social critic, Michel Maxwell Philip.[47]

Despite the fact that the "policy of the magazine was really the absence of one,"[48] the reading public focused on Gomes's outrageous brand of militant rhetoric, and *The Beacon* faced libel threats, police harassment, and vitriolic attacks from church pulpits. Its concern for the plight of the poor, and its sometimes explicit "local nationalism"[49] earned the journal an unflattering editorial in the island's newspaper of record, the Trinidad *Guardian*: "Letters protesting against the obscenities of the Magazine have been pouring into the *Guardian* office during the past week. One is from a Boy Scout who says: 'Its disagreeable implications cast unwarrantable aspersions on the fair name of our beautiful island.'"[50]

The circle around Gomes and Mendes thrived on controversy, with Gomes later remembering that they "were held together by a common bond of detestation of the hypocrisy, obscurantism and general claustrophobia of Trinidad society . . ."[51] Certainly the brouhaha surrounding *The Beacon*'s more controversial editorials was unlikely to have impeded James's career. During the 1920s he was clearly a "young man with a future"—a budding writer with good personal connections, a mostly supportive family, and a cozy niche in Trinidad's emergent literary subculture. A biographical note in *The Beacon* described him as a fiction-writer who "has had some success, but is tired of hearing them said over and over again."[52] As an advocate of modernist ideas in the spheres of literature and criticism, he was also something of a bohemian, with a mild disdain for social convention. For several years he lived in the Belmont section of Port of Spain, where he wrote, entertained friends, and listened to records. An acquaintance from this period remembered his room as being "simply appointed: a table, a large orthophonic cabinet record player, and a bed placed diagonally across the room on which were always two opened books."[53] It was during this Jazz Age period that he read all six volumes of Havelock Ellis's *The Psychology of Sex*, which provided him with a "scientific" understanding of sex and sexual relations.[54]

Standing at six feet three inches tall, versed in the canon of Western civilization, the young C. L. R. was an avid consumer of records and books who spent a great deal of time walking and discoursing on the cosmopolitan streets of Port of Spain. An athlete and an aesthete, he was perhaps more socially aware than many of his associates, but less politically awakened than others. Like others in his sophisticated circle, he no doubt found the prevalent system of government flawed and archaic; and he was quite aware of the limitations that colonial society placed on young men such as himself. But he apparently did not go so far as to call for national independence, and in no way was he a socialist. His main energies were concentrated on teaching, writing fiction, and playing cricket, although he later recalled that "the real *magnum opus*" of his Trinidadian literary career was to be a second novel, a novel that was never written.[55] He also dabbled in poetry; the one extant poem, "Pascall Bowled," memorably described a mythical encounter that pitted Learie Constantine's uncle, the bowler Victor Pascall, against the world's greatest cricket batsmen.[56]

The one novel that did get composed was *Minty Alley*, written "purely to amuse myself one summer [1928]. I had nothing to do in August and I wrote a chapter a day."[57] It narrates the fortunes of Mr. Haynes, a young bookstore clerk who moves into cheap lodgings at no. 2 Minty Alley to see something of the world and experiment with life. Inevitably, Haynes (whose inquisitive yet bookish character was not so unlike that of the author's) is drawn into the life of the neighborhood. The other residents look up to Haynes on account of his status as a white-collar worker, and he tries to give advice that will minimize conflict in the Alley. Haynes conveniently discovers a crack in his bedroom wall which enables him to watch the nearby goings-on. His eavesdropping is richly symbolic of the author's own sense of distance from everyday life, as James can only describe from behind a wall of text the meaning of life for the urban poor. Haynes's spying is not meant to betray a superior attitude on the part of the youthful character. Indeed, Haynes becomes firmly impressed that the Alley dwellers were far more interesting than the snobbish friends of his deceased parents. He found himself sitting, "waiting to see the household set about its daily tasks. The stage, he felt, was set for a terrific human drama."[58]

Drama arrives as a passionate, sexual affair erupts between Haynes and Maisie, a spirited young woman. Haynes stops being the voyeur and becomes an active participant in his own life. The possibility is raised that the young lodger might, in some way, choose the lifestyle of Minty Alley, severing his ties to a more respectable past. But Haynes (and the author?) is not ready for such a sharp rupture with conventional society. Maisie runs off to America, a deep unhappiness settles in the yard, and the property is finally sold by the destitute landlady. Haynes returns to his own people. Even Minty Alley as a physical structure changes, as gentrification upgrades the buildings in the yard, returning as Haynes does to their original status. The novel ends with the protagonist back where he started: a passive bystander. "[H]e stood outside, looking in at the window and thinking of old times."[59]

As in "La Divina Pastora," and "Triumph," James explores the tempo and vernacular of the barrack yard. Although he doesn't identify the sources of Trinidadian poverty, he vividly depicts the affliction of material scarcity, and he carefully dissects the social and class divisions. The characters' dialects seem natural, and the tone is sympathetic without being maudlin. Haynes and a neighborhood man, Benoit, have a drink:

> "Well, how do you like your new life?" said Haynes.
>
> "Not bad." But he avoided Haynes's eye. "Of course we haven't settled down yet. The nurse out working and I have to fix up at home, you know. But we will move soon and get a servant—by the New Year, you know."
>
> If there was money he wasn't getting much of it. He hadn't a cent in his pocket and let Haynes know as much.
>
> "You have cigarettes?"
>
> "No," said Haynes, feeling his pocket. Benoit asked him to get some.
>
> "Let's have another beer."
>
> "Yes, man. Liquor is helpful."[60]

A little earlier a resident gossip describes Benoit's wedding:

> Miss Atwell began. "The church was full o' people. A lot of idlers. I
> suppose they had come to see the Jezebel [Benoit's new wife] mar-
> ried at last—'cause everybody know what she is, you know, Mr.
> Haynes. And people was only whisperin' about the way the snake
> come into you' house and take the man away. There was a strange
> woman next to me and we was talking about it all the time . . . The
> bride was in white with a lot of beads,' she continued, 'but although
> the cloth was expensive she didn't look well." Miss Atwell shut her
> eyes, shook her head and repeated, giving emphasis to each word:
> "She didn't look well. And one foolish little hat on 'er head, and as
> for he, in the old grey suit. I look to see what kind o'shoes 'e had on,
> if was new ones in truth, but where I was sittin' I couldn't see. They
> ring the bell little bit when they was goin' away, but the whole thing
> was tame, tame, tame. You could see it was a pick-up wedding."[61]

As these passages suggest, the author's perspective on the Alley is
sympathetic but a little standoffish. At the same time, James is slightly
detached from his own literary stand-in, Haynes, whose own sense of
remoteness is the target of a clement critique. As Michael Gilkes
argues, the novel is an "indictment of the pallid middle class who
uphold status at the expense of genuine living."[62] But Gilkes goes on
to argue that *Minty Alley*'s least convincing aspect is the easy interaction of Haynes with the yard folk. It is a relationship free of antagonism: Haynes is consulted and respected, and he expresses no ill feelings about the occasional beatings and other acts of cruelty that take
place around him. As Gilkes rightly suggests, Haynes's relationship to
his neighbors in the novel is idealized, and the ending is a little pat,
with Haynes wistfully recalling the good old days.

    Minty Alley was published without fanfare in London by Secker
and Warburg (George Orwell's publisher) in 1936. It was one of the
very first indigenous novels of the West Indies, and it explores
themes—the emotional distance between educated and uneducated
blacks, the impact of violence on urban life, sexual relations among
the poor—that are recurrent in modern Caribbean fiction. Comparable works written by James's contemporaries include two novels by
Alfred Mendes, *Pitch Lake* (1933) and *Black Fauns* (1935), as well as
R. A. C. de Boissiere's splendid *Crown Jewel* (1952) and *Rum and Coca
Cola* (1956). Traces of the earlier generation's modernist and cau-

tiously experimental influence can be detected in postwar fiction such as Merle Hodge's *Crick Crack Monkey* (1970), and Samuel Selvon's *The Lonely Londoners* (1956), as well as in the better-known work of George Lamming, Wilson Harris, and the early novels of V. S. Naipaul.

The residents of Trinidad's barrack-yards, portrayed in *Minty Alley* as being largely indifferent to social concerns, had in fact begun a process of politicization by the 1920s. The circle around *The Beacon* was particularly intrigued by the role that the nation's first authentically mass-populist movement, led by the flamboyant Arthur Andrew Cipriani, had begun to play in arousing political awareness. Having served as Commander of the British West India Regiment in World War I, Captain Cipriani traded on his personal popularity in order to pursue an unorthodox career in West Indian politics.[63] His political instrument became the Trinidad Workingmen's Association (TWA), a reformist organization founded in 1897 and which he came to head in 1923 at the age of forty-eight. It was as President of the Trinidad Workingmen's Association that Cipriani successfully contested the 1925 general elections for a position on the Legislative Council.[64]

Cipriani, a French Creole, agitated on behalf of the "unwashed and unsoaped barefooted man"—that is, the Benoits of *Minty Alley* and the Matthew Bondmans of Tunapuna—and received over fifty percent of the votes cast in the capital city. For Cipriani, Trinidad and Tobago was a colony "being bled white and the worker defrauded, pilloried and exploited."[65] Through the TWA's newspaper, *The Labour Leader*, published between 1922 and 1932, Cipriani and his comrades vigorously challenged the Crown Colony system of government and advanced a curious amalgam of Garveyism and British-style Labourism. Guided by these seemingly incompatible doctrines, the paper agitated on behalf of universal male suffrage, the recognition of trade unionism, free primary and secondary education, and a federation of the West Indies. But Cipriani's populism was not as inclusive as some may have wished. For one thing, unlike many of his newspaper's journalists (such as Gomes, Mendes, and de Boissiere), he opposed the relaxation of divorce legislation. More significantly, the Corsican-born Cipriani drew a careful distinction between West Indians and "tribalized Africans." He never called for full national independence from Britain. "All demands for social and political reforms were made within the imperial framework," notes the political historian Selwyn Ryan.[66]

Cipriani was the first of a succession of West Indian nationalists
who would base their organizations and programs around the struggles of the urbanized Afro-Caribbean masses, particularly the industrial working class. He was still on the scene in his capacity as leader
of the Trinidad Labour Party when a wave of social unrest shook
many parts of the Caribbean in the second half of the 1930s. Sugar
workers in St. Kitts and British Guiana went on strike in 1935, and
smaller numbers of workers subsequently engaged in industrial
action and street protests in St. Lucia and St. Vincent.[67] In Trinidad,
oil workers struck for higher wages in 1937. These workers, led by
the immensely popular Uriah Butler, a Barbadian-born oil worker,
were joined in their strike by agricultural laborers and public employees.[68]

Trade union organizations, youth leagues, and other nationalist-
leaning forces experienced considerable growth in this period. Cipriani himself was appointed President of the British Guiana and West
Indies Labour Congress (eventually renamed the Caribbean Labour
Congress), a body that underwent something of a revival in the aftermath of the strike wave of the late 1930s. A number of those who
were to later help build the People's National Movement and similar
organizations in the West Indies came to political maturity during
this period. In retrospect, it seems that Cipriani's labor-based, Afro-
Caribbean-centric, party-building strategy was to become a model for
the type of institutions and tactics that were to emerge both in the late
1930s and in the period just prior to independence.

Partly as a literary exercise, James drafted a biography of Cipriani
in the late 1920s. As we shall find, James found the genre a useful
instrument for exploring the tension between political authority and
popular mobilization. Through his studies of a wide variety of Pan-
African figures—including Cipriani, Toussaint L'Ouverture, George
Padmore, and Kwame Nkrumah—James sought to distinguish
between authoritarian rule and beneficial leadership. While he was
largely uninterested in identifying the biographical origins of political greatness, he was strongly concerned with describing the complex
relationship that can develop between a movement and a given revolutionary leader. For James, what was interesting about Cipriani was
his capacity to excite the political passions of the Trinidadian masses.
Cipriani's obvious limitations and idiosyncracies remained secondary
to his role in activating the hitherto untapped energies of the urban
poor.

As a still-youthful resident of Port of Spain, James sympathetically followed the remarkable progress of the TWA, and it seems likely that he contributed at least a couple of articles on sport to Cipriani's newspaper.[69] In the process of writing this biography, he became convinced that Cipriani's reformist populism did not go far enough, and that progress toward self-government was long overdue. The book thus became a formal attack on the whole philosophy of colonial rule, although it had little to say about colonialism outside of the Caribbean. Entitled *The Life of Captain Cipriani: An Account of British Government in the West Indies*, the study offered a broadbrushed survey of politics and society in Trinidad and Tobago, placing special emphasis on the role of the Trinidad Workingmen's Association in awakening the consciousness of subordinate social groups. James referred in particular to the powerful impact that Cipriani's rallies had on "the agricultural labourers and the artisans, the masses of the people . . ." and he reported that the people were now "alive to politics as at no other time in the history of Trinidad."[70]

The book also drew attention to the problematic character of racial tensions and divisions within Trinidadian society, and ended by calling on the British to grant self-government for the West Indies. Yet John La Guerre suggests that the book contained little that was new, claiming that it "expressed very much the customary criticisms of Crown Colony Government . . ."[71] The historian Robert Hill reports, however, that *The Life of Captain Cipriani* "came to play a significant role in orienting many individuals when the widespread labor riots broke out in 1937–1938."[72] These protests, kindled by a strike of Trinidadian oil workers and fueled by the international Depression, suggested that the events of 1919 were not anomalous. A few of the strike leaders may have read the biography, finding in its call for self-government an echo of their own incipient radicalism.

The peerless cricketer Learie Constantine helped arrange and finance the biography's publication when the author arrived in England in 1932. The book was the subject of some controversy in the West Indies; Albert Gomes said that its "method of criticism is not very significant or sound," and wrote that it is "good in parts, bad in others and, as a whole, formless and devoid of any real value to the student." Gomes went on to chide James for failing to call for "a classless society, a communist society."[73] Another reviewer, the writer and labor activist Ralph Mentor, attacked the book for failing to address the economic roots of racial discrimination. "Mr. James seems to cherish," Mentor wrote, "the notion that Crown Colony rule is responsible for the prevalence of race prejudice in the West Indies. He is entirely wrong. Racial prejudice will exist under any system. It is a barbaric relic of slavery days . . . It has its roots in the slave trade of the fifteenth century, thrives on ignorance and a vicious economic situation."[74]

Just weeks after the maligned biography had been privately issued as a full-length book, Leonard Woolf, of Bloomsbury fame, published an extract under the title *The Case for West-Indian Self-Government*. Although this pamphlet circulated far more widely than the biography, it also made clear the limitations of its author's analysis of colonialism. James based his case for political self-determination on the grounds that there were sufficient numbers of educated blacks in the West Indies to assume the tasks of administrative and political leadership. Moreover, "the bulk of the population of these West Indian islands" had internalized the values and aspirations of Western culture. [I]n language and social customs, religion, education and outlook," he wrote, West Indians "are essentially Western and, indeed, far more advanced in Western culture than many a European community."[75] Consequently, the British Crown Colony system of government "was useful in its day but that day is now over." At an earlier point the author finds fault with West Indians, who "live in the tropics, and have the particular vices of all who live there."[76] No criticisms are raised concerning the effects of slavery, or the conditions prevalent on the sugar plantations and other commercial estates. The emphasis instead is on the "Westernness" of the black middle class, the fact that they were finally ready to inherit the mantle of enlightened self-rule.

The publication of *The Life of Captain Cipriani* prompted one local writer, C. H. Archibald, to produce a thoroughgoing analysis of the man he termed "Trinidad's best known author." Published in the literary journal of Queen's Royal College, *The Royalian*, Archibald's provocative critique may be said to constitute the earliest known contribution to the secondary literature on C. L. R. James. Archibald opened his piece by acknowledging that his subject was a talented individual. "He had the reputation," Archibald wrote, "before he left Trinidad, of being one of the best read men on the island. He studied literature; he studied art; he studied music with the aid of the gramophone. And he wrote."[77] Yet he goes on to argue that James was all too often facile in his writing, and more than once had "slavishly copied a method which has obviously pleased him and which he felt must please everyone."[78] Archibald judges James's best work to be his least ambitious—his short fiction, and his sports journalism, as opposed to his longer essays, or his biography of Cipriani. He expresses sorrow that "when reading Mr. James I have felt that what he has set down is not what he is absolutely convinced is the truth . . . sometimes, it seems he shrugs the truth aside."[79] Archibald's final assessment was rather damning: "I do not think he will produce something to startle the world into applause."[80]

As Archibald reluctantly acknowledged, however, and as both *Minty Alley* and *The Life of Captain Cipriani* demonstrated, James was maturing as a writer, becoming technically adept at handling a variety of styles and voices. By the mid-1920s he had assumed the industrious work habits of a serious author, laboring daily to perfect his craft. The obvious question was whether Trinidad offered a suitable environment for this sort of career. To reach a larger and more cosmopolitan audience—to make a living as a writer—he decided to settle abroad. As he later recalled in a letter to Constance Webb:

> Thirteen years ago, 1930, I was 29, married and in the West Indies. I had been practicing writing. And I said "enough of this. I shall save two hundred pounds. I shall go to London and take my chance, come what may. I'll make it." I didn't do exactly what I intended to do. But I found my way to myself and my place in the world.[81]

Or, as he wrote in *Beyond a Boundary*, "I was about to enter the arena in which I was to play the role for which I had prepared myself."[82]

In this retrospective judgement, his early years in Trinidad were a dress rehearsal for a metropolian literary career. The clear implication is that he had always known that he would move on. It is uncertain whether he communicated this to his wife Juanita Samuel James (nee Young), a woman of Spanish descent from Venezuela whom he married in 1929. Theirs was a placid, traditional marriage marked by a conventional division of household labor. Juanita, who worked as a stenographer at a law firm, was, in James's mind, "not interested in the World Revolution." He claimed there "was some sort of arrangement whereby she was to come to meet me in England, but she saw after a time that I did not really need her and her pride rebelled . . ."[83] Apart from these passing references in an early letter to Constance Webb, James almost never referred to his first marriage, and there is little evidence to suggest that Juanita enjoyed a critical influence on his overall development. But neither did he share his own inner feelings with his wife. "My virtues as a husband," James later admitted, "were entirely negative. I didn't pay attention to my wife as a human being sharing a life with me."[84]

The allure of the European metropolis was strong for all of *The Beacon* circle, as it would be for later generations of West Indian writers. But Albert Gomes remained in Trinidad. Many years later James and Gomes talked about this:

> Albert Gomes told me the other day: "You know the difference between all of you and me? You all went away; I stayed." I didn't tell him what I could have told him: "You stayed not only because your parents had money but because your skin was white; there was a chance for you, but for us there wasn't—except to be a civil servant and hand papers, take them from the men downstairs and hand them to the man upstairs."[85]

When he sailed for England in March 1932, James was a cordial critic of the system that would have generously allowed him to shuffle papers. A keen student of human affairs, a lover of fine music, he was widely touted as a local writer of real promise. If we group *Minty Alley* with the short fiction that appeared in *Trinidad* and *The Beacon*, we can see that he had considerable potential, that he was comfortable with the discipline and challenge of being a writer. But apart from a brief foray into dramatic theater (and a few children's stories), he never wrote fiction again. *Minty Alley*, for all of its strengths, was not the inevitable culmination of his literary endeavors, and it certainly does not reflect everything that the cerebral cricketer had absorbed after spending three decades in the West Indies. There is no reason to suppose that he would not have generated other, more accomplished novels and short stories had he stayed in Port of Spain. But he wanted to fulfill his calling as an Anglicized intellectual. The centrality of British and European high culture had, after all, been a key presupposition of his formal education.

At the juncture of 1932 and the future James was in a real sense still growing as an individual. He had become an accomplished journalist, but his intellectual capabilities were still to be fully explored and developed. He had only begun to consider explicitly political issues, and his theoretical training was almost rudimentary. The future was unknown.

CHAPTER TWO

Modern Politics

THE OPPORTUNITY TO MOVE to Britain arrived in the form of an invitation from Learie and Norma Constantine to stay with them and their four-year-old child in their new home on Meredith Street in Nelson, Lancashire. After spending a few adventuresome weeks in London during the spring of 1932, Nelson became James's primary place of residence during the first segment of his extended visit to England.[1] Although James was by nature polite and well behaved, he must have been something of a burden as a house guest. The Constantines lived in a small, four-room house with no garden, and James "kept late hours, read intensely and was deeply interested in politics."[2]

Because of his personable nature and masterful athletic abilities, Learie Constantine was already a local celebrity. Playing the part of an older brother (even though he was the younger of the two by several months), Constantine subsidized James's writings and encouraged him to develop his incipient critique of colonialism. In Nelson they collaborated on Constantine's *Cricket and I*, a personal history of West Indian cricket.[3] While the text focuses mostly on sports, one quintessentially Jamesian passage makes reference to their place of origin:

> there are few more cosmopolitan little places in the world and one has the opportunity of hearing all sorts of languages and seeing at first hand the style and manners of some of the most important races in the world. Trinidad is a Crown Colony, that is to say it is governed by the Colonial Office officials in England, and a movement for throwing off this yoke is gathering strength.[4]

James later described this work as "the first book ever published in England by a world-famous West Indian writing as a West Indian about people and events in the West Indies."[5] As he wrote in *Beyond a Boundary*, "henceforth the West Indies was speaking for itself in the modern world."[6]

Although Learie Constantine shared many of James's pre-Marxist views, he generally refrained from commenting on political matters in public. The scion of a local family which had a long history of accomplishments on and off the cricket pitch, Constantine was a firm believer in progressive reform and mutual respect between different social and ethnic groups. Temperamentally, he was courtly and generally moderate; as far as politics was concerned, he was anticolonial but not explicitly antiimperialist. Together he and James spoke to a variety of audiences in northern England about cricket, the conditions in the West Indies, and the prospects for independence. "By the winter [of 1933], we were in full cry all over the place."[7] In the same year, James was asked to speak on a BBC program commemorating the centenary of the abolition of slavery in the British colonies. He pressed home the idea that because of their training and outlook West Indians were ready for self-determination. Some listeners were clearly appalled. "Colonial officials in England, and others, began their protests to the BBC almost before I had finished speaking," he later wrote in *Beyond a Boundary*.[8]

Learie and Norma Constantine were not the only influences operating on the youthful critic of colonialism. Nelson itself was in many ways an ideal locale for James's intellectual development. An industrial town of some forty thousand inhabitants that was notorious for the militancy of the weavers who worked in its mills, Nelson had been dubbed "little Moscow" in the 1920s.[9] Learie Constantine introduced his guest to some of the town's trade unionists. Many of the men Constantine knew were members of the Independent Labour Party (ILP), a radical organization that had disaffiliated from the larger Labour Party in 1932.[10] These activists vigorously attacked the paternalistic assumptions embedded in *The Case for West-Indian Self-Government*, and James later reported that these "humorously cynical working men were a revelation and brought me down to earth."[11] Perhaps the most influential of these sharp Northerners was Harry Spencer, a local activist and autodidact with whom James spent a great deal of time.[12] The startling impact of personal conversations with working-class leftists was complemented by the ambitious nonfiction reading program that James undertook in Nelson. Starting with Leon Trotsky's *A History of the Russian Revolution* and Oswald Spengler's *Decline of the West*, he found it "necessary to read the relevant volumes of Stalin. And, of course, I had to read Lenin in order to trace the quarrel. And thereby I reached Volume One of *Das Kapital* and the *18th Brumaire* of Marx himself."[13]

It seems almost inevitable that James would sooner or later have encountered socialist ideas and attempted to make sense of the Marxist tradition. Given the wider context of economic and political crisis, as well as James's specific interest in the development of the West Indian urban working class (as evidenced by his early fiction) and his exposure to trade union militancy in Port of Spain and Nelson, it is little wonder that his initial response to Marxism was so favorable. He quickly embraced Marxism's emphasis on class and social conflict as the motor of history. Marxism may also have helped to make sense of the root causes of the international Depression, the emergence of fascist movements, the spread of European colonies in the nineteenth and early twentieth centuries, and so on. The Marxist tradition could also take credit for the October Revolution, an event which proved to be a tremendous inspiration to many First and Third World intellectuals for several decades. Historical materialism offered a holistic approach to the problems of the world economy and to interrelations between class, race, economics, and politics. For a variety of reasons, then, both biographical and intellectual, the young Caribbean writer had succumbed to a committed Marxist position by the conclusion of his stay in Nelson, Lancashire.

The reading program encompassed more than Marxist, Stalinist, and Spenglerian texts, however. In addition to unraveling the controversies of classical Marxism, James read extensively in the French and British literature on Toussaint L'Ouverture and the San Domingo slave revolution of the late 1800s. This preoccupation with Haiti's colonial past arose not only out of a general interest in world history, and in the concrete dynamics of revolutionary change, but also out of a concern for integrating black diasporic history and revolutionary politics. As leader of the Haitian rebellion, Toussaint L'Ouverture conveyed a literate, capable, and, as we shall see, tragic quality that would have appealed to a radicalized graduate of QRC. Toussaint L'Ouverture, it may be suggested, successfully negotiated the difficult transition that Mr. Haynes backed away from: to leave a comfortable sinecure (Toussaint worked as an animal steward on a large farm) and actively participate in the struggles of the barefooted masses. By 1934 James had decided to write a book on Toussaint and San Domingo. This project dovetailed nicely with his deepening attachment both to Marxism and to the cause of full independence for colonial nations. Moving to London at the very beginning of 1934, James bade farewell to his friends in northern England and prepared to find a suitable role in the British capital in the context of Depression-era politics.

◆◆◆

As a resident Briton, Nello seems to have been blessed with good fortune. One of the people that Constantine introduced him to was Nelville Cardus, the Manchester *Guardian*'s chief cricket correspondent. Soon James was covering county and test matches for the *Guardian*, the Glasgow *Herald*, and a number of other publications. Employment as a cricket correspondent enabled him to engage in political and intellectual pursuits. The fact that professional cricket had a lengthy but finite season meant that James could afford to spend one or two winters in Paris, researching the history of San Domingo at the National Archives. In London he joined the Independent Labour Party, and fraternized with a wide circle of literary and leftist types which included novelists, anarchists, West Indian and African students, publishers, and other intellectuals, such as the brilliant German Marxist theorist, Karl Korsch.[14]

London was an international crossroads of Pan-African thought and activism in the interwar period. International events, particularly those involving colonial issues, helped to propel the city's exiled blacks into political activity. By the end of World War I, colonialism encompassed twenty percent of the globe's land mass and over ten percent of the world's population. The conquest of African and other Third World territories in the nineteenth and early twentieth centuries by the major European powers constituted the most intensive period of imperial expansion in world history. Movements for political and socioeconomic self-determination, many of them led by intellectuals who had resided in Europe's capitals at one time or another, emerged as a militant response to the Age of Imperialism.

A key event in the development of anticolonial agitation in this period was fascist Italy's 1935 blitzkrieg invasion of Abyssinia (present-day Ethiopia), a bid for national glory and imperial conquest. Those who "thought that the era of gunboat diplomacy was at an end, that imperialism was just a schoolboy phrase from the past, suddenly now saw for themselves how it operated with a nation hacking its way towards empire at the costs of everything sacred."[15] The symbolism of an assault on independent Abyssinia shocked and galvanized racially conscious blacks across the globe; Benito Mussolini's military aggression was viewed with alarm not only by rival European powers, but by the *de facto* enemies of the European order.[16]

In London, a number of individuals came together to mobilize against fascist aggression in Africa. Among them were Amy Ashwood Garvey, Jomo Kenyatta, T. Ras Makonnen, I. T. A. Wallace-Johnson, and one or two others, including C. L. R. James. The organization they founded was the International African Friends of Abyssinia, whose aim was to rally the British around the Abyssinian cause. Garvey and company were joined in their efforts by Sylvia Pankhurst, the great suffragette, as well as by George Padmore, the son of Alphonso Nurse. By this time, Padmore had already broken with the international Communist movement in protest against the "pragmatic" drift of Communist strategy during the Popular Front period. During the 1920s, Communists had loudly insisted that colonialism was an enemy of socialism. By the mid-1930s, at the direction of Stalin, and in the aftermath of Hitler's rise to power, the international confederation of Communist parties, the Comintern, decreed that Western liberal democracy was on the whole preferable to authoritarian nationalism. As a result of this new policy of cooperation, communist parties suddenly clamped down on all unauthorized forms of anticolonial zeal within their sphere of influence.

As James remembered, Padmore arrived early one morning at his front door to express his dismay over the new line. "Padmore strongly opposed any attempt to downplay the struggle against British, French, and Dutch colonialism. As he complained: 'But how can I do that?' He said: 'Germany and Japan have no colonies in Africa. How can I attack them? Britain and France are the ones with colonies in Africa. And America is the most prejudiced country in the world.'"[17] As a result of Communism's tacit alliance with the West, Padmore broke with the movement and lent his considerable talents to groups like the International African Friends of Abyssinia. The group also benefitted from the contribution that George Padmore's companion, Dorothy Padmore, made to its intellectual and organizational development.

As a leading member of the organization, James publicly offered
to enlist in the Abyssinian army. He later explained his motives in the
pages of the Independent Labour Party's *New Leader*:

> My hope was to get into the army. It would have given me an oppor-
> tunity to make contact not only with the masses of the Abyssinians
> and other Africans, but in the ranks with them I would have had the
> best possible opportunity of putting across the International Social-
> ist case . . . I did not intend to spend the rest of my life in Abyssinia,
> but, all things considered, I thought, and still think, that two or
> three years there, given the fact that I am a Negro and am especially
> interested in the African revolution, was well worth the attempt.[18]

By the time this offer had been made, however, Abyssinia's anti-
quated military forces had been routed on the battle front. Amy Ashwood Garvey joined James, Padmore, Kenyatta, Makonnen, Wallace-
Johnson, W. E. F. Ward, and Fitz Braithwaite to form a successor organization, the International African Service Bureau, or IASB, with the
aim of furthering the cause of anticolonialism. Active membership in
the Bureau was restricted to people of African descent; "non-Afri-
cans" who wanted to "demonstrate in a practical way their interest in
Africa and the cause of the Colonial peoples" were invited to become
associate members.[19] In an advertisement that appeared in the leftist
monograph series *Fact*, the IASB billed itself as "primarily an African
organisation, run solely by Africans." The ad went on to say that the
Bureau "serves as a clearing house of information on matters affecting
Africans and people of African descent. It supplies speakers to organ-
isations, convenes meetings and discussions. It publishes pamphlets,
books, memoranda, etc. It is anti-Imperialist in character and outlook."[20]

Members of the International African Service Bureau gained considerable agitational experience by writing letters and articles for outside publications, and by organizing several small marches in the
spring of 1938 against British imperialism.[21] They organized a study
group, and also managed to produce a journal, *International African
Opinion*, that appeared on an irregular basis, containing short articles
on a variety of topics pertaining to anticolonial movements and
events organized by the Bureau.[22] Perhaps their most characteristic
activity was addressing skeptical audiences at Hyde Park's famed
Speakers Corner. Different members of the Bureau took turns in

declaiming on behalf of black rights; Ras Makonnen liked to start his speech by calling for "war," because "it's the only way we are going to get our rights."[23] The others could be equally brazen in their rhetoric, but James was the only Marxist. He would often walk to the nearby Trotskyist soap-box and rip into Stalinism after lecturing on the coming collapse of the British Empire for the Pan-Africanists.

The IASB was undoubtedly the most militant of the various black organizations operating out of Britain. For example, the London-based League of Coloured Peoples, founded in 1931 by a Jamaican, Harold Moody, sought to "make representations to government authorities, hospital managements, medical faculties, commercial concerns," and other influential bodies "on behalf of coloured people in Britain."[24] Similar organizations included the African Association, founded in 1897, and the African Progress Union, founded in 1921. Although James contributed to Moody's publication, *The Keys,* and gave a formal presentation on developments in the West Indies to members of the League, his own sensibility was more accurately reflected by the IASB's impatient agenda.

The active core of the IASB was comprised of a remarkable circle of West Indian intellectuals and future leaders of postcolonial Africa. The group's advocacy of African independence was both honorable and prescient, as Pan-Africanism was to become a potent force for change by the late 1940s. Pan-Africanism had been first proposed as a political philosophy emphasizing black unity, consciousness, and autonomy by a Trinidadian lawyer, Henry Sylvester-Williams, at the end of the nineteenth century. As a doctrine it served to underscore the dispersed character of the African peoples, the inherently unjust nature of slavery and oppression, and the need for an independent black leadership that could establish a black-centered agenda. The hope was that Pan-Africanism—as a philosophy and as a social movement—could generate a distinctive perspective on the black condition that would ultimately transform world politics.

Sylvester-Williams brought together thirty West Indians, African-Americans, and Africans in London in 1900 for the first of six (thus far) Pan-African congresses. One of the delegates, the prominent sociologist W. E. B. DuBois, organized three further conferences in the 1910s and 1920s. Initially, the rhetoric of Pan-Africanism was less militant than Marcus Garvey's "back to Africa" movement. Refusing to adopt the oppositional tone of Garveyism, the first four Pan-African congresses called on the West to disengage from colonial practices out of a sense of both fair play and self-interest. The fifth Pan-African congress, organized in 1945 by George and Dorothy Padmore, pushed the movement leftwards when it issued a call for the ousting of the colonial authorities through the popular mobilization of the African and Caribbean masses. By preparing the intellectual and organizational groundwork for an anticolonialism based on a more radical, grassroots perspective, the Padmores and the IASB helped shape the language and tactics of postwar anticolonialism. The sixth Pan-African congress, which furnished additional evidence of Pan-Africanism's evolution in a militantly populist and leftist direction, was held in Africa in 1974, partly at James's urging.

The possibility of linking revolutionary politics in Europe and the colonies was perhaps uppermost on James's mind as he worked on a manuscript that encompassed all of the important questions facing the Pan-African and revolutionary movements: the San Domingo revolution. At the end of the eighteenth century, San Domingo was a jewel in the crown of French colonialism. A highly organized and finely stratified society, San Domingo was one of several Caribbean colonies to make a decisive contribution to the making of the modern world economy. Over half a million slaves worked on the plantations and farms that dotted the island. In 1791, inspired by the radical republicanism of the French Revolution, and aided by the sharp political divisions that had emerged within the ranks of the local elite, large numbers of slaves rose up in revolt, taking over farms and sending whites fleeing to port cities on the island's western edge. Out of the chaos of localized revolt emerged a number of armed gangs and factions consisting primarily of exslaves. Under the astute leadership of Toussaint L'Ouverture, a forty-five-year-old former head steward on a large estate, several of these gangs merged to form a mobile army. This fighting force engaged a succession of European military expeditions in combat and came to provide a measure of political stability and cohesion in many areas of San Domingo. Toussaint L'Ouverture took responsibility for designing a legal code, appointing regional administrators, reorganizing the system of taxation, and reviving the plantation economy on the basis of free labor. In 1803, Toussaint's army decisively defeated Napoleon Bonaparte's final invasion force, and so on January 1, 1804 the new state of Haiti (*Ayiti* being an Arawak Indian word for mountains) was born amid the wreckage of French colonialism.

As the world's only successful slave revolution, the San Domingo uprising was above all a dramatic event. Indeed, James first presented the fruits of his historical research in the form of a play, entitled *Toussaint L'Ouverture*, which was performed in 1936 in London with the renowned American singer Paul Robeson in the title role.[25] The play focused on the complicated diplomatic maneuvers that took place between the revolutionary generals, led by Toussaint L'Ouverture, and the elegant French, British, and American ambassadors. While Toussaint was courteous in his dealings with the emissaries of colonialism, his aide General Dessalines was more blunt: the diplomats, he suggested, only wanted "land for plantations, and slaves to work."[26] The play notes that Toussaint was eventually imprisoned on Napoleon's orders—he was abducted onto a French warship and transported to France, where he was imprisoned and later died—and that General Dessalines was compelled to lead the San Domingo exslave army to victory in Toussaint's absence. Indeed, Dessalines was crowned Emperor Jacques I, the first sovereign ruler of Haiti, in October, 1804. The themes of the later *The Black Jacobins*—the movement toward self-emancipation on part of the slaves; the strained relations between slaves and mulattos; the fragile links between the West Indian freedom fighters and the partisans of the French Revolution; the conjunction of diplomacy and mass insurrection—were all richly dramatized for a London theater-going audience.[27]

Within two years, Secker and Warburg had brought out *The Black Jacobins*.[28] The book's central thesis concerns the centrality of the slaves' purposive action in undermining slavery and the plantation system in San Domingo. The aim of the book was to show how West Indian slavery was abolished not by humanitarian gestures or legislative decrees but by the collective mobilization of slaves, particularly those in revolutionary Haiti. It was the threat of similar revolts, James argued, that compelled Europe's politicians and civil servants to finally outlaw slavery. As a crucial passage in the book asks: "But when did property ever listen to reason except when cowed by violence?"[29] This is not to suggest that James regarded violence as a panacea. He goes out of his way to emphasize that Toussaint's skills encompassed the arts of negotiation, mediation, and compromise, and the fact that from its inception Haiti was handicapped by Toussaint's captivity and death as an exiled prisoner of the French state. Toussaint's absence, and the eclipse of radical republicanism (i.e., Jacobinism) in revolutionary France, helped deprive an independent

Haiti of the leadership it required, or of any substantial outside economic or technical assistance.

The text is peppered with references to the prospects for analogous uprisings in modern Africa. In a 1975 interview James said that *The Black Jacobins* was written to show "how the African revolution would develop."[30] The book's conclusion emphasizes that "those black Haitian labourers" have "given us an example to study":

> Despite the temporary reaction of Fascism, the prevailing standards of human liberty and equality are infinitely more advanced and more profound than those current in 1789. Judged relatively by those standards, the millions of blacks in Africa and the few of them who are educated are as much pariahs in that vast prison as the blacks and Mulattoes of San Domingo . . . Imperialism vaunts its exploitation of the wealth of Africa for the benefit of civilisation. In reality, from the very nature of its system of production for profit it strangles the real wealth of the continent—the creative capacity of the African people. The African faces a long and difficult road and he will need guidance. But he will tread it fast because he will walk upright.[31]

The book's preoccupation with the question of African independence may be explained, in part, by a point that James emphasized in its 1963 appendix:

> *Before they* [West Indians] *could begin to see themselves as a free and independent people they had to clear from* [their] *minds the stigma that anything African was inherently inferior and degraded. The road to West Indian national identity lay through Africa.*[32]

Although this point was only made explicit in an essay written a quarter-century after the book was first published, we must assume that even in the late 1930s James was broadly sympathetic to the notion that, as he so elegantly put it, the "road to West Indian national identity lay through Africa." Yet in this earlier period, sub-Saharan Africa represented above all a strategic linchpin in the international revolutionary process. It would be misleading to suppose that James was as interested in the question of "national identity" in the late 1930s as he would later become in the early 1960s. His uppermost concern in the earlier period would have been in the political

dynamics of, and prospects for, world revolution. While the formation of a West Indian national identity was not an entirely separate
issue for James, it was at this juncture far from being his top priority.[33]

It was a hallmark of Pan-African thought to draw connections
between struggles in the Old World and the New. By its very nature,
Pan-Africanism was concerned with linking movements across the
diaspora, and with the exchange of ideas, personnel, and tactical
advice across national and regional boundaries. In this sense, Pan-
Africanism shared an internationalist character in common with
Marxism. Decisively shaped by the author's newly acquired Marxism
and Trotskyism, the radical internationalism of *The Black Jacobins*
vividly distinguished it from comparable works. As Cedric Robinson
notes, other Pan-African texts published in the 1930s and 1940s—he
cites George Padmore's *How Britain Rules Africa* [1936], Eric Williams's *The Negro in the Caribbean* [1942], and Jomo Kenyatta's *Kenya:
Land of Conflict* [1945]—"were addressed to the colonial powers." In
contrast, *The Black Jacobins* "was a declaration of war for liberation."[34]

In addition to being a manifesto and primer for the coming African uprising, *The Black Jacobins* was intended to demonstrate the
applicability of Marxist analysis and Marxist categories to social
change in what later became known as the Third World. The book's
chapter titles—"The Owners," "The San Domingo Masses Begin,"
"And the Paris Masses Complete," "The Bourgeoisie Prepares to
Restore Slavery," etc.—confirm the author's conflict-centered, class-
analytic perspective. In addition, the centrality of international capitalist relations in shaping political relations in the colonies is
assumed. Following Marx's own approach, capitalism is described in
the book as a dynamic and totalizing system which imposes its profit-
maximizing logic on both states and individual actors. Furthermore,
questions of political and military organization and leadership—a
salient dimension of Lenin and Trotsky's interpretation of Marxism—
are considered in great detail. An essentially dialectical relationship is
posited between the spontaneity expressed by the San Domingo
masses and the forging of a revolutionary vanguard under the leadership of Toussaint L'Ouverture. James's one criticism of this "master of
the art of war, and skillful negotiator"[35] was that Toussaint failed to
trust the masses with his inner thoughts. "He ignored the black
labourers . . . and to bewilder the masses is to strike the deadliest of

all blows at the revolution."[36] As a biographer, James saw this lack of trust as Toussaint L'Ouverture's tragic flaw. As Edward Said writes: "Toussaint is drawn by James as an admirable man, nonvindictive, immensely intelligent, subtle, and yet perfectly responsive to the sufferings of his fellow Haitians. 'Great men make history,' says James, 'but only such history as it is possible for them to make.' Toussaint rarely took his people into his confidence [however] . . ."[37]

The evidence makes it clear that Toussaint remained faithful to the example, and to the declared representatives, of the French revolution. It is Toussaint, rather than his army, who is the authentic "Black Jacobin." Yet one of the book's central themes concerns the way in which a wider link opened between the most radical elements of the French Revolution and the San Domingo rebellion. In the midst of social and political upheaval, an objective connection was disclosed between two very different subordinate groups in two distinct contexts. The events in France provided the slaves of San Domingo with an opportunity—fissures within the local white elite—and with an ideological rationale, that is, republicanism. At the same time, the slave rebellion in San Domingo was an inspiration to radicals in France. The cause of Haitian independence was aided considerably when the French assembly, under pressure from the radical Jacobins, abolished slavery or "the aristocracy of the skin" in the French colonies. James wrote:

> On August 11th, the day after the Tuileries fell, Page, a notorious agent of the colonists in France, wrote home almost in despair. "One spirit alone reigns here, it is horror of slavery and enthusiasm for liberty. It is a frenzy which wins all heads and grows every day." Henceforth the Paris masses were for abolition, and their black brothers in San Domingo, for the first time, had passionate allies in France.[38]

It was only with the overthrow of Jacobinism, which commenced on the day of the Thermidor (July 27th, 1794), that the connection between the two revolutions would be severed. Henceforth France would once more take up arms to defend her "property." It was under the leadership of the great consolidator Napoleon Bonaparte that the French military attempted to restore slavery in her most recalcitrant colony—with no success.

James's emphasis on the international repercussions of civil war was written in the spirit of Marx's own comparative historical sociology. But *The Black Jacobins* specifically drew on Leon Trotsky's analysis of "permanent revolution," which stipulated that successful rebellions in the developing nations would quickly pass through the stage of bourgeois democracy to the "dictatorship of the proletariat." While revolutions in "backward" nations, in Trotsky's view, could play a catalytic role vis-a-vis developments in advanced nations, isolated revolutions would fail as long as they lacked material and political support from workers in the West.[39] What the Haitian events suggested was that revolutionary alliances fashioned across national (and racial) boundaries were a genuine historical possibility. It was, James believed, the degeneration of the French Revolution—rather than of the San Domingo Revolution—which deprived Haiti of the resources that it needed to protect itself against an international system predicated on primitive capitalist accumulation. *The Black Jacobins* should not be read as saying that a global socialist order could have been created at the close of the eighteenth century. But its author certainly meant to suggest that the general dynamics identified by the theory of "permanent revolution" came into play in an epoch when slavery and capitalism were most closely intertwined.

While *The Black Jacobins* was not specifically concerned with the nexus of slavery and capitalism, it did help inspire Eric Williams's *Capitalism and Slavery*, which was published in 1944, two years after Williams's first book, *The Negro in the Caribbean*, appeared in print. Based on a dissertation Williams defended in the late 1930s at Oxford University, *Capitalism and Slavery* focused on British colonialism and sought to demonstrate that slavery was ended not by abolitionism but by rational self-interest. Williams met with his former tutor on numerous occasions when both were living in Britain, and it seems that James both read drafts of the dissertation and had a significant role in formulating the book's primary thesis.[40] Of all of Williams's works, this was the book that registered the greatest impact on both scholarly and popular audiences.[41] However, it should be noted that Williams's approach differs from his tutor's in several important respects. Williams's account stresses purely economic factors, in particular the substitution of tenant and industrial labor for slave labor as a function of economic calculation. Unlike *The Black Jacobins*, *Capitalism and Slavery* does not survey its historical terrain from the perspective of the masses, and its author effectively discounts the role of self-emancipatory struggles in undermining slavery. Given their subsequent personal histories (one a socialist and internationalist, the other a postcolonial politician), this contrast between the two books is revealing.

Their stylistic and political differences were underscored by the publication of a short companion volume to *The Black Jacobins* that surveyed black protest movements in Africa, the United States and the Caribbean, entitled *A History of Negro Revolt*. Williams would have been incapable of producing such a class-conscious document, and his fastidious empiricism probably would have prevented him from advancing the kinds of sweeping claims that James makes throughout this book. It is doubtful, for example, that Williams would have dismissed Marcus Garvey's doctrines as "pitiable rubbish"; declared that between the blacks and Indo-Caribbeans of Trinidad "there is no racial ill-feeling"; or suggested that the sectarian creed of the Watch Tower Movement (Jehovah's Witnesses) "primitively approximates to the dialectic of Marx and Lenin."[42] While *A History of Negro Revolt* contained a mass of information that would have been new to its readers, and makes a strong case for the ubiquity of black resistance, the pamphlet is marred by a distracting degree of sloppiness both at the level of presentation and theory.

Nevertheless, through public speeches, books, and articles, James made a singular contribution to the Pan-African cause in the 1930s. What distinguished his voice from that of, say, Jomo Kenyatta, whose rhetorical militancy masked a refusal to engage in socialist politics, or even George Padmore, who retained a broad commitment to socialist ideals, was that it bore the hallmark of a consciously historical materialist and Trotskyist conception of politics and history. In the early 1930s, the maverick Trotskyists offered a pugnaciously Marxist alternative to Communism, anarchism, and social democracy. But how did James reconcile Pan-Africanism, with its proto-Third Worldist approach to politics, with Trotskyism? Revolutionary socialism may have seemed far removed from Pan-Africanism, but for James the two were complementary. Trotskyism anticipated the emergence of new revolutionary movements in the coming period, and it placed a critical emphasis on the importance of linking and extending radical struggles across national borders. Permanent revolution, Trotsky's theory of the interpenetration of radical movements in the core and periphery of the world system, conveniently (and, for James, persuasively) arranged world-historic forces in such a way as to allow for the complete and secure abolition of colonialism and imperialism.

Trotsky's own remarkable biography and corpus proved to be tremendous assets to the Trotskyist movement in its efforts to attract new members. The Russian-born theorist of permanent revolution was, after all, more than just another antibourgeois utopian. Leon Trotsky had written penetrating histories of the Russian revolutions of 1905 and 1917; he had commanded the victorious Red Army; he was an astute literary and social critic; and he had been the leader of the Petrograd Soviet in 1905. He was as widely known for his brilliant oratory as for his support for the *soviets*, the workers' councils of 1905 and 1917. Trotsky was also a steadfast opponent of Stalinism who had been deported from the Soviet Union in January 1929, stripped of his citizenship, and placed in great physical danger. Trotsky's personal charisma was great, and the Old Man's magnetism only increased on the printed page. For someone like James, who was new to the revolutionary movement, Trotskyism promised to fuse theory and practice through the creation of a genuinely revolutionary international vanguard that could decisively intervene in the struggles of the day. The fact that the Trotskyists oriented themselves around the movements of the industrial working class was wholly acceptable to James, since he had been impressed by the militant and democratic trade unionism he saw put into practice in the West Indies and England.

When James moved to London in 1934 he came into contact with Trotskyists in the Hampstead branch of the Independent Labour Party and quickly joined their ranks. Because of his erudition and political skills, he was catapulted into the leadership of the Marxist Group, one of the smaller British Trotskyist groupings, within a matter of weeks. At that time, the organization had a few dozen members concentrated in London.[43] The strategy of the Marxist Group was to dominate the left-wing of the Independent Labour Party and steer that organization in a revolutionary direction. Trotsky had initially endorsed their strategy, which went by the name of "entryism," as in "entering" a larger, non-Trotskyist formation to recruit new members or take over the organization. The ILP, with its 17,000 members, had been targeted by the Trotskyists as the party was turning leftwards during the early years of the Depression. By 1935, however, Trotsky was urging his followers to pull out of the ILP, on the grounds that its leaders were wedded to parliamentary politics.[44] Despite Trotsky's advice, the Marxist Group remained active in the Independent Labour Party—but the group was expelled in November 1936 for publishing its own factional paper, *Fight*.

James was fast becoming a well-known figure in this period. Several of his pieces for the ILP's *New Leader* caused a stir among progressive circles. His first article for the ILP, "Is This Worth a War? The League's Scheme to Rob Abyssinia of its Independence," represented an important intervention in the debate about the left's response to Italy's military aggression. The debate hinged on the question of whether to support the League of Nations' call for economic sanctions against Italy. While the Labour Party supported sanctions, the ILP was sharply divided over the issue. Many ILPers argued that under the rule of Hailie Selassie, Abyssinia, like Italy, was a dictatorship. They therefore took a neutral position on the question of sanctions. The Marxist Group, on the other hand, called for independent proletarian action in defense of Abyssinia. James was largely responsible for articulating the Group's position, and in one article he exclaimed: "Workers of Britain, peasants and workers of Africa, get closer together for this and for other fights. But keep far from the Imperialists and their League and covenants and sanctions. Do not play the fly to their spider."[45]

At the Independent Labour Party's annual conference in 1936, he played a leading role in converting the Party to the Marxist Group's position on sanctions. Drawing on the precepts of Pan-Africanism, James promised the ILP that Italy's invasion would spark an international opposition movement of immense proportions:

> It is necessary to support the anti-Imperialist mass movements arising among "coloured" peoples in all countries in connection with the Abyssinian crisis, and to create a firm alliance between the international working-class movement and suppressed peoples.[46]

James also took his message of "class struggle Pan-Africanism" to Independent Labour Party meetings in south Wales, where he drew large and enthusiastic crowds.[47] Given his growing prominence within the ILP, it is no wonder that the British historian Duncan Hallas has observed that James "found that staying in the ILP, as it was, in many ways suited his talented but individualistic personality."[48]

James's public reputation was cemented by his writings. He wrote a preface to a moving account of the Spanish Civil War written by two

English anti-Stalinists (one of them the surrealist poet Mary Low), and contributed several pieces to *Controversy*, an ILP-sponsored journal that maintained a broad-minded editorial policy. In addition, his book *World Revolution: 1917–1936* (which was dedicated to the Marxist Group) left a lasting impression on the non-Communist left, and in a letter to Trotsky, James explained that he hoped to stir up trouble inside the Communist ranks: "We shall have a good basis for putting across our line. The CP here is terribly frightened by the prospect [of publication] for they, more than anyone else, know all that is to be said about their criminal policy during the last few years."[49] One Communist reviewer did acknowledge that *World Revolution* was "a masterpiece—of political dementia."[50] The book was banned by the British colonial authorities in India shortly after its publication.[51]

World Revolution presents a scathing and comprehensive critique of the Comintern's foreign policy under the leadership of Joseph Stalin. Calling particular attention to "crimes" and "blunders" committed by the leadership of the international Communist movement in the context of revolutionary crises in Germany (1919–1921), China (1927), and Spain (mid-1930s), its central theme is that with the consolidation of Stalinism the Soviets placed a greater priority on their own national security than on promoting anticapitalist movements abroad. The book consequently proposes a variety of ways in which the revolutionary impetus could be restored inside the Soviet Union. It emphasizes above all the need to provide for working-class control over the state apparatus through the formation of democratic workers' councils. By revitalizing the institutions of class power, the Soviets would be far more likely to conduct a genuinely revolutionary foreign policy. The book argues that the Communists should open their ranks to the expelled Trotskyists, and otherwise overhaul their internal structures. In the absence of such sweeping reforms, the Soviet Union would stray further from the socialist path and would begin to function as an essentially counterrevolutionary force in world affairs.

The book was arguably the most "orthodox" text that James ever produced. As he acknowledged in the introduction, the principles advanced in the text were firmly based on "the fundamental ideas of Marxism," specifically its Trotskyist variant. "How much the book owes to the writings of Trotsky, the text can only partially show,"[52] he wrote. The truth of this statement is confirmed throughout the text, as when the author defends Trotsky's characterization of the Soviet Union as a "degenerated workers' state." (In later writings, as we shall

find, he would take strong exception to this thesis.) The book's
Trotskyist lineage is also corroborated by its stress on the importance
of building a new, revolutionary international to defend the gains of
October and forge new revolutions in the advanced countries. The
last chapter, titled "A Fourth International is the Only Hope," views
such an International as the "only hope" not only for revolutionaries,
but for the future of the quasisocialist Soviet Union. "The USSR,"
James flatly predicted, "cannot survive without a revolutionary international."[53] As he wrote a few pages on: "If the Third International
loses its last stronghold, in France, and Fascism conquers in that
country, then unless the workers of the world can create another
international organisation . . . the Workers' State of Soviet Russia is
doomed."[54] Following Trotsky, James argued that the coming period
would produce a cataclysm on the scale of what was known as the
Great War, and that this war would both test Stalinism's viability and
create new avenues for revolutionary action. Something of the flavor
of James's cataclysmic but ultimately hopeful assessment of the overall political situation was expressed in the first chapter ("Marxism"):

> We may well see, especially after the universal ruin and destruction
> of the coming war, a revolutionary movement which, beginning in
> one of the great European cities, in the course of a few short months
> will sweep the imperialist bourgeoisie out of power, not only in
> every country in Europe, but in India, China, Egypt and South
> Africa. With an organised international revolutionary socialism
> could face the future without dismay. The task of rebuilding such
> an international has been begun. It is a race with time.[55]

In his autobiography, Fredrick Warburg wryly observed that the
Trotskyists "loved the USSR as children love their mother, but they
knew that the wicked father, Stalin, had debauched her and produced
a miscarriage."[56] His Oedipal analysis was tempered by the recognition that the author of *World Revolution* and his intransigent comrades had a valid argument to make about Stalinism: "The Trotskyists
pointed out, with maddening persistence, that the Russian worker
was poor, bullied by bureaucrats, the subject of an awesome tyranny,
spied upon by a secret police. The state in Russia, they claimed, far
from withering away, as Marx expected, had become more omnipres-
ent than ever."[57] Warburg, the book's publisher, went on to term
World Revolution "the bible of Trotskyism." While this may have been

a slight overstatement, the work did cover a great deal of material that was of vital interest to the movement. Trotskyists promoted the book in their press (in North America, Europe, and elsewhere) and used it to familiarize recruits with their indictment of international Stalinism. Apart from Trotsky's own writings—many of which were as yet untranslated and otherwise inaccessible—*World Revolution* was the only critique available of the Communist International from a leftist, non-CP perspective. Because of the controversial nature of the subject matter and the diverse range of cases under consideration, there were not even academic studies that covered the same ground from a less openly partisan perspective. Interested readers would have had to choose between James's revolutionary analysis and unreliable Communist tracts.

Despite its orthodox stance, Trotsky found fault with *World Revolution*, arguing that the book's account of the consolidation of Stalinism was "formalistic" in that it situated Stalin's rise to power primarily in terms of exogenous factors—such as the failure of proletarian revolution to spread throughout Western Europe, and the economic and military pressures placed on the Bolshevik government by liberal-democratic regimes in the West—rather than recognizing the endogenous factors at work, such as Stalin's relationship to the bureaucracy, and the political and physical exhaustion of the working class in the 1920s.[58] Although he valued the book's contribution, Trotsky strongly believed that a proper understanding of the decline of the revolution and of the Communist International required a more probing look at political and socioeconomic conditions inside the Soviet Union during the years of the revolution's "degeneration." While both men agreed that the Russian experiment had been irreparably damaged by the lack of outside support, Trotsky was far more inclined than James to link the rise of Stalinism to the nation's underdeveloped or "backward" character.

Even as he was helping to define the meaning of orthodox Trotskyism, James became engaged in a surprisingly suspect project, one that attested to his inherent openmindedness. Through friends in Paris, James had come into contact with Boris Souvarine, a nonconformist intellectual who had served on the Central Committee of the French Communist Party before being expelled for "Trotskyite" deviations in the mid-1920s. For a short period after his expulsion Souvarine had become active in the international Left Opposition before breaking with Trotsky in the early 1930s. His scathing biography, *Sta-*

lin: A Critical Survey of Bolshevism, was published in France in 1935, and James translated the book from French into English.[59] Souvarine's book documented for the first time the mediocrity of Stalin's career as a Bolshevik in the pre–1917 period, and went into painful detail concerning Stalin's despotism in the period following Lenin's death. Instead of maintaining a broadly Leninist perspective, as Trotsky did, Souvarine embraced a pluralistic, "democratic socialist" political viewpoint that emphasized the protection and defense of individual civil liberties under socialism. After the book received favorable reviews in a few liberal publications in Europe and North America, Trotsky coined the term *Souvarinism* as a term of abuse to describe democratic leftists who posited some form of continuity between Leninism and Stalinism.

Stalin laid the blame for the degeneration of the Russian Revolution in two places: in the objective circumstances, particularly the absence of successful socialist revolutions in Western Europe, and in Leninism's organizational premises. Souvarine did not believe that Lenin was insincere in his ultimate goals, but he did maintain that the Leninist concept of the "vanguard party," with its hierarchical and secretive organizational principles, inevitably fostered a one-party state. In one passage, he argued that the tendency of the Bolsheviks to "organize and to act as a disciplined army capable of carrying out orders" was evident within months of the 1903 split with the Mensheviks. This quasimilitary sense of discipline, Souvarine suggested, left the Bolsheviks "always at the mercy of an error on the part of their leader and in danger of sinking into an intellectual passivity contrary to their theoretical mission as vanguard and model."[60] By the early 1920s, the Leninist party had effectively provided Stalin the means to usurp power and dominate the new Soviet bureaucracy without having to cope with a democratic mass opposition. Thus Souvarine could write of the "miscarriage of Bolshevism." "Democratic socialism," he mournfully concluded, "is almost everywhere allowing itself to be led, circumvented and compromised by dictatorial communism. The death agony of socialist hope in the world thus opens up an immeasurable ideological crisis."[61]

Despite signs that its preeminent black recruit was willing to entertain unorthodox opinions, James was one of two British delegates at the founding conference of the Fourth International, which was held in Paris in September 1938. Trotsky believed that the coming war would create a real opening for revolutionary socialists, and he worked hard to convince his followers that Trotskyism should be launched as a formal movement with its own International—the Fourth International. Many Trotskyists, such as the writer Isaac Deutscher, strongly opposed Trotsky's proposal, however, on the basis that it was premature and tactically unwise. The 1938 *Transitional Program*, penned by Trotsky (who was unable to attend the conference), laid out the rationale for this move, and it served as the central document at the Paris conference. The *Transitional Program* featured a list of "transitional demands" which, while not explicitly socialist, were unattainable under capitalism in its current epoch. The demands included calls to "open the books," that is, for employers to reveal the state of their finances to trade union representatives, and "thirty for forty," a call for a thirty-hour work week for all workers at full pay. Through the application of transitional demands and the formation of unified Trotskyist parties, the Fourth International could take advantage of the coming crisis and rally the international working class around a genuinely socialist platform. The hallmark of Fourth International politics became its insistence that capitalism's periodic crises would undermine the Communist movement and mobilize mass numbers of workers under the banner of Trotskyism.

The conference's minutes record that James made five remarks to the gathering. The first four were more or less perfunctory in nature. The final comment, however, was quite suggestive. "In view of the fact that . . . the present congress had dealt explicitly with the Colonial question," he stated, "the congress should officially instruct the English section [i.e., the speaker] to work out a program on the Colonial question and to suggest to the Executive Committee a definite plan for an International Colonial Bureau which the EC would be empowered to establish."[62] What would he have had such a Bureau do? We can safely assume that its work would have had administrative *and* political dimensions—circulating and translating documents, promoting the formation of new Trotskyist groupings in colonial countries, prodding European Trotskyists to create alliances with expatriated anticolonialists, and revising Trotskyist doctrine to more adequately encompass colonial issues. An agenda similar to this would be developed when James traveled to Mexico in 1939 to confer with Trotsky on the issue of black politics in the United States. What is conveyed here is James's forbearance regarding the Trotskyists' sometimes less-than-impressive commitment to the anticolonial cause. For the time being, despite whatever private reservations or concerns he may have had, James appeared on the surface at least to be a loyal Fourth Internationalist.

As was true of his involvement in Pan-Africanism, James's rhetorical commitment to Trotskyism was matched by deeds. Ajit Roy, a law student at the London School of Economics, later described what it was like collaborating with James in the Marxist Group after their expulsion from the ILP:

> James and I got together and we took a flat in Boundary Road, where James had another great devotee, a chap from the East End called Stanton. Our main task was to bring out the *Fight* and to make open propaganda in street corner meetings. We built a portable platform and the three of us, James, a tall West Indian, Stanton, a very Jewish-looking chap from the East End, and myself, an Indian, taking the portable platform to the shopping centres all over London, regarding ourselves as the vanguard of the British proletariat! It is all very amusing—but people did listen—probably the very strangeness of it gave us an audience. But once James started speaking he always got a crowd.[63]

Fredrick Warburg offered further testimony to James's unflagging political commitment:

> Night after night he would address meetings in London and the provinces, denouncing the crimes of the blood-thirsty Stalin, until he was hoarse and his wonderful voice a mere croaking in the throat. The communists who heckled him would have torn him limb from limb, had it not been for the ubiquity of the police and their insensitivity to propaganda of whatever hue. If you told him of some new communist argument, he would listen with a smile of infinite tolerance on his dark face, wag the index finger of his right hand solemnly, and announce in an understanding tone—"we know them, we know them"—as of a man who has plumbed human wickedness to its depth and forgiven it, since man even in his wickedness is pitiable.[64]

Another engaging memoir of these times is Ethel Mannin's *Comrade O Comrade*, a humorous, thinly fictionalized account of radical politics in England in the 1930s, subtitled *Low-Down on the Left*. In one chapter, Mary Thane, the author's stand-in, serves tea to James and two comrades as they discuss revolutionary politics. "The eminent Trotskyist was an extremely handsome young Negro. He arrived with two white friends," she writes. "The Trotskyists arrived punctually at four and they left punctually at five, and in that hour Mary uttered exactly twelve words." (These are "Hullo," "This is Larry Lanaghan, from Ireland," "Sugar?" "More Tea?" "Cake?" and "Goodbye.") The conversation is dominated by James's "rich dark voice" that "flowed like music"; the content concerns the thesis that "Permanent Revolution and International Socialism must form the basis of all revolutionary strategy."[65] A separate account of this odd social engagement, which appears in the autobiography of Ethel Mannin's husband, Reginald Reynolds, confirms the essential facts outlined in her novel. He writes:

> Ethel had long hoped to meet C. L. R. James, whose intellect and good looks were praised by all except the Stalinists. She had invited him to tea one Sunday and he arrived unexpectedly with two of his friends a week later, when the house was already full of guests . . . they arrived in the middle of a deep discussion which they had begun two hours earlier, in Hyde Park, continued it with no apparent attention to anybody or anything else, and eventually walked down the garden path, still arguing—without, as Ethel said afterwards, any sign that they even knew where they'd been.[66]

How much had James's character changed in this period? Not as much as one might suppose. Obviously he had a far greater interest in politics than before, and his new-found Marxism may have given him a somewhat more somber and determined outlook on life. There was nothing dilettantish about his commitment to Trotskyism. At the same time, he retained his characteristic blend of inner confidence and public volubility. He continued to express himself in a lucid, crisp prose, and *The Black Jacobins* in particular reflected its author's steadfast love affair with the English language. In his dealings with comrades, political opponents, and strangers, James remained faithful to the public school code of his youth. (Not least among the crimes of the Communists, in James's eyes, was their lack of a sense of fair play.) While some family members and childhood friends may not have understood or sympathized with his uncompromising radicalism, they would have surely recognized the romantic figure described by his publisher:

If politics was religion and Marx his god, if literature was his passion and Shakespeare his prince among writers, cricket was his beloved activity . . . I can hear today the opening words of *Twelfth Night*, delivered beautifully from his full sensitive lips: "If music be the food of love, play on; give me excess of it." Excess, perhaps, was James's crime, an excess of words whose relevance to the contemporary tragedy [totalitarianism] was less than he supposed.[67]

Yet this almost lurid portrait of a passionate devotee of poetry and language may be somewhat overstated. A nice corrective image is provided in his notes for his unfinished autobiography, where James describes a "pub crawl" with Eric Williams in London in the mid-1930s: "I am a cautious man and on quite a few evenings Williams and his friends went pub crawling, accompanied by me with Marx, Jane Austen or H. G. Wells in my pocket which I faithfully read during the pauses. At the end I got into a cab with Williams and saw him safely home to my flat."[68] Which composite is likely to have a greater basis in fact—the voluble conversationalist, or the abstinent bookworm? No doubt the answer is more complex than the question allows. Certainly he could be dazzling in public, at ease with himself and his ability to put others at ease. At the same time, he nurtured a private self, loathed fatuousness and frivolity, and retained an almost Victorian sense of reserve and decorum.

At Trotsky's request, this "cautious man" prepared for a six-month visit to the United States between the months of the cricket season. Trotsky was particularly interested in having James supervise the "Negro work" of the Socialist Workers Party (SWP), although he may also have been hoping to remove an awkward sectarian from the troubled British Trotskyist movement. What is certain is that during his years of exile, Trotsky had become concerned with what was known at the time as "the Negro question." From his fortified estate in Coyoacan, Mexico, the great revolutionary sought to exhort the Socialist Workers Party to recruit black workers, sharecroppers, and intellectuals into the party. As a talented West Indian orator and polemicist, James could attract nonwhites into the Trotskyist camp. He could also help educate SWP members about the strategic importance of black politics in the United States. As Trotsky wrote to James Cannon, leader of the Socialist Workers Party: "The party cannot postpone this extremely important question any longer. James's sojourn in the States is very important for the serious and energetic beginning of this work."[69]

James's willingness to leave Britain may have reflected not only his redoubtable political commitment, but also the unhappy state of his personal life. Trotsky's suggestion came just as he was recovering from a failed romance. James later referred in private correspondence to his having fallen in love in 1936 to "Candide," a Dutch woman,

> a ravishing blonde, small but carrying herself like a queen. She was married . . . we had wonderful times—finding out good and cheap restaurants, talking, going to book-shops and fiddling around with books—she was fluent in English, French, Dutch and German— she had a wonderful eye for people and when she said she didn't like a person, I learnt to be very careful of him. Well, it ended. I was sick for a year at losing her but then I came to America.[70]

When James set sail for New York City in 1938, he had achieved in only thirty-seven years what some might hope to accomplish in a lifetime. During his stay he had forged a career as a playwright, Pan-Africanist, cricket correspondent, and Trotskyist. He made a powerful impression on a wide stratum of British society, and he had taken up a gamut of fascinating topics—African decolonization, Abyssinia, Haiti, Soviet foreign policy, the British labor movement, the relationship between Leninism and Stalinism, and the game of cricket. His intellectual debt to Trotsky was deep but not binding; he continued to read widely and develop his own political identity.

Driven by restlessness, curiosity, and ambition, James brought with him on the boat to America his charitable but strict moral outlook, his good humor, and his volumes of Shakespeare, Thackeray, Marx, and Lenin. It was the year of the reprieve: within twelve months Europe would be at war. Intending to return to Britain by May 1939 for the opening of the cricket season, he would end up staying in the United States for fifteen years.

PART TWO

Let us not forget that in the Negro people, there sleep and are now awakening passions of a violence exceeding . . . anything among the tremendous forces that capitalism has created. Anyone who knows them, who knows their history, is able to talk to them intimately, watches them at their own theaters, watches them at their dances, watches them in their churches, reads their press with a discerning eye, must recognize that although their social force may not be able to compare with the social force of a corresponding number of organized workers, the hatred of bourgeois society and the readiness to destroy it when the opportunity should present itself, rests among them to a degree greater than in any other section of the population of the United States.

—C. L. R. James, "The Revolutionary Answer to
the Negro Problem in the USA" (1948)

■
Education, Propaganda, Agitation

HAVING DECIDED TO TEMPORARILY relocate to America to serve the movement as a Trotskyist troubleshooter, C. L. R. James went on to become a central player in the country's peripheral far left. The bulk of his writing in this period was aimed at a relatively narrow audience—the "reading public" and periphery of the radical left, those who subscribed to *The New International*, *Labor Action* or who somehow became aware of the pamphlets of James's own semi-Trotskyist faction, the Johnson-Forest tendency. For over a decade he seemed to drop altogether the notion of being a traditional type of "writer" or "intellectual," concentrating instead on cajoling and organizing a tiny, radicalized minority of American workers into adopting a militant, socialist perspective.

The main incentive for taking this approach lay in the heroic expectations he quickly developed for his new homeland. For James, America held great promise on account of its brash people, lofty idealism, and dynamic popular culture. Independent movements of black, industrial and women workers enjoyed a special vitality and would, he wagered, play a pivotal role in the creation of a "new society." James saw the coming war—World War II—as a bellwether for an even bigger conflagration between capital and labor. In Trinidad, he matured as an individual and as a writer; in London, he had emerged as a political thinker and activist. As a West Indian New Yorker, James fashioned an idiosyncratic radicalism that was simultaneously Hegelian, Marxist, populist, and cultural. The importance of this period for James's intellectual and personal development cannot be overstated.[1]

As Scott McLemee has suggested, James's relocation to America "marks a profound shift in the coordinates of his personal identity."[2] New York may have been geographically closer to Port of Spain than London, but for a product of British colonial schools and Afro-Caribbean culture, the mannered English way of life would have been more familiar than the individualistic American. The United States—unlike Trinidad and Tobago, or Britain—lacked a viable social democratic movement or party. Even during the Depression, the socialist left enjoyed only a marginal presence in the country's benighted political culture. American politics reflected the country's exceptional ethnic, regional, and racial cleavages and conflicts. Perhaps the most obvious point of contrast was that in spatial terms the United States was apparently boundless, and in many places almost devoid of human settlement. It therefore seemed to lack the sort of social cohesion that characterized both West Indian and English society. The weight of history would have undoubtedly seemed slighter, and a tremendous sense of possibility and indeterminacy was likely to have struck the expatriate intellectual.[3]

As his personal letters reveal, the experience of traveling across the country and meeting ordinary Americans made a lasting impression on James. Anna Grimshaw and Keith Hart write: "Having already escaped from the confines of a small Caribbean island, he was now freed from the claustrophobia of a decaying Europe."[4] They go on to cite a passage from *Mariners, Renegades and Castaways* where he describes "my first journey from Chicago to Los Angeles by train—the apparently endless miles, hour after hour, all day and all night and the next morning the same again, until the evening. I experienced a sense of expansion which has permanently altered my attitude to the world."[5] This "sense of expansion" was accompanied by a sense of excitement and intellectual stimulation. Living in such a buoyant and chaotic society appealed to his imagination, to his ambition, and to his anthropological curiosity.

Far from being an America-basher, James harbored a deep attachment to the country's popular culture—its movies, comic strips, genre fiction, radio plays, and popular music. Even after a grueling internment on Ellis Island, at the height of the anti-Communist scare, he told two of his American friends that "at the present moment the feeling that I have and the memory of life in the United States are expressed most concretely in gramophone records, jazz records in particular and movies. Real, ordinary commonplace movies."[6] Partly as a result of his uncertain status as an illegal alien, James was more cloistered than before in the sense that his writings and lectures were almost exclusively aimed at the cognoscenti. At the same time, however, his work and activities in this period displayed an uncommon openness to new ideas and new experiences. His commitment to and understanding of socialist politics and philosophy deepened at the same time that his admiration for the world's most capitalistic nation grew. It was an unrequited love affair; the always cosmopolitan Trinidadian was able to make only the faintest imprint on a society that was essentially impervious to the most supple of Marxisms.

"It was only when I went to the United States," James later claimed, "that I really became active in those issues"—that is, comprehending and confronting racism.[7] As strategically critical as it no doubt was, the struggle against colonialism in the Caribbean did not necessarily invoke the same social dynamics as the struggle against racial segregation in the United States. Although James did not abandon his primary emphasis on class and class conflict, his experiences in the U.S. led him to revise—more than once—his conception of the dialectics of class, race, and capitalism. As a resident of the world's most populous free society, James was able to gain a firsthand sense of the intolerable conditions under which most blacks lived. For a period of time during the war he lived on 125th Street in Harlem, and for five months during 1941 he assisted striking sharecroppers in southeast Missouri. While on a lecture tour for the Socialist Workers Party in 1938 he met with members of the National Association for the Advancement of Colored People (NAACP) and lunched with journalists at the black-owned Pittsburgh *Courier*; after the 1939 visit with Leon Trotsky in Mexico he returned to New York City by bus from New Orleans. What appears to have struck him most was the unresolved character of race relations in America, the underlying resentment of the black population, and at the same time the need for institution building and consciousness raising among all oppressed sectors of society.

James also commented, in private correspondence, on "the feeling of uncertainty" (read: anxiety) that his first direct contact with the American South provoked within him. Arriving into the New Orleans harbor on a Mexican steamer, he revealed his concerns in a letter to Constance Webb:

There are taxis for white and taxis for black, and as few blacks travel
by this boat there will be no taxis for them and I shall have to tele-
phone for one. So that is my introduction to the South. People have
been warning me and I said, "Oh, I'll manage," perhaps with too
much confidence. If I were an American citizen I wouldn't care, but
if I get into any trouble with the police bang go my hopes for a further extension of my visa and re-entry after a little trip abroad.
Strange, as I near the actual contact, I begin to feel a slight nervous-
ness. I shall get through of course, unless someone goes out of his
way to annoy me, but the feeling of uncertainty shows me how terribly the minds and characters of Negroes must be affected, especially those with no experience or political or historical background
to help them, or no consciousness of a way out.[8]

As someone who had the requisite Marxist training, James was
already familiar with the history of black nationalist movements that
had flourished in the early years of the twentieth century. He knew,
for example, about how radical veterans had organized a revolution-
ary-nationalist organization, the African Blood Brotherhood, in the
years following the end of World War I. The Brotherhood's newspaper, the *Crusader*, publicized the organization's armed defense of
Tulsa's embattled black community during the race riots of 1920.

Although James may not have met ex-Brotherhood activists, he
did speak with former members of Marcus Garvey's Universal Negro
Improvement Association, an organization whose avowed aim was
the establishment of a "universal confederacy among the race, to promote race pride and to administer to and assist the needy."[9] Garvey, a
Jamaican-born journalist and orator, built a Pan-African organization
which, by the mid-1920s, boasted of having over one thousand
branches on five continents. James was later to write that Marcus
Garvey made "the Negro people and the people of Africa an integral
part of world history, where they have remained ever since." It was
"the greatest propaganda feat of the twentieth century . . ."[10]

The very existence of an African Blood Brotherhood or the United
Negro Improvement Association suggested that in one form or
another black nationalism was a constant factor in African-American
politics. It was as a U.S. resident that James became cognizant of this
fact. He also became aware of the ambiguous legacy of the left's position on the "race question." He knew, for example, that Eugene Debs,
the charismatic leader of the pre-World War I Socialist Party, insisted

more than once that "we have nothing special to offer to the negro worker."[11] In a similar vein, the journalist John Reed told Comintern officials in 1920 that "the Negroes do not pose the demand for national independence. A movement which aims for a separate national existence like for instance the Back to Africa movement that could be observed a few years ago is never successful among the Negroes."[12] What Debs and Reed were reluctant to admit was that nationalistic slogans, such as calls for repatriation or autonomous homelands, were rooted in both symbolism and a material desire for political and social equality. "Back to Africa" was a metaphor as well as a program; a set of images as well as an agenda. Working-class unity, the traditional mantra of the American left, was no substitute for a historically grounded conception of the specific dynamics of black oppression and black politics.

Under Trotsky's and James's prodding, the Socialist Workers Party began to seek opportunities to intervene among black workers and intellectuals. The SWP had already achieved some success in the areas of union politics and New York intellectual life.[13] In 1938 the party had nearly one thousand adult members and several hundred supporters in the Young People's Socialist League. The party was able to attract thousands of people to hear the author of *The Black Jacobins* speak on the topic of "The British Empire." Martin Glaberman remembered the tour's first stop as a resounding success: "He was an honored visitor, a fabulous speaker . . . I remember the first time I ever saw him—it was a lecture at a hotel ballroom in New York, where he spoke for about three hours on the British Empire, walking back and forth across the stage without notes or anything else."[14] Frank Lovell, a longtime SWP member, wrote that James was "an impressive speaker with his British accent and his poise . . . It was as if he were a great actor delivering a famous oration."[15] *Socialist Appeal*, the party's weekly newspaper, boasted that "Scores of New York Negroes turned out to listen to one of the outstanding lecturers of their race . . ."[16] Constance Webb, who heard James speak in Los Angeles when she was a teenager, was as dazzled as anyone:

> He was over six feet two inches; slim, but not thin, with long legs. He walked easily, with his shoulders level. His head appeared to be on a stalk, held high with the chin tilted forward and up, which made it seem that his body was led by a long neck—curved forward like that of a racehorse on a slip. Shoulders, chest, and legs were

powerful and he moved decisively. But, as with highly trained athletes, the tension was concentrated and tuned, so that he gave the
impression of enormous ease. He was without self-consciousness,
simply himself, which showed in the way he moved, and one recognized a special quality.[17]

The tour gave this remarkable specimen a firsthand impression of
the American comrades in action; although he was impressed with
the youth and determination of those he met, he found the party deficient in terms of its understanding of "the Negro question." In a private letter he wrote,

> I am now certain that no one in America, none in the party, has ever
> seen the Negro question for the gigantic thing it is, and will increas-
> ingly be. L.T. [Leon Trotsky] sees it, I was groping towards it. I begin
> to see it now, everyday more clearly. The American Negroes touch
> on the one side the American proletariat, on whom so much depends
> in the present period; on the other they and not the British or French
> proletariat form the link with the African revolution; and they can
> form a link with the millions of Indians and Negroes and half-castes
> who form so much of the population of Spanish-America.[18]

Trotsky was to readily assent to James's essentially negative characterization of the party's Negro work when they spent several days
together in Coyoacan, Mexico, in 1939. In his preliminary remarks,
Trotsky said he believed that

> the first question is the attitude of the Socialist Workers Party
> towards the Negroes . . . The characteristic thing about American
> workers' organizations is their aristocratic character. It is the basis
> of opportunism. The skilled workers who feel set in the capitalist
> society held the bourgeois class to hold the Negroes and unskilled
> workers down to a very low scale . . . under this condition our party
> cannot develop—it will degenerate.[19]

In order to properly orient the party around this question, James
made several suggestions. Drawing up a program of internal education, he proposed that party members familiarize themselves with
black history and culture. He was particularly interested in the work
that the Communists had undertaken inside the black community,

and he recommended that party members become familiar with the research that Communist historians had done on slavery and the abolition movement.[20] The key point he wanted to get across was that the Trotskyist movement would have to concentrate more resources on the Negro question. After all, the black masses would play a critical role in the construction of a revolutionary alternative. As he outlined in a paper written for the Coyoacan meeting,

a) the Negro represents potentially the most revolutionary section of the population;
b) he is ready to respond to militant leadership;
c) he will respond to political situations abroad which concern him;
d) he is today more militant than ever.[21]

To bring large numbers of blacks into the party's orbit, James urged that the SWP take the lead in establishing an independent, all-black organization that would fight for civil rights. Blacks "have followed similar movements in the past," and "*are looking for a similar movement now,*" he argued. A new organization "has the possibility of setting the Negro masses in motion."[22] Through persistent activity around basic democratic and humanitarian demands—the right to vote; the integration of jobs, unions, schools and stores; and so on—such an organization could transform the American political landscape. Its formation would also heat up the class struggle and bring credit to the SWP, which would eschew a vanguard role in favor of a strategic alliance with a mass movement.

It should be noted that the Socialist Workers Party and its predecessors had never quite undertaken a project of this type before. In common with other small parties founded on Leninist principles, the SWP had established various "front groups" and had collaborated with nonparty forces around specific issues, such as strike support and antifascist mobilization. But James was proposing that the party should commit its resources to a long-term strategy where few immediate gains were likely. The point of such an exercise would be to facilitate the autonomous self-activity of the most militant section of the community, not to simply recruit more members into the SWP. It was a "transitional program" of another kind. To his credit, Trotsky agreed that the party's policy could not involve "simply passing through for a few weeks. It is a question of awakening the Negro masses . . ."[23] Far from being opposed to James's program, Trotsky was intrigued by the prospect of party members taking a bold initiative in this area. At the same time, he raised the practical matter of whether the SWP itself had the human resources to launch such a movement. "The question remains," he noted, "as to whether we can take upon ourselves the initiative of forming such an organization of Negroes for Negroes—not for the purpose of winning some elements to our party but for the purpose of doing systematic educational work in order to elevate them politically."[24]

The War, and a 1940 split inside the Socialist Workers Party, derailed any specific plans. But the Trotsky-James discussions had a salutary effect on the movement's appreciation for the need to develop a specific approach to black politics. The party's press began to cover issues of particular concern to African-Americans (partly through James's own column, "The Negro Question"), a Negro Department was set up and the party's political program was revised in accordance to the agenda discussed in Coyoacan. The fact that the SWP later sought to find common ground with Malcolm X, in the early 1960s, reflected Trotsky's sympathetic attitude toward black nationalism and his efforts to prod the party into action around the question of racism and white supremacy. SWP leader George Breitman played a particularly critical role in developing and clarifying the party's position along the lines suggested by the Trotsky-James dialogue.[25] Yet James brought an unorthodox perspective on the role of socialists in the struggle for African-American liberation. Trotsky unknowingly lent his imprimatur to a policy which would open the door to a sweeping assault on the Leninist theory of the vanguard party.

As the transcript reveals, Trotsky and James conducted an animated and friendly series of exchanges. Although their conversations focused on black politics, James and Trotsky also discussed the latter's criticisms of *World Revolution 1917–1936*, and the prospects for the fledgling Fourth International. However, the transcript of their conversation gives little indication of James's impending break with Trotskyism. Even a year after their meeting, James eulogized Trotsky in the following terms:

> [T]o appreciate his powers and his past, the enormous force of this many-sided and yet perfectly integrated personality, and to see him listening patiently to some inexperienced comrade putting forward his inexperienced ideas, to read letters in which he took up some apparently minor point and elaborated it meeting all possible objec-

tions one by one, was to have a great lesson in the difference
between the superficial arrogance which often characterizes essentially sensitive men, and the ocean of strength, patience and resil-
iency which can come from complete devotion to a cause.[26]

However consistent with the viewpoint expressed in *World Revolution*, this tone was hardly in keeping with what would become a pronounced antipathy to Trotsky's political method and legacy. This
more critical perspective emerged in the early 1940s, in the context
of the collaborative work he undertook in developing an independent
Marxist conception of social emancipation. James was later to claim
that "Trotsky, who had isolated himself from Lenin's *concrete* struggle,
made *no* contribution to the struggle for international socialism. On
every serious point he was wrong."[27] In another context, he conceded
that "Trotsky understood as few men have ever done the creative
power of the proletariat in revolution," but went on to observe that
"the full, the complete significance of the creative power of the proletariat in the construction of the socialist economy always eluded
him."[28] As we have seen, this was not his attitude in 1939. There is
every indication that during their conversations in Mexico James was
attentive to the nuances of Trotsky's analysis. But his objections to
specific aspects of Trotskyist politics would soon become apparent.

Returning to New York, James began writing for *Socialist Appeal*
and the SWP's theoretical journal, *New International* ("a monthly
organ of revolutionary Marxism"). His articles played a significant
role in articulating the party's opposition to the war, which James
regarded as an interimperialist quarrel over the contours of political
power in the second half of the twentieth century. Neither the Allies
nor the Axis powers were fighting for the liberation of industrial
workers or Third World peoples. "Democracy," he averred, "has
nothing to do with this war," and nothing good would come out of it:
"A worldwide crisis, thirty million unemployed, fascism and imperialist war—that is what they the capitalists have to offer. They must be
broken, and only the workers' revolution can break them."[29] The
Trotskyist position was one of "revolutionary defeatism"—a call for
soldiers, sailors, and workers to turn their weapons against the bourgeoisie of all countries. As appalling as Hitler and the Nazis were,
their kind could only be defeated through a European-wide uprising
"from below." Implicated in the evils of colonialism, racial segregation, and capitalist exploitation, the Allied powers could not be

expected to carry out the sweeping changes needed to wipe out the scourge of fascism. The role of the Trotskyists would be to link the war against fascism to the struggle against capitalism.

The Socialist Workers Party's ability to implement a policy of revolutionary defeatism was severely handicapped by a damaging internal faction fight that led to the formation of a rival Trotskyist group, the Workers Party, in 1940. The chief issue at stake concerned the class character of the Soviet Union and the appropriate attitude that revolutionaries were supposed to adopt toward the world's only self-proclaimed "workers' state." While Trotsky urged Fourth Internationalists to offer a resolute "defense" of the Soviet Union (not for its internal policies but in the event that the USSR was attacked by the capitalist states), many of his followers were leery of lending any sort of support to the Communist camp.

In fact, differences over "the Russia question" had been simmering for several years, as had personal tensions between party leaders James P. Cannon and Max Shachtman. However, Cannon had managed to maintain an acceptable level of party discipline throughout the 1930s by appealing to Trotsky's personal authority and by building up a cadre of militants who were steadfastly loyal to the party regime. Cannon's efficient but sometimes heavy-handed leadership style quickly became a central issue in the faction fight. A more conciliatory approach on Cannon's part might have prevented a profound rupture in what was at the time the world's largest Trotskyist formation. Yet Cannon and Trotsky were united in their belief that it was critical that the party hold fast to its "orthodox" position on the Russia question.

The emergence of an anti-Cannon faction inside the SWP was more or less given once events in the real world ensured that ideological cracks within the party could no longer be papered over. Specifically, the Hitler-Stalin Pact (which Trotsky had predicted), and the Soviet invasion of Finland of 1939, seemed to undermine Trotsky's view that the Soviet Union was a progressive historical force vis-a-vis liberal capitalism. Led by a triumvirate with deep roots in the radical movement—Max Shachtman, a noted orator, James Burnham, professor of philosophy at New York University, and Martin Abern, a longtime party officer—the Socialist Workers Party minority argued that the USSR could no longer be characterized, as Trotsky maintained, as a "degenerated workers' state." Although James was initially critical of both factions, on the grounds that a split would be "irresponsible,"[30] he soon sided with the Shachtman minority and traveled to Los Angeles "to present the minority viewpoint to the western comrades."[31] It was during this period that James began working with Raya Dunayevskaya, a dedicated and brilliant Russian-born intellectual who had served as a translator and personal secretary to Trotsky and who encouraged James to stay in the United States and work on developing a state capitalist perspective on the Soviet Union and an independent perspective on revolutionary strategy.

While many of the party's trade union cadre sided with Cannon, most of the younger members joined the minority camp. The minority was particularly successful in attracting a sizable number of young Jews who were in and around the milieu of the so-called New York Intellectuals.[32] Compelled to devise a positive alternative to the orthodox Trotskyist position (which he had developed strong doubts about by 1937–1938), Shachtman helped to clarify the theory of "bureaucratic collectivism," which described the Soviet Union as an antidemocratic regime of a new type, neither capitalist nor socialist. The two sides could now be clearly differentiated on the basis of their incompatible perspectives on the Russia question. Furthermore, all sides believed that it was vital that a revolutionary organization maintain a proper attitude with regards to this question. This consensus made a split of some kind almost inevitable. But Cannon insisted that the main issue was not the minority faction's hastily formulated position on the USSR, but was that faction's dubious class character—specifically, its roots in the urbanized middle strata with weak links to the proletariat. He warned that, "with the approach of war Trotskyism as a doctrine and as a movement began to lose its 'respectability'," and emphasized the fact that "our party membership consists in part of petty-bourgeois elements, completely disconnected from the proletarian class struggle . . ."[33]

This effectively reduced the split to a question of objective class relations. But of course Cannon's implicit identification of the "proletarian class struggle" with the Socialist Workers Party majority was nothing more than a tired conceit. He seemed to acknowledge no role for honest intellectual debate in the sphere of revolutionary politics. The uncompromising Trotskyist leader was right, however, to suggest that the coming war would drastically alter the political climate in America. Despite the Constitution's First Amendment, eighteen SWP leaders, including Cannon, would be imprisoned in 1944 under the Smith Act for their antiwar stance. (The Communist Party enthusiastically gave its blessing to this and other government clampdowns on wartime dissent.)

Motivated by a desire to build a "small mass party" that could ultimately replace the Communist Party as the main force on the left, hundreds of "petty-bourgeois" members of the new "Shachtmanite" organization took blue-collar jobs during World War II. Their strategy, known as "proletarianization," was to place their cadre in the core sectors of the economy, especially where the methods of production had collected together the largest concentrations of workers (such as shipyards, auto plants, steel mills, and so on).[34] Shachtman's Workers Party had been formally inaugurated in April 1940 at a conference attended by some eight hundred people. Walking out of the SWP, the Shachtman-Burnham-Abern minority ended up taking nearly half the organization with them. At the party's first convention, it was agreed that the Workers Party would constitute the foundation of a new revolutionary socialist party, one that was internally democratic, principled in its opposition to the war, and equally critical of Western capitalism and Soviet bureaucratic collectivism. The new, neo-Trotskyist organization attracted a throng of intellectuals and writers who had been previously in the orbit of the SWP, such as Saul Bellow, Hal Draper, James T. Farrell, Irving Howe, and B. J. Widick. Draper, Howe, and Widick were all active in the new organization. For a short period, Dwight MacDonald, the essayist and an editor of *Partisan Review*, lent his support to the Workers Party after having become disillusioned with the small-mindedness that characterized the orthodox Trotskyists:

> I must confess I often felt like Alice. Comrade Cannon has some resemblance to the Caterpillar Alice found sitting on a mushroom serenely smoking a hookah:
>
> "Are you content now?" said the Caterpillar.
>
> "Well, I should like to be a little larger sir, if you wouldn't mind," said Alice. "Three inches is such a wretched height to be."
>
> "It is a very good height indeed!" said the Caterpillar angrily, rearing itself upright as it spoke (it was exactly three inches high).[35]

James was far more committed to the utopia of a communist revolution than either Burnham or MacDonald, whom he dismissed as a "counterrevolutionary songbird."[36] Indeed, he disdained all but the youngest and most radical of the Workers Party's intellectuals, and effectively turned his back on the world of *Partisan Review* and the New York Intellectuals. Characterized by an attachment to Freudian analysis, a fundamentally liberal-Left sensibility, and an ever-deepening connection to the literary establishment, this celebrated subculture seemed to have left him cold. He maintained friendly relations with a handful of individuals—such as Meyer Schapiro, the erudite Marxist art critic—but his relationships with others, particularly the pugnacious Irving Howe, deteriorated over time as political differences became transformed into personal animosities. With regard to some of the less self-consciously political members of the *Partisan Review* crowd, such as the poet Delmore Schwartz, he seemed largely indifferent.[37]

His evident preference was to collaborate with the theoretician Raya Dunayevskaya, auto worker Martin Glaberman, and a small number of others. Eschewing the intelligentsia's "little magazines"— and also mass market publications—he concentrated on generating articles for the Trotskyist press as a way of circulating his ideas. After James's visa ran out, he was forced to go underground and was effectively barred from speaking at public gatherings. One of his very last public addresses was delivered for the Workers Party in the winter of 1940, shortly after France had been overrun by the Nazis. It appeared that Germany would soon control all of Europe—and despite the WP's antiwar perspective, party members were of course horrified at the spectacle of a European fascist juggernaut. Shachtman asked James to talk about what was happening in Europe. Conrad Lynn, a black lawyer who was later active in the civil rights movement, remembered this talk vividly many years later:

> C. L. R. James was the only speaker, and he was magnificent. His address lasted seventy-five minutes, and he seemed equally at home in English, Yiddish [!], and French . . . Never had I witnessed such a performance. James proved despite all appearances Hitler could not win.
>
> The meeting unanimously delegated to James the authority to write the entire next issue of *New International*. It was entitled "Capitalist Society and the War" and it must be a bibliophile's prize now.[38]

Another bibliophile's prize is *"My Friends": A Fireside Chat on the War*, by "Native Son" which the Workers Party issued in June 1940 and which sold for a penny. The author's alias, one of James's more obscure pseudonyms, was taken from Richard Wright's novel *Native Son*, while the title makes reference to President Roosevelt's famous radio broadcasts. A fierce polemic aimed at black workers, the pamphlet opens with a stirring poem by the West Indian writer Claude McKay ("If We Must Die"),[39] and is written from the standpoint of a married "black working man" whose "people were here as early as the family of President Roosevelt."[40] Posing the question "Is America in Danger?," Native Son answers that the real danger comes from within, from "Senator Bilbo, Vice-President Garner, all of them aided by you, President Roosevelt for all of you are in one Party together, the Democratic Party . . ."[41] As the author goes on to insist: "When we have defeated the enemies of democracy here, then we can give Hitler a beating."[42] This passionate but odd and strangely disingenuous pamphlet ends on the following note: "I went to the last war. I was treated like a dog before I went. I was treated like a dog while I was there. I was treated like a dog when I returned. I have been played for a sucker before, and I am not going to be played again."[43] On the next page, an advertisement for the Workers Party summarizing the party's position on Negro equality.[44]

It was in this period that C. L. R. adopted "J. R. Johnson" as his primary *nom de plume*. He seemed almost proud of his marginal, underground existence, evidently shedding whatever interest in broad influence or literary prominence he may have once had. At the same time, he felt thwarted by the fact that he could no longer address public meetings, as much of his intellectual inspiration had previously come from lecturing to diverse audiences. His status as a semifugitive served to confirm the seriousness of his commitment to Marxism, but it also meant that he had little money or personal security. James sounded a little conflicted when talking about his own life in a letter written to Constance Webb in 1943:

> These last three years have been the most exciting intellectually of my life . . . I have aged a little—grayer in the temples, a little thinner, not much, a little more serious, a few lines in my face; my hands are more nervous than before, but I am much the same, quieter externally, more explosive inside; and very sure of what I am doing politically—of myself as a person, doubtful and more than a little worried as to my future.[45]

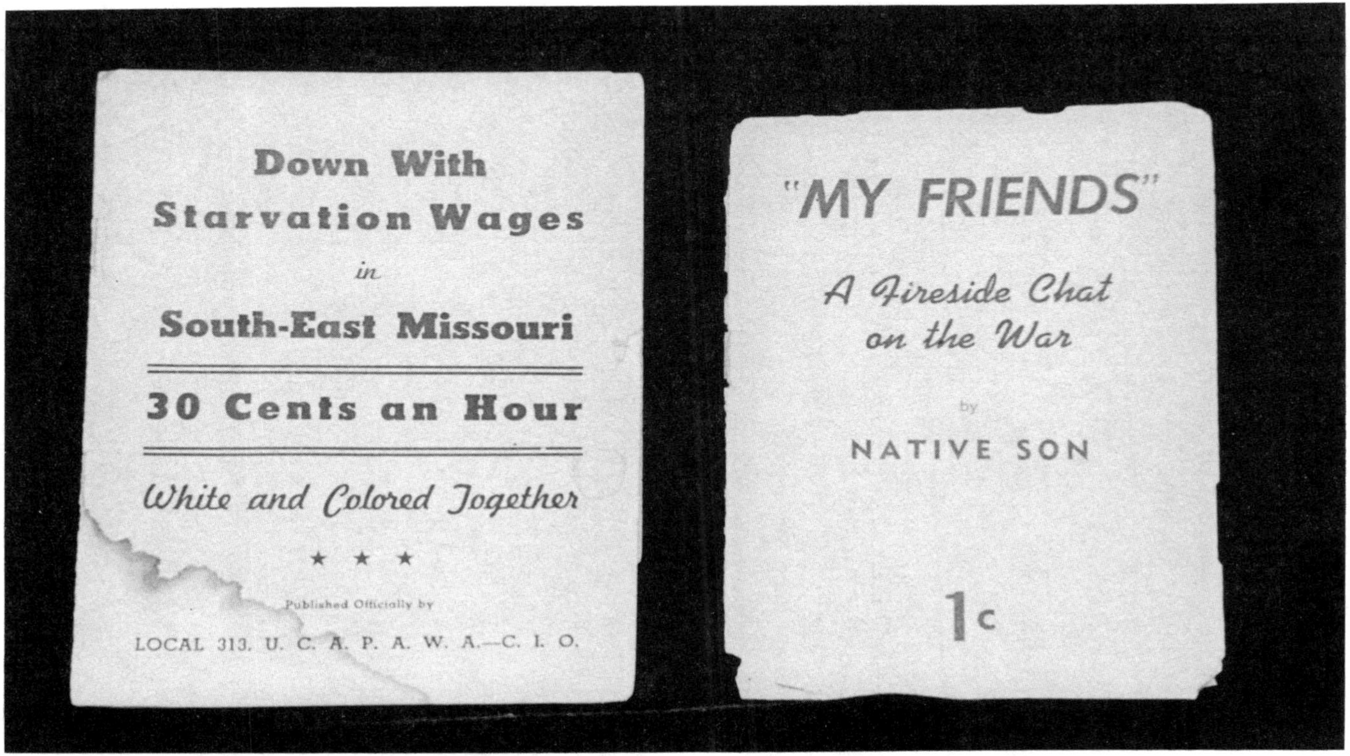

"MY FRIENDS"

A Fireside Chat
on the War

by

NATIVE SON

1c

Down With
Starvation Wages

in

South-East Missouri

30 Cents an Hour

White and Colored Together

★ ★
★ ★
★ ★

Published Officially by

LOCAL 313. U. C. A. P. A. W. A.—C. I. O.

Pamphlet covers—1940 to 1941
Photo: Jon Anderson

In an earlier letter he sounded somewhat fierce, and sly:

> I am a rather unusual combination, I am 40 odd and have obviously
> traveled and seen the world and read a great deal—and at the same
> time in my attitude to life and my outlook I am quite young, do not
> live in the past at all and haven't the faintest trace of complaint
> against the world though I know it for what it is.[46]

One senses that James was more open about his private feelings
with Constance Webb than with other comrades and friends. Constance played an absolutely pivotal role in James's life in this period;
their correspondence, which began in 1939, generated literally hundreds of letters and thousands of pages of handwritten text, by the
late 1940s. As Selwyn Cudjoe has noted, "[w]hen one realizes the
physical pain James underwent when he used a pen . . . it dawns on
the reader that writing these letters was a monumental task of love
and devotion."[47] Although many of the letters addressed questions of
political theory or literature, James used his considerable composi-
tional skills to flatter and court the young woman, who was just starting out on a career as a model, actress, and writer. Vowing to be a
good husband and to instruct her in the inner workings of the dialectic, James married Constance Webb in May 1946 and again in 1948,
when the divorce from Juanita Young James was officially recognized
by the U.S. immigration authorities. Apart from rare exceptions such
as those noted here, however, James rarely reflected on his own
mood, preferring instead to adopt the famous reserve of the hard-bit-
ten revolutionary (and, not coincidently, of the English gentleman).

Life was never more uncertain than when James spent five
months in Missouri engaged in strike support work. The Workers
Party's St. Louis branch had made contact with a handful of black
sharecroppers and union activists in the southern part of the state. By
1941 a strike was likely, and James traveled from New York to cover
the story for the WP newspaper *Labor Action*. In late May, some 8,000
members of Local 313 of the United Cannery, Agricultural, Packing
and Allied Workers of America went on strike for thirty cents an
hour, forty-five cents an hour for tractor drivers, and time-and-a-half
for overtime (after ten hours). The standard rate of pay in the fields
had been a desultory $1.25 per day. Despite the reasonableness of the
strikers' claims, the Cannery union's national leadership was at best
lukewarm about the strike. Like that of other left-led Congress of

Industrial Organizations (CIO) unions at that time, the union's leadership was aligned with the Communist Party, which was committed to the war effort and was strongly inclined to oppose disruptive strikes. This gave James and the Workers Party an interesting angle to pursue as they labored to help the strikers.

James had written that "the Negroes try to organize themselves and must be aided in the attempts to prepare a strike force."[48] He had meant this generally, but could now apply the idea in practice. Forging the all-black organization that Trotsky had supported was hardly in the cards, but black discontent still existed, and it could be inflamed. James described a meeting he had with the activist leadership of Local 313:

> I called some of the leaders together and said, "We have to publish something, for everyone to read about it." They said yes. So I sat down with my pen and notebook and said, "Well, what should we say?" So (I used to call myself Williams) they said, "Well brother Williams, you know." I said, "I know nothing. This is your strike." . . . and I went to each of them, five or six of them; each said his piece and I joined them together.[49]

Hundreds of copies of the resultant pamphlet, *Down With Starvation Wages in Southeast Missouri*, found their way to sharecroppers, union activists, church leaders, and other concerned parties throughout the middle West.[50] Small enough to fit into a back pocket (the pamphlet was only six inches long and four and a half inches wide), *Down With Starvation Wages* was written in an accessible, anecdotal style. It sold for a penny. A section addressed to rural preachers read:

> All the Preachers must get their flock together and preach to them about the union and solidarity in the struggle. If a preacher is not with us he is against us. That is the voice of scripture. Also the laborer is worthy of his hire. That is scripture also . . . Solidarity in the union, that is the way to get the Kingdom of Heaven upon earth.[51]

The section labeled "To The Merchants" hit a plaintive note:

> We say to the merchants: Why don't you support us? Every penny we get we spend with you. We cannot save anything. If we get 30

cents an hour it means we are able to buy a little more lard, a little
more bread, a piece of meat once a week while the money lasts. After
that we'll starve again. But it all goes to the merchant, to raise his
income. So we look to the merchant, especially the little merchant,
to support us, and stand by us if we are compelled to strike. If during
the strike we ask for a little credit, then the merchant must give it.[52]

But winning the strike took more than polemics. The national union
was grudging in its support, the Farm Security Administration was
sympathetic to the cotton landlords, and the local press was openly
hostile to trade unionism in any form. Despite the forces arrayed
against them, however, the strikers won their demands after eleven
weeks. The cause of their victory was the fact that the landlords were
desperate that the crops be harvested before abundant weeds stran-
gled the fields of cotton. Local 313 had secured the first rank-and-file
union victory since the start of the war. *Labor Action's* on-the-scene
reporter returned to New York a hero among comrades.[53]

The sharecroppers' strike seemed to confirm the wisdom of the
perspective James had outlined in his meetings with Trotsky. The strike
suggested that certain sectors were ready to channel their frustration
and anger into class-based mobilization. Of great symbolic significance
was the fact that James had written down the sharecroppers' words,
rather than formulating their demands. The strike's successful conclusion seemed to validate his overall approach. The sharecroppers—
overwhelmingly but not exclusively black—forged alliances with
trade unionists in St. Louis as well as Protestant congregations across
Missouri. In a small way the strike "intervened with terrific force upon
the general social and political life of the nation."[54]

The trip to Missouri also confirmed what had been obvious since
Coyoacan: James's Pan-Africanism had devolved into a specific concern with African-American politics and culture. This is not to suggest that James was no longer a Pan-Africanist, since the question of
the history and social movements of American blacks were important
from the standpoint of the entire African diaspora. But in America he
was more than a New York-based correspondent for *International
African Opinion*—although he informally served in that capacity until
the International African Service Bureau's journal folded as a result of
wartime paper shortages[55]—he was a serious student of black America. This became evident not only in his discussions with Trotsky and
work in Missouri but in the voluminous documents he generated on

the subject for *Labor Action* and the WP's journal *New International*. (After the 1940 split, the SWP launched a new journal, *Fourth International*, while the Shachtmanites retained control over the *New International*. James contributed over twenty articles to the postsplit *New International* between 1940 and 1947.)

James's journalism was animated by the same optimistically "proautonomy" framework that characterized his whole approach to the race question in America. In his regular column "One Tenth the Nation" (also called "The Negro Fight") he discussed novels, segregation, industrial relations, relations between the sexes, and whatever else happened to be in the news. A recurrent motif was that American society was due for a major shakeup. Nothing was static. Blacks were arriving at a new stage of self-awareness, and sooner or later would move in the direction of independent political action. Certainly the Democrats seemed incapable of providing any kind of leadership in the area of civil rights. Through concrete activity, blacks would discover their collective power and find their natural allies. The logic of the struggle would teach African-Americans about politics, about class politics, and about socialism. In effect, the multifaceted movement toward freedom—and not the vanguard party—would produce the next generation of revolutionaries, black and white.

James recognized that many obstacles lay on the road to social and political equality. One of his characteristic themes was that racial prejudice was deeply ingrained in the culture. "In books and magazines," he pointed out, "all grace, strength, beauty, nobility, courage are automatically attributed to members of the white race . . . If he [the black man] is included, he is placed in his usual menial position, made the butt of jokes or at best portrayed as a good and loyal servant."[56] Other articles concerned important figures in black history. Given the formative impact of the *Negro World* on his political development, and his overall sympathy for all-black organizations and programs, it seems surprising that he engaged in a bitter polemic against Marcus Garvey:

> Garvey, however, was a race fanatic. His appeal was to black against white. He wanted purity of race. A great part of his propaganda was based on the past achievements of blacks . . . With that disregard of facts which characterizes the born demagogue, he proclaimed that there were 400 million Negroes in the world, when there are cer-

tainly not half as many. What does this remind us of? Who but
Adolf Hitler?[57]

Despite his sympathetic theoretical framework, he had never adopted
a black nationalist approach, and had always been critical of Garvey's
political practice. James offered a more characteristic view of Garvey's
contribution many years later, however:

> Marcus Garvey was not a scholarly man, he was careless in the
> things he said. He used to say "400 million Negroes"—multiplying
> the number by two. That is okay with me; he could have multiplied
> by three as far as I am concerned. He was saying something that had
> to be said.[58]

One of the ingredients that went into James's work on black politics was his frank anti-Stalinism. Unlike later historians of the so-
called revisionist school,[59] or indeed many minorities in the United
States and elsewhere who were then active on the left, James regarded
the policies of the Communist Party as an unmitigated disaster, especially for blacks and workers. As he wrote in *The New International*,
the "policy of Stalinism in regard to the working masses everywhere
is universally recognized as a policy of *manipulation*."[60] The party
trained its cadre to lie to outsiders and to bully new members; the
party falsely claimed that there was no racial prejudice in the Soviet
Union; and the party represented bureaucratic tyranny as socialist
liberation. As the branch office of an international conspiracy, the
American CP stood for ideological conformity, the betrayal of the
working class, and the political economy of state capitalism. For
James and others on the anti-Stalinist Left, Communism remained a
"pernicious"[61] impediment to the development of a genuinely radical
alternative. In this view, the fact that the party curbed its rhetoric in
favor of a tacit alliance with liberals through the stratagem of the Popular Front changed nothing. The Popular Front was itself a cynical
deception that had nothing to do with empowering the masses and
everything to do with considerations of international relations and
statecraft.

   As a result of his unblemished anti-Stalinism, James was characteristically suspicious when it came to the influence of the CP in the
literary, arts, and black communities. An admiring review of Richard
Wright's *Native Son* (1940) suggests the tenor of James's approach. As

a novelist, Wright clearly exhibited tremendous potential, and James went out of his way to praise the young author's somber, naturalistic work. But James also warned that Wright's talents would be "blighted" if he continued to participate in the activities of the Communist Party. "Wright is a Stalinist," he wrote, and in that "evil garden, nothing creative flourishes. The artist in uniform soon ceases to be an artist. The Stalinists are past masters in the art of enveloping, suborning, corrupting. It will be a pity if they succeed in perverting and blighting this splendid talent."[62] These gloomy lines were penned at a time when the Communist Party was approaching the peak of its influence in the United States—as a political organization, and as a constitutive element in the "progressive" current in the fields of literature, culture, and the media. Yet once he became famous, Wright's party membership represented a special coup. The evident appeal of the Communist movement for figures such as Wright and Paul Robeson must have been grating for an anti-Stalinist like James. A bittersweet interest (some would argue obsession) in the party's malign impact on the cultural community was to become a hallmark of the Workers Party itself.

Richard Wright had joined the Communist Party in Chicago in 1934, at the height of the Depression, and he was active in a couple of Communist literary groups, although he was never entirely reconciled to the party's dogmatic and authoritarian style. Wright's private break from the party finally came in 1942 and was announced with the publication of "I Tried to be a Communist," which appeared in the *Atlantic* magazine in the summer of 1944.

Not coincidentally, this was the same period that Constance and C. L. R. spent a great deal of time in the company of the ex-Communist author and his wife, Ellen. The Wrights introduced Constance and her future spouse to the group Richard called his "thinking coterie,"[63] whose members included sociologists Horace Cayton and St. Clair Drake,[64] novelists Ralph Ellison and Chester Himes, and others such as Manet Fowler, E. Franklin Frazier, Lawrence D. Reddick, and Melvin B. Tolson.[65]

By the mid-1940s, Constance Webb had become interested in her own writing projects. One project drew on these new friendships and took the form of an untitled, 150-page pamphlet that Constance and C. L. R. circulated in 1944. The pamphlet came in two parts: (a) "a hitherto unpublished manuscript by Richard Wright, being a continuation of *Black Boy*"; and (b) "notes preliminary to a fuller study of the work of Richard Wright by Constance Webb."[66] While *Black Boy: A Record of Childhood and Youth* had been published by Harper and Brothers in 1945, this edition contained only the first half ("Southern Night") of a longer manuscript, *American Hunger*, that was eventually published in its entirety in 1977. Webb's 1944 pamphlet made available to a select few a lengthy extract from the second half of Wright's manuscript, which Wright titled "The Honor and the Glory," and which recounted the author's experiences in Chicago and with the Communist Party. It had been excised from the 1945 edition after editors at the Book of the Month Club had objected to the manuscript's length.

Webb's preliminary notes chart Wright's lonely passage from Communism to existentalism, locating interesting parallels between his early fiction and that of Chester Himes, who, at that time, seemed to express a greater openness to the ideals of revolutionary socialism. Her main argument is that Wright's unhappy turn toward existentialism reflected a wider difficulty, one facing a number of black secular intellectuals who had become disenchanted with Communism. She writes:

> The Communist Party gave Wright the first sustained relationships to his life. They showed him the ideals of future collective living embodied in an immediate community life with other members. And more important than anything else, they linked up the collective life on a local scale with the lives of millions of rebellious and persecuted people all over the world . . . [But] [t]hey crushed every hope they had awakened. Unlike white liberal intellectuals who rejoin society when they become disillusioned, Wright the Negro has nowhere to go; he retreats into himself. Into the circle of absolute loneliness; the area of dread, anguish and psychic pain.[67]

With its references to "dread," and "psychic pain," this passage very likely draws on conversations that Webb herself had with the novelist. But the counsel proffered in the pamphlet—that Wright should find a way to align himself with the cause of organized labor—artlessly presupposed that working-class politics constituted the only true path to personal happiness.[68]

It was in this period that Wright and his friend Horace Cayton talked about launching a journal of black opinion, which Wright wanted to call *American Pages*, with the subtitle: *A Magazine Reflect-*

ing a Minority Mood and Point of View. Nonpartisan, non-political, espousing no current creed, ideology or organization.[69] To raise interest in the project, they talked to a number of friends and potential contributors, such as James, Ralph Ellison, James T. Farrell, Bernard Wolfe, and others.[70]

The prospective editors started from the assumption that black writers and readers needed an independent outlet for their diverse opinions, one that was not affiliated with either the Communist or Democratic parties. At the same time, the journal would also have been aimed at enlightened whites, such as James T. Farrell. As Webb noted in her biography of Wright, *American Pages* was to have featured a Jamesian-style compendium of "fiction, articles, essays, poetry, cartoons, profiles of individuals who lived 'the American way' such as Frank Sinatra, Gene Krupa, Frances Farmer; surveys on race tensions, popularly written, excerpts from novels which revealed the American scene, studies of crime and criminals, black and white."[71] The lengthy subtitle given to *American Pages* connotes the opinion-and-culture blend pioneered by the newspaper *Correspondence*, which James, Dunayevskaya, and several dozen of their supporters produced after leaving the Trotskyist movement in the early 1950s. Richard Wright and Horace Cayton also talked to Ralph Ellison and James about working together on a book project, to be titled *The Negro Speaks*.[72]

Although Richard Wright never expressed any interest in joining the Workers Party, he was certainly friendly with one of its leading (albeit dissident) members. Their proposed collaborations never really got off the ground, however, in part because of Ellen and Richard's restlessness, which led to their departure for Paris in 1947.[73] Financial considerations similarly constrained the circle's ambitions. An additional factor was the fact that some of James's political associates feared that these projects would distract him from the more important task of reconstructing Marxism. Finally, Wright may have come to appreciate that the gulf between his own existentialism and James's Hegelian neo-Trotskyism, was virtually insurmountable.

Although in one way or another James was spending a considerable amount of time observing the African-American community and immersing himself in black culture, he was unable to find a way of addressing a mass black audience. The closest he came was via the Workers Party's newspaper, *Labor Action*, which enjoyed a circulation of tens of thousands of copies—it was distributed free of charge at dozens of factories throughout California, the industrial Midwest, and the Northeast—and whose wartime readership reflected the incomplete integration of large-scale manufacturing.[74] James's more theoretical contributions, however, published in *New International* and in internal bulletins, reached only a few hundred people.

Yet his interventions inside the American Trotskyist movement allowed James to refine the analysis that he had first advanced in Coyoacan. Two interventions are of particular note. The first took place in 1944, when the Workers Party sponsored an internal debate over whether racial integration or James's pro-autonomy perspective was the correct revolutionary position. The circle around Max Shachtman were concerned that James had a tendency to push the "independent organization" perspective on black politics too far. These leaders wondered what the connection was between autonomous black struggles and the goal of forging a multiracial revolutionary organization. *Labor Action* adopted the slogan "black and white, unite and fight!" whereas the position of James and his comrades inside the Workers Party—the Johnson-Forest tendency, which had been constituted in 1941 as a result of the collaborations of James ("Johnson") and Dunayevskaya ("Forest") to advance the theory of state capitalism and develop Marxist theory and practice—was that blacks would have to form their own, black-led organizations to advance their particular interests.

Arguing on behalf of the traditional socialist approach was Ernest McKinney, a journalist who had been politically active for several decades. McKinney, who was black, had extensive experience with the trade union movement, and was employed by the party on a full-time basis to work on labor issues. Writing under the *nom de plume* "David Coolidge," McKinney argued that racial animus would slowly dissipate as the U.S. workforce was integrated through the application of capitalist technology. He further asserted that struggles for civil rights had no intrinsically leftist or revolutionary character. As McKinney wrote:

> Under the present leadership, white or Negro, the struggle is and will be carried on entirely within the framework of bourgeois democracy and capitalism. The program of this leadership does not include a struggle against capitalism now or in the future . . .

He warned:

> The WP is not unaware that Negroes have been indoctrinated with ideas of racial separation, racial sufficiency, and racial autarchy. These dogmas have paraded under a banner labeled "race consciousness." The most extreme form of this is promulgated by the advocates of black chauvinism or Negro-Nationalism.[75]

The harshness of McKinney's contribution (which was reprinted in *New International*), reflected his concern that the "Johnsonite" position sanctioned a kind of reverse racism which romanticized black movements and downplayed the class struggle. He was pessimistic as to whether blacks would come to an anticapitalist perspective unless they were guided by an explicitly socialist organization armed with a revolutionary program, such as the Workers Party. And he saw civil rights leaders as wielding a troublesome influence on black consciousness. Along with other WP cadre, McKinney believed that autonomous black struggles constituted a particular type of threat to the task of consolidating revolutionary forces in America.

James's views were quite different. Building on the 1939 conversations with Trotsky, McKinney's adversary predicted that "To the degree that the Negroes are more integrated into the unions [and industry] their consciousness of racial oppression and their resentment against it become greater, not less." Race-based discrimination would not end with the integration of America's work places. *Pace* McKinney, the apparently prosaic struggle for civil and political rights had a revolutionary dimension: "the Negro struggle for democratic rights is not a concession that Marxists make to the Negroes. In the United States today this struggle is a direct part of the struggle for socialism."[76]

In tackling unjust laws, backward attitudes, and discriminatory practices, black protesters would find themselves challenging the very edifice of American capitalism. The "natural excess of the desire for equality" that James identified in black nationalist ideology contained the seeds of a far-reaching indictment of American society. If McKinney was right, then virtually any expression of black pride hindered class unity; the job of socialists would be to work inside the trade union movement and push for the integration of industry. On the other hand, if James was right, then even an imperfect black nationalism could ignite and deepen social antagonisms and thereby contribute to "the struggle for socialism." The implication of the latter perspective was that Trotskyists would have to learn how to work

alongside an entire constellation of groups and movements struggling for social emancipation.

Two years after this inconclusive debate took place, the grouping
around Dunayevskaya and James bolted from the Workers Party, and
after a few months of independent activity, applied to join the Socialist Workers Party in late 1947. (A good percentage of the group's
members had been active in the SWP before the 1940 split, and were
familiar with the strengths and weaknesses of Cannon's organization.) James, Dunayevskaya, and the others convinced themselves
that in its own, somewhat crude fashion the SWP was still committed to revolutionary politics. After the war had ended the SWP had
predicted that a new upsurge in union militancy and social conflict
was on the way. This was also the position of the Johnson-Forest
tendency, and the Socialist Workers Party had been making secretive
overtures to the embattled WP faction for some time—even as it was
considering a merger with the Shachtmanites. SWP leaders were particularly concerned about the difficulty the party was having in
recruiting and retaining black members. With James's expertise on
the question of black politics and with their natural interest in adding new members, inducting the Johnson-Forest tendency into the
party was an especially attractive prospect to the Cannonites. Martin
Glaberman characterized the SWP in this period as "going through a
tremendous crisis on the Negro question, so they . . . really welcomed James, who gave the report on black politics at the next convention."[77]

James's convention document, "The Revolutionary Answer to the
Negro Problem in the USA," is one of the most stimulating and exciting documents to come out of the American far left. The report syn-
thesized the conversations with Trotsky, the work in Missouri, the
debate inside the Workers Party, and its author's personal experiences
and relationships. In it, James argues that black struggles are rooted
in the soil of American democracy, that they enjoy a lasting and profound impact on American society, and that they can inspire, instruct,
and transform working-class politics. Black protest would "exercise a
powerful influence upon the revolutionary proletariat and . . . is in
itself a constituent part of the struggle for socialism."[78] The report
described a nascent movement of religious, secular, local, and
national black forces gathering momentum and preparing for victory.
It presented a perspective on politics that was more pluralist than
Leninist: virtually every black-run church, newspaper, and neighbor-

hood group in America, James suggested, "is dominated by the idea that each organization must in some manner or another contribute to the emancipation of blacks from capitalist humiliation."[79]

Although one critic complained that "it is difficult to find in this coldly incisive analysis the sense of permanent hurt,"[80] the reaction of one of the party's few black members, a Southern-born auto worker, was quite different:

> He said the workers are the ones we must rely upon. But that didn't mean that the Negroes must not do anything until the labor movement actually came forward. The Negro struggle would help bring the workers forward. That was complete for me. I couldn't see how I would ever think of leaving after hearing him. I was tied and wedged into the party . . . [81]

This particular member, Charles Denby (Si Owens), joined the Johnson-Forest tendency soon after hearing this speech, and left the Socialist Workers Party in 1951 along with the majority of the James-Dunayevskaya group. Denby sided with Raya Dunayevskaya during a split within Correspondence that took place in 1955, and he went on to edit the eponymous newspaper of Dunayevskaya's News and Letters group. But the impact of James's 1948 report was felt beyond his immediate circle. His unorthodox approach, the product of intensive study and close observation, offered the Marxist left an imaginative perspective on the relationship between class politics and social movements under advanced capitalism. The idea that autonomous social movements were in themselves a positive good seemed to anticipate a range of campaigns that gained momentum in the late 1950s and 1960s, including the civil rights movement, the anti-Vietnam war movement, and the women's movement. His approach captured the flavor of much of what was to come. But in the final analysis his work on black America was only one aspect of the tendency's overall analysis of revolutionary politics in the epoch of world capitalism.

CHAPTER FOUR

Mariners, Renegades, and Castaways

THE EMPHASIS IN THE PREVIOUS chapter was on James's contribution to leftist debates over the role of black struggles in the construction of a revolutionary movement. The cause of social equality
and democratic rights for black Americans, James believed, occupied
the center ground of U.S. politics. The black community, in its very
essence an oppositional, counterhegemonic force, was brimming
with militancy. Inevitably, he concluded, any mass movement for a
democratic and revolutionary socialism in America would be obli-
gated to come to terms with the nationalistic and "autonomistic"
dynamics of black politics. There would be no subsuming the Negro
question under the rubric of a fictive proletarian or Leninist univer-
salism.

James's radical, democratic sensibilities concerning this question
of race and politics carried over to other issues that were of concern
to socialists in the 1940s. His independent Marxism emerged in a
very specific context—that of factional activity within two rival
American Trotskyist organizations. His positions were staked out not
by way of a leisurely meditation on moral, aesthetic, or metaphysical
subjects, but in the midst of furious sectarian arguments over the
Correct Line on Everything. This meant that the issues James,
Dunayevskaya, and the Johnson-Forest tendency took up—the
Negro question, the nature of the Soviet Union, the prospects for
world revolution, the Leninist party, specific episodes in American

history—were not chosen out of thin air. They were seen as central to the task of extirpating capitalism. From the Johnson-Forest perspective, Marxism offered the basic framework for understanding the modern world; but it would have to be emended in light of the constant transformation of capital and labor, of states and societies. This process of ideological rectification was designed to enhance the capacity of socialists to increase their effectiveness and accomplish their goals.

It seems remarkable—given the exotic circumstances of its birth—that by the 1950s James's *weltanschauung* would be characterized above all by its humanist, democratic, and populist hues. For all of its political bravura, the Johnson-Forest tendency was in many respects grounded in the arcane protocols of the Trotskyist movement. It thus appears paradoxical that after more than a decade of intensive factional activity James would have gone on to write *Mariners, Renegades and Castaways* (1953), and *A Preface to Criticism* (1955). To unravel this paradox, one must remember that although its polemics were couched in the strident language of Trotskyism, the tendency identified itself with a radical tradition emphasizing the possibilities inherent in democratic self-emancipation. They understood socialism to mean a freely chosen, participatory, and nonexploitative society, one compatible with the approaches of Rousseau, Kant, and the early Marx. Furthermore, the group's theory of state capitalism was intended to distinguish their conception of revolutionary democratic socialism from actually existing Communism. It should also be noted that James's concerns went beyond those of Johnson-Forest. He retained from his childhood and early adult years a keen awareness of cultural and psychological dimensions of social organization. He quickly came to appreciate not only America's industrial unions and black nationalists but also the country's literary traditions and even her show business personalities. At the same historical moment that he was advancing a critical analysis of Trotskyism, then, James was savoring the vibrancy of everyday life in America.[1]

It would be a mistake, however, to draw too sharp a distinction between James's own political and intellectual evolution in this period, and that of the Johnson-Forest tendency. James no doubt found it extremely helpful to have on hand, from 1941 onwards, a highly motivated and expanding circle of individuals committed to renovating socialist theory and practice along the lines suggested by his own writings. In many respects the tendency functioned like "an advanced seminar in Marxist theory,"[2] with individual members taking assignments and reporting their findings back to the group. At the same time, however, the group operated as a political faction, and also as a social network. Because it combined so many functions and because the overall intellectual project was so exciting, the organization's membership came to expect great things from what was, in the final analysis, a small leftist clique. The highly problematical character of members' expectations probably contributed to the intense outpouring of anger and frustration that emerged when the tendency's successor organization split apart in 1955 and again in 1962.

From James's perspective, the most important feature of the group may have been the way it made possible an intensive process of intellectual and political collaboration with a small number of talented individuals. Martin Glaberman, for example, was knowledgeable about various aspects of American history and labor politics. Freddy Paine had worked in a number of different factories; her husband, Lyman Paine, was a Harvard-trained architect. Together they helped to subsidize the group and contributed to shaping its perspective. A younger member, Philomena Daddario (Finch), immersed herself in the poetry of Shakespeare. One of the most promising members was Morris Goelman (otherwise known as William Gorman), who had written on the American civil war in the 1940s and who later planned a book on the capitalist state. Goelman's legendary inability to complete writing projects was a source of considerable frustration for the entire group.

Two individuals were of particular importance to the group's development—Raya Dunayevskaya and Grace Lee. With her extensive background in leftist politics, her knowledge of Russian, and her training as a political economist, Dunayevskaya brought many rare gifts to the organization. Although it seems that Dunayevskaya and James arrived at the "state capitalist" perspective independently of each other, they began collaborating on this and other issues by 1941. It was Dunayevskaya who did most of the work in terms of developing the state capitalist thesis, but James's intervention was instrumental in using the thesis to give coherence to the group's overall assessment of the world situation. By the mid-1940s, James had also come to depend on Grace Lee in her capacity as a revolutionary intellectual. Fluent in German and a skilled writer, Lee had a good overview of Western philosophy. For the first few years, at least, Dunayevskaya-James-Lee enjoyed a happy and productive partnership, and their intensive collaborations broke new ground in several areas of Marxist theory. Their partnership never quite engendered a process of collective leadership, however. Despite his evident respect for Dunayevskaya and Lee as Marxist theorists, James continued to regard himself as the group's sole leader.[3] The centralization of leadership under one individual (combined, as I have suggested, with what proved to be the tendency's immoderate expectations about the prospects for social revolution in the United States) no doubt contributed to the factionalism that ultimately debilitated American "Johnsonism."

Were it not for the Johnson-Forest tendency, James's break with Trotskyism may not have taken such a deliberative and theoretically self-conscious form. The break was a collective endeavor, and required considerable energies. As he emphasized in a passage in *Beyond a Boundary*:

> As early as 1941 I had begun to question the premises of Trotskyism. It took nearly a decade of incessant labor and collaboration to break with it and reorganise my Marxist ideas to cope with the postwar World. That was a matter of doctrine, of history, of economics and politics. These pursuits I shared with collaborators, rivals, enemies, and our public.[4]

As we have seen, James's history was one of working in association with others on literary questions (in Trinidad) and political questions (in Britain). This orientation toward small groups of like-minded individuals was a critical aspect of James's praxis, and his work in the post–1953 period may have suffered as a result of his inability to locate himself within such an environment. Of his various collaborative ventures, Johnson-Forest was the longest running and in certain respects the most fruitful. We shall find, however, that in many ways it was also the most enervating and ultimately disheartening project that James was ever involved with.

More than the Trotskyist milieu in general, Johnson-Forest provided James with a forum where he could develop his particular gifts. In the short run at least, it also offered a comforting perch in what was otherwise an unsettled and insecure period of his life. During its ten-year existence—Johnson-Forest was superseded by the independent Correspondence group in the early 1950s—the tendency carved out for itself a distinctive program and intellectual agenda. Lodged inside the Shachtmanite Workers Party from 1941 to 1947, the group issued a steady stream of polemics on black politics and on the state-capitalist nature of the Soviet Union. In addition, James wrote numerous articles for the Workers Party press on a range of topics, such as fascism, the Labour Party in Britain, trade union politics in America, Wendell Wilkie and the Republican Party, and Edmund Wilson's political writings.

The hallmark of the tendency was its sense that factory workers were in the process of moving in a broadly socialist direction. James argued that the war was accelerating the tendency for capitalism to forge a revolutionary working class at the point of production, a class with a capacity to define itself and to defend its class interests. Moving beyond traditional Marxist categories, he also saw great potential in the "bottom-up" struggles of a variety of multiclass sectors (women, young people, blacks) to transform society. On behalf of the tendency, James argued that what was required on the part of the Workers Party was an "Americanization" of "Bolshevism." The party, he maintained, would have to speak the language of ordinary workers and to learn to grasp the connection between popular culture and political mobilization. And the party would have to somehow provide a positive alternative to the chicanery of the Communist-inspired Popular Front. While drawing a stark contrast between liberal capitalism and Stalinism on the one hand, and "socialism from below" on the other, was characteristic of the Workers Party, unguarded confidence in the imminent triumph of the latter over the former became a defining feature of the "Johnsonite" current.

It is worth noting that countless Western intellectuals had come to the conclusion that capitalism was on its way out during the 1930s and 1940s. A number of developments, such as the social unrest associated with the Depression, the "Five Year Plans" in the Soviet Union, and the application of neo-Keynesian macroeconomics in Western Europe and North America in the 1940s all seemed to point to the obsolescence of nineteenth-century laissez-faire doctrines and to the triumph of state-led modernization strategies. The chief difference, of course, between popular front, liberal, and technocratic conceptions of the future, and that of the Johnson-Forest tendency, was that the latter stressed the self-activity of the working class and the importance of overturning bureaucratic arrangements in favor of decentral-

ized institutions and the free association of individuals. Far from
viewing the expansion of the state as either a positive end, or as a step
toward "socialism," the tendency regarded 1940s-style state intervention as a stop-gap measure, as an ultimately futile effort to empower
capital over labor.

Having started out with a handful of individuals, the tendency
consisted of nearly seventy members concentrated in New York and
Detroit by the war's end. They were by far the largest political minority in the Workers Party, which had shrunk to 400 members by 1946.
Despite the fact that WP leaders heaped scorn on what Irving Howe
dubbed the group's "soviets in the sky" perspective, the "Johnsonites"
somehow managed to recruit new members every year.[5] By late 1947,
when it formally joined the Socialist Workers Party, the tendency had
supporters scattered around the country. The Morgantown, West Virginia, branch was a rare case of an SWP branch that was dominated
by the Johnson-Forest tendency. It was a highly active branch, whose
members included: "an intellectual from the coal area and his wife, a
radical youth from Detroit . . . Frank, an army veteran who had lost
his leg in Germany, and Raymond, a navy veteran who had been born
and raised in a mining community in southwest Pennsylvania . . . an
ex-miner and two others from the southern part of the state, and two
ex-servicemen from the Morgantown area."[6] In sociological terms,
the Morgantown branch may have been unusual by the standards of
the Johnson-Forest tendency. But it is important to remember that
not everyone active in Johnsonite politics—or, indeed, in the Workers Party and in the Socialist Workers Party—were intellectuals or
students or expatriots of one kind or another. The Trotskyist movement attracted a wide array of personalities and social types, with a
far greater concentration of working-class (and middle-aged) activists than would have been typical, for example, of New Left groupings
during the late 1960s or early 1970s.

During its three-month hiatus from organized party politics in
1947, the group advanced and clarified its unorthodox Marxism
through an impressive array of publications. These included *The
American Worker* and James's important essay, *Dialectical Materialism
and the Fate of Humanity. The American Worker* contained two essays,
one by Paul Romano (Phil Singer) and the other by Grace Lee.
Romano's piece offered an autobiographical account of the conditions
in a postwar General Motors plant. In painstaking detail, he depicted
the "dirt and oil" of the assembly line:

> It is commonplace to put on a clean set of clothes in the morning
> and by noon to be soaked, literally, with oil. Most workers in my
> department have oil pimples, rashes and sores on their arms and
> legs. The shoes become soaked and the result is a steady case of ath-
> lete's foot. Blackheads fill the pores. It is an extremely aggravating
> set of effects. We speak often of sitting and soaking in a hot tub of
> water to loosen the dirt and ease the infectious blackheads.[7]

Romano went on to describe "what the workers are thinking and
doing while actually at work on the bench or on the line." In this context, he discussed the company's incentive system, speed-up tactics,
shop-floor management, health and safety issues, probation, company "stool pigeons," race and gender relations, the role of veteran
workers, and "the attitude toward radical workers." The final result
is a piece of masterful industrial sociology. As Lee writes in her
accompanying piece, "[t]o read Romano's description of the life in
the factory is to realize with shocking clarity how deeply the alienation of labor pervades the very foundations of our society. All the
preoccupation of the intellectuals with their own souls and with economic programs for 'full employment' and a higher standard of living,
fade into insignificance in the face of the oppressive reality of the lifetime of every worker."[8]

The essay on "Dialectical Materialism" took up this theme of the
intellectual's irrelevancy by counterposing those who "bog down in
the chaotic disintegration of the modern world" with those who pos-
sess the revolutionary clarity of the "dialectical materialist."[9] As distinct from the intellectual, the latter fully appreciates that the "great
millions, very often unorganized in unions . . . have their own ideas
and in the continuous crisis and catastrophic decline of society, they
have in recent decades repeatedly entered upon the field of history
with world-shaking effects."[10] These "effects" include continental
Europe's revolutionary crises in the period from 1917 to 1923, and
the emergence of the Congress of Industrial Organizationsx in the
United States in the 1930s. The "great millions" are moved to political action not by their commitment to particular intellectual systems
but by their desire to achieve a measurable degree of freedom and
equality in their own lives. James called this search the "mass quest
for universality in action and in life," and announced that "history
has reached a climax because this quest has reached a climax."[11] The
"bankruptcy of bourgeois civilization" ensured that the masses had

The American Worker

$1

THE
INVADING
SOCIALIST
SOCIETY

by
C.L.R. JAMES, F. FOREST
and RIA STONE

one dollar

Pamphlet covers—1947
Photo: Jon Anderson

few other options but to attempt to reconstruct society in their own interests. For the first time in recorded history, humanity's fate lay in the hands of the majority.

Nineteen forty-seven was the year that the group issued *The Invading Socialist Society*, a blistering critique of bureaucracy and statism which argued that the "achievement of state capitalism is at the same time the beginning of the disintegration of capitalism as a social system . . ."[12] Much of the authors' polemical fire was directed at "Germain," a pseudonym for the Belgian Marxist economist Ernest Mandel, who eventually established himself as the authoritative spokesperson for the postwar Fourth International movement. While Mandel attempted to apply Trotsky's analysis of the Soviet system to Eastern Europe, James and company were eager to proclaim that the "self-mobilization of the masses is the dominating social and political feature of our age."[13] The same trio also drafted an introduction for the first English language translation of major extracts of the young Marx's economic and philosophical manuscripts.[14] *State Capitalism and World Revolution*, prepared by James, Lee and Dunayevskaya for the 1951 World Congress of the Fourth International, offered a bold recapitulation of the state capitalist thesis, and James and Lee's *Facing Reality*, published in 1956, represented a definitive restatement of the Johnson-Forest perspective.

In retrospect, 1947—a high-water mark in terms of postwar labor conflict and of Communist influence in the trade unions—may have been the Johnson-Forest tendency's finest hour. At the level of Marxist theory, virtually everything that the group had to say was in *The Invading Socialist Society*; and the tendency's essentially workerist, "autonomist," and post-Trotskyist politics were expressed in an admirably down-to-earth fashion in *The American Worker*. After 1947, rifts started to appear in the small circle of "state caps." While the Socialist Workers Party provided the group a safe political harbor in the late 1940s, the Correspondence group was composed of only sixty or so members when it was launched at the start of the Cold War.[15] James was effectively expelled from the country in 1953 (he left a few weeks before the date by which he had been ordered to leave), and a majority led by Dunayevskaya broke off from Correspondence to form a new, "Marxist-Humanist" group, News and Letters, in 1955. After the 1955 split, the remaining Johnsonite current was barely able to maintain a viable organizational presence on the American left. Although such Jamesian motifs as a heavy emphasis on the spontaneous self-activity of workers, the importance of lending nonsectarian support to black organizations, and the centrality of integrating culture and politics in both theory and practice enjoyed a modest influence on the New Left of the 1960s and 1970s, these themes were largely conveyed via indirect and nonorganizational means.

Within the ranks of the North American and European far lefts, the tendency was best known for its state-capitalist analysis of the Stalinist regime, with Raya Dunayevskaya in particular responsible for analyzing developments within the sphere of Soviet political economy.[16] As we have seen, the Soviet question was regarded as the most critical and divisive question facing the left in the postwar period. Trotskyists believed that the transformation of the postrevolutionary state into a dictatorial leviathan constituted a fundamental betrayal of the historic promise of 1917, and Trotsky himself devoted a great deal of energy to the task of comprehending the revolution's degeneration. His book *The Revolution Betrayed* (1936) depicted an unstable regime relying on surveillance and terror to control a demoralized population. Trotsky predicted that the regime would probably not outlast the war. Although the Soviet Union was governed by an antidemocratic elite operating on the basis of self-interest, it was not a capitalist society. The capacity of the Soviet leadership to extract wealth from the population reflected

> the fact that the present transition structure is still full of social contradictions, which in the sphere of *consumption*—the most close and sensibly felt by all—are extremely tense, and forever threaten to break over into the sphere of production . . . The basis of bureaucratic rule is the poverty of society in object of consumption with the resulting struggle of each against all.[17]

From the Trotskyist standpoint, the Soviet regime was progressive in comparison to capitalism in that it rested on top of a system of collectivized property that had its origins in a proletarian revolution. The Trotskyists therefore called for a "political revolution" to resurrect genuine Bolshevik principles inside the Soviet Union. After Trotsky's death in 1940 the movement was faced with the troubling and divisive question as to whether the regimes in Eastern Europe that had been established after the war were themselves progressive in this comparative sense. Eventually many Trotskyists came to describe the Eastern European party states as "deformed workers' states," with the distinction being that, unlike the Soviet case, these regimes had never degenerated from a more or less healthy starting point. Again, the underlying idea was that a collectivized system of property relations, even one imposed through military and bureaucratic fiat, was more "advanced" than liberal capitalist democracy.

Drawing on resolutions prepared by Joseph Carter, a reclusive intellectual who belonged to Workers Party's "secondary leadership," Max Shachtman expounded the theory of bureaucratic collectivism as an alternative to Trotsky's approach. Shachtman wrote in 1940:

> In the Stalinist state, production is carried on and extended for the satisfaction of the needs of the bureaucracy, for the increasing of its wealth, its privileges, its power. At every turn of events, it seeks to overcome the mounting difficulties and resolve the contradictions which it cannot really resolve, by intensifying the exploitation and oppression of the masses.[18]

At its first convention, the Workers Party voted to reject the degenerated workers' state thesis on the grounds that it "covers up the class nature of the Stalinist bureaucracy and the reactionary character of the regime." The party described the regime as "counterrevolutionary," led by a "particularly brutal gendarme converting 'inequality into a whip for the spurring on of the majority', and steadily accentuating the inequality in favor of the ruling class . . ."[19] Those who held the bureaucratic collectivist position agreed with Trotsky that capitalism had not been restored in the Soviet Union, but proposed to distinguish between two types of collectivist property relations—socialist and nonsocialist. Shachtmanites regarded the Soviet Union, obviously, as being in the nonsocialist camp. The Stalinist regime (and, later, its Eastern European counterparts) was an entirely reactionary phenomenon. As Shachtman insisted in the introduction to a collection of his essays on bureaucratic collectivism:

> The Stalinist bureaucracy in power is a new ruling, exploitative class. Its social system is a new system of totalitarian exploitation and oppression, not capitalist and yet having nothing in common with socialism. It is the cruel realization of the prediction made by all the great socialist scientists, from Marx and Engels onward, that capitalism must collapse out of an inability to solve its own contra-

dictions and that the alternatives facing mankind are not so much capitalism or socialism as they are: *socialism or barbarism*. Stalinism is that new barbarism.[20]

The Johnson-Forest position represented a third pole in the debate over the Soviet Union. Unlike the orthodox Trotskyists, who described the regime's leadership as a "caste," the Johnsonites argued that a new ruling class had usurped power inside the USSR. In contradistinction to the Shachtmanites, the tendency argued that the Soviet Union could be analyzed using many of the categories contained in Marx's *Capital*. For James and Dunayevskaya, the Stalinist system represented an unanticipated manifestation and extension of capitalism rather than an entirely new form of social organization. For the Johnson-Forest tendency, the key difference between Western capitalism and Soviet state capitalism was that in the USSR capital was generated and reproduced through a single value-maximizing organization, the state, whereas in the West capitalism was defined by the clash of rival economic units. While institutional and political arrangements within the two blocs may have differed in ways that would be significant to students of comparative government, the underlying reality in both blocs was one of alienation and exploitation. As James asked in an early contribution to the debate, "Why is the total national capital any less capital because it exploits the workers under unified control instead of in separate conflicting parts?"[21] In both cases the production and reproduction of capital was deeply implicated in processes of class exploitation, and was sure to generate mass, class-based resistance.

The state-capitalist perspective complemented the characteristic optimism of the Johnson-Forest tendency, and James, Lee, and Dunayevskaya insisted on the importance of linking a class analysis of the Soviet Union to a wider conception of "the capital-labor antagonism in the context of the world market."[22] The gist of their perspective was that state capitalism represented a new and final stage of the development of historical capitalism. In essence, history had entered a phase where the decisive conflict was between bureaucratic capitalism and "the invading socialist society" of the masses. In a climate of heightened class struggle, it was expected that Stalinism would "collaborate with American imperialism for the maintenance of the condition of their joint existence—the suppression of the world proletarian revolution."[23] Since the obdurate logic of capital would itself tend to generate a socialist consciousness among industrial workers, the prospects for socialist advance were viewed as good-to-excellent.[24]

Despite their fierce critique of Trotsky's theory of the degenerated workers' state, then, the Johnson-Forest tendency's belief in the imminence of the European revolution (and in mass rebellion in America's industrial heartland) echoed Trotsky's prewar revolutionary optimism.[25] As of the early 1940s, the American labor movement had "suffered none of the drastic blows which have fallen upon the European proletariat during recent years . . . [and] is conscious that its great battles are before it."[26] In the same period, he steadfastly maintained that, despite the "absence of working-class organization, soviets [workers' councils] could be formed in European factories within hours."[27] As Buhle notes, "James's circle had an almost unique sense of actual optimism within or outside the Shachtman group." The Johnson-Forest tendency, Buhle rightly suggests, "based its hopes not on Allied victory and postwar Russo-American cooperation in a state-regulated world order, but rather in the instinctive rebellion against that order."[28] This emphasis on the concrete possibility of antibureaucratic revolutions in the midst of world war or during the economic reorganization of the late 1940s was a hallmark of Johnsonism and earned the tendency considerable ribbing and derision from the more pragmatic Shachtmanites.

From a Johnsonite perspective, the fact that orthodox Trotskyists continued to maintain the fiction that the Soviet Union was a degenerated workers' state reflected their innate ideological conservatism. At the same time, the bureaucratic collectivist stance adopted by the Workers Party's spoke to that formation's loss of confidence in the international proletariat. The Shachtmanite notion that the USSR was regressive in comparison to Western capitalism seemed to symbolize the political demoralization that had impelled the Johnson-Forest tendency to reject the Workers Party and join the more rhetorically militant Socialist Workers Party in late 1947. But neither party, the Workers Party or the Cannonite SWP, was prepared to recognize the main fault line in international class relations—that dividing the world bourgeoisie from the world proletariat.

Although the tendency was in the process of breaking with Trotskyism, its leaders strenuously maintained that they were still operating from a more or less Leninist perspective. In private letters to Constance Webb, James made clear his devotion to what he defined as "Bolshevik" principles—organizational discipline, intensive Marxist study, the necessity of appealing to workers in a consistent and well-organized manner, and so on.[29] He retained those principles even after *Notes on Dialectics* and *State Capitalism and World Revolution* announced his break with the Leninist conception of the vanguard party, insisting that the Johnson-Forest tendency and the Correspondence group were functioning in a manner that was consistent with the spirit of Lenin's own writings and practice. Even in the 1960s and 1970s James had nothing but the highest regard for Lenin as a political leader.[30] A pronounced sympathy for Lenin's own method and practice did not, it seems, preclude a break with a core proposition of Marxist-Leninist politics.

The Johnson-Forest critique of the vanguard party was several years in the making. Initially the tendency focused on encouraging the Workers Party to "Americanize" its "Bolshevism." In an internal document on "Education, Propaganda, Agitation: Postwar America and Bolshevism" (1943), James wrote forcefully about the WP's declining membership and internal divisions. First and foremost he invited the party to consider the possibility that an upsurge in union militancy would soon lead to the formation of a labor party: "Soon to be freed from the restraints of the European war, and with the great experiences of 1939–1944 to help it, it now faces a political development which . . . will in all reasonable probability be as violent and all-embracing as was the industrial development of the CIO."[31] To influence this "political development," the Workers Party should "gather a nucleus of a few thousands, of whom seventy-five percent will be American workers, men and women, instinctively hostile to bourgeois society, who are workers, have been workers and have no other prospect in life except to be workers."[32] But how was this nucleus to be formed? The cadres of the WP had to somehow grasp that capitalist modernity was in the process of fostering a "mass society":

> Today the whole organization of society is moving rapidly towards mass collective action of a grand scale. Workers in any numbers are repelled from small insignificant groups. The perspectives of one-by-one building up of a party to have an effect in ten or twenty years make little sense to a worker in a country where organized labor is 14 million strong, and the NAACP has half a million members.[33]

The Workers Party had to accommodate itself to the new realities by taking such steps as publishing a daily newspaper and otherwise intervening in the nation's political debate. "*Life* writes on the free market? Good," wrote James. "We write the Marxist view of the free market. The *Saturday Evening Post* writes about cartels and monopolies? Next week, we write one or two articles on monopolies and cartels exposing their superficiality and preaching our own view."[34] From now on, the debate had to be cast in terms of American realities, and had to respond directly to ideas expressed in mass-circulation magazines and other popular outlets. It was no good hiding behind European certainties or abstract political formulations. The Americanized Marxist party would have to "get down and dirty" as it took on the "superficial" ideology of the American Century.

By the late 1940s, the Johnson-Forest tendency had rejected this conception of building a "small mass party" in favor of emphasizing the masses' capacity for independent mobilization. Yet this did not preclude socialists from building independent Marxist organizations, as long as they acknowledged the centrality of autonomous social movements to the revolutionary project, and shunned the practice of "substitutionism," which entailed the sectarian imposition of socialist or Marxist leadership on mass social movements. As James argued in *State Capitalism and World Revolution*, socialist groups could become an important ingredient in working-class and popular uprisings aimed against all forms of bureaucracy and exploitation. But, for the Johnsonites, workers' struggles against capitalism would not require monolithic vanguard parties, or "indirect methods of representation,"[35] as the Trotskyists believed.

This conception of socialists working in tandem with autonomous social movements further distinguished the Johnsonites from other tendencies on the American left. One is tempted to describe their position as "spontaneist" and "post-Leninist"—in other words, worker centered and Marxist, emphasizing the self-activity of the masses and renouncing the project of constructing a revolutionary party that would smash the capitalist state and lead the working class to victory. In some respects their approach shared certain features in common with anarcho-syndicalism, but their ideas, training and discourse were rooted in the Trotskyist and Marxist traditions. At the same time, while they had broken with Leninism as it was and is commonly defined, they had not moved in a social-democratic or liberal-democratic direction.

Informing or complementing the Johnson-Forest tendency's distinctive positions on the Negro, Soviet and organizational questions was the group's ongoing engagement with the philosophical underpinnings of Marxism. Throughout the mid- and late 1940s the group's leaders exchanged dozens of letters that concerned the contemporary relevance of Hegel's dialectical system. A selection of James's letters on philosophy were circulated privately in 1948 and finally published in 1980 under the title *Notes on Dialectics*.[36] The tendency's interest in philosophy was plainly antischolastic. Dunayevskaya, James, and the others regarded Hegel's writings, along with those of Marx and Lenin, as an integral component in the socialist armory. They self-consciously turned to Hegelian philosophy in the same spirit as Lenin had at the outbreak of World War I: to make sense of a new epoch in the development of capitalism and the international workers' movement. Over time, Johnson-Forest documents became saturated with Hegelian-sounding phrases and concepts. The tendency's immersion in European political theory further distinguished the group from the other main Trotskyist currents, which leaned more toward pragmatism (the Shachtman group) or dogmatism (the Cannon group). None of these three groups, however, was ever able to complete the task of "Americanizing Bolshevism."

The tendency's leaders saw Hegel's writings as providing a philosophical method and language that could illuminate history's inner meaning and trajectory. In particular, Hegel's dialectic offered Johnson-Forest a philosophically structured way of thinking about the social crisis of capitalist modernity and the role of working-class self-emancipation as the new and possibly final "category" of history, making possible the reconciliation of the subjective and the objective. Drawing on Hegelian constructs, James attacked the Trotskyists for clinging to the degenerated workers' state thesis, and thus giving tacit support to the Stalinist one-party state. Because they equated socialism with state ownership of the means of production, Trotskyism had effectively come to pose an obstacle to the universal movement of Reason. "God help you if your concept, your notion of a workers' state in 1917, remains static, while everything else around you changes," James exclaimed.[37]

James's enthusiasm for Hegelian categories was accompanied by a celebration of the creative power of spontaneous social activity. In the age of the American Century, that is, the era of Fordism, a faith in the masses' capacity to engage in spontaneous rebellion could be substituted for the type of party building favored by Marxist-Leninists. As James wrote in *Notes on Dialectics*, "[o]rganization as we have known it is at an end. The task is to abolish organization." For the Johnsonites, the Trotskyists and others seemed to privilege the deliberations of their National Committees above the potentiality of working-class self-activity. But they should have been concentrating on what was going on beyond their fiefdoms in lower Manhattan. "The task today," James wrote: "is to call for, to teach, to illustrate, to develop *spontaneity*—the free creative activity of the proletariat." James then emphasized that the "proletariat will find its method of proletarian organization."[38] This was a point he was to return to on innumerable occasions, as when he wrote many years later, in the context of the postwar movement for West Indian independence, that the "people must organise themselves according to the best methods of the day which they find suitable for themselves."[39]

As we have seen, the constitutive elements of the Johnson-Forest tendency's program included a critique not only of Soviet-type systems but world capitalism as a totality, along with an appropriation of Hegelian concepts and a belief in the power of spontaneous popular mobilizations to generate a more democratic society and culture. The group's analysis of the political and economic conjuncture in the period just after World War II led them to expect a degree of social unrest that one would later identify with the civil rights movement and the campus protests of the 1960s. By the late 1940s, however, trade union militancy and leftist-inspired political activity were threatening to give way to the era of the so-called silent generation. While the theory of state capitalism seemed on target in many respects, the group's appraisal of the domestic political scene appeared undertheorized and somewhat preposterous. Yet some of the most interesting and suggestive work that James was able to do in the immediate postwar period concerned not Marxism or the Soviet Union but the intellectual history of the American Republic. Curiously, a wildly optimistic prognostication regarding the dynamics of American politics went hand in hand with an astute appreciation for the strengths and weaknesses of the dominant strands in American political culture.

Thus we find that at the same time that he was assessing midcentury America from his perch as leader of a theory-soaked Marxist sect, James was also acquainting himself with the nation's history, geography, and popular culture. Occasional references to American novelists and intellectuals in his articles for *New International* and *Labor Action* only hinted at James's interest in the country's traditions, mores, and inhabitants. In a letter written to Constance Webb in the early 1940s, he explained that, "I have sat for hours in America, listening to people, all sorts of poor working people, telling me all about themselves. It is indispensable for any understanding of anything. It must go side by side with the books."[40] Conversations with all types of ordinary Americans represented one way in which James sought to become, in his words, a "neighborhood man."

Despite its intensely private and personal nature, the relationship with Constance Webb provided James with a treasured window onto the "real" America. As we have seen, Constance had first seen C. L. R. speak in 1938 in Los Angeles, when she was a teenager. A strong advocate of racial equality and a native Californian, Constance Webb studied history, literature, and other subjects at Fresno State College and later at the University of California at Berkeley. Before she married James she had a career as a model and later worked as an actress in Los Angeles and New York. She had also been through two previous marriages, neither of which had been completely satisfying. The seasoned revolutionary was clearly enchanted by her personal warmth, intellectual openness, and straightforward manner. "But I believe in you, young America," he wrote in one letter. "You have the confidence of ten generations of pioneer ancestors and achievement. I admire you immensely."[41]

To ensure that their 1946 marriage was legally valid, James traveled to Reno, Nevada, in 1948 to clear up legal complications connected with the divorce from Juanita James that had been originally filed in Mexico. The task of obtaining a legally valid divorce took several months, partly because Nevada had a six-week residency requirement for those seeking divorce, but mainly because key documents took weeks to arrive from the West Indies. In the end, James was made to pay Juanita nearly a thousand dollars to achieve a proper settlement. Written during what was clearly an unhappy period of his life, James's letters from Reno are full of pathos. Writing to Constance Webb, he describes lunching on giblets and rice (for seventy cents) at a "Negro place"—one of "two or three places set aside for Negroes . . ."[42] A similar bleak sense of racial segregation was expressed in another letter, where James describes drinking and driving around Lake Tahoe with a group of locals. "All we did," he writes, "was to drive 'round it—about eighty miles. We stopped three or four times for whiskey and coke. They had brought half-a-bottle . . . The lake was lovely, the drive splendid. It should have been a perfect outing." But it wasn't, because "there were no colored people in sight. We were excluded. All 'round there were houses, people, cabins, cars, people bathing. But Negroes were out. The exclusion was always present. It did not ruin the day but it poisoned it. You and Dick [Richard Wright] between you have taught me much about the Negro question."[43]

After spending several lonely weeks in Reno, James found a job working as a handyman, kitchen helper, and gardener at a motel in Pyramid Lake, thirty-five miles outside of Reno. While he lost that job after a few weeks, he continued to stay at the motel for $40 a week, including meals, which he had to eat in the kitchen. In the town he dubbed "the back of beyond,"[44] James passed the time by reading Hegel's *Science of Logic* and by translating his friend Daniel Guerin's acclaimed two-volume study of the French Revolution (*La Lutte de Classe dans la Premiere Republique*, 1944) into English.[45] It was in Reno that he came up with the idea of writing a book on American civilization, one that could reach a large audience and earn an advance from a major publisher. As a temporary resident of Nevada he also lost money playing the slot machines.[46] While he desperately wanted Constance to travel from New York to join him in Reno (Constance was by that time pregnant with their only child), they were both concerned that as an interracial couple they would make an easy target for racial bigots.

Although Constance and C. L. R. obviously felt passionately about each other, their marriage—his second and her third—was on the rocks by 1949 and crumbled only a year or two later. A number of factors conspired to ensure that their courtship was more successful than their brief marriage. Harassed by the Federal Bureau of Investigation on political grounds, they found only a handful of places to go as an interracial couple. Constance feared, rightly or wrongly, that several of the "heavies" in Johnson-Forest disapproved of her high-profile career, and she never really felt comfortable operating within the tendency's febrile subculture. There was also the issue of James's emotional detachment and reserve. Constance injected the following when she later edited one of James's letters:

> Rather than have any disagreement, Nello's method was to simply retreat behind an impenetrable wall. He could not express his emotions. Instead, he walked about the Bronx carrying on lengthy, furious arguments with me and with himself—all inside his own head. Then he would come home and discuss politics, literature, any-

thing but what was troubling both of us. If asked a personal question, he changed the subject . . . And I was spoiled, not only because of the attention that actresses receive but because the eight years of letters from Nello had made me feel like a princess. Suddenly, I was Cinderella; the ball was over and I was relegated to cleaning the kitchen for cruel step-sisters.[47]

An interesting light on their failed relationship is cast by a letter dated July 16, 1984, where an elderly James wrote about his feelings to his ex-wife, admitting "[t]he lack of consideration and the feeling that the woman is there for his own convenience and his own affairs . . . that is how I lived with the various women with whom I was associated; and I was not crude or conscious that I was maltreating them in any way, but simply that is the view that men have and work on instinctively . . ."[48] Despite the collapse of their marriage, the woman he dubbed "Saint Monica" remained for James both an emblem of the "new society" and a romantic ideal. Having identified with both Marxism and revolution, and yet immersed in American values and American culture, Constance Webb was the first—and one of the truest—of the American Johnsonites.

One of the activities C. L. R. did share with Constance was his avid appreciation for popular art forms. Even as the New York Intellectuals and exiled affiliates of the Frankfurt School were bemoaning the very existence of "mass culture," James insisted on the importance of the comic strip, the gangster movie, and the theatrical musical comedy. After Constance moved to New York in 1944, she was his regular companion as he set out to explore the subliterary realms. They agreed that while the high arts in America were largely derivative of European prototypes, the country possessed a dynamic and imaginative popular culture. Grimshaw reports that James

> began to go regularly to popular films such as *Stormy Weather*, *That Uncertain Feeling*, and *Cabin in the Sky*, as a distraction from his political work. Initially he had rather despised them; but he soon found himself reflecting on this new art form which he saw as one of America's most distinctive contributions to the twentieth century.[49]

Inevitably he began to formulate ideas about the movies he watched as a curious spectator. In a letter to Constance, James posed the following question:

Why the popularity of the Western? Because young people who sit cramped in buses and tied to assembly lines terribly wish they would be elsewhere; if even, not consciously, yet when they see it they respond. That is the fundamental principle. Like all art, but more than most, the movies are not merely a reflection, but an extension of the actual, but an extension along the lines which people feel is lacking and possible in the actual. That my dear, is the complete secret of Hegelian dialectic. The two, the actual and the potential, are always inseparably linked; one is always giving way to the other. At a certain stage a crisis takes place and a complete change is the result.[50]

A handful of associates gradually became aware of his interest in film and popular culture.[51] While his infatuation with the culture was severely tested by his de facto expulsion from the country in 1953, his enthusiasm nevertheless continued to generate sparks well into the 1980s.[52]

As we have seen, the reference to "Hegelian dialectic" was characteristic of the Johnson-Forest tendency. Whereas Dunayevskaya and the others mostly confined their theoretical investigations to the sphere of politics, however, James sought to apply Hegelian metaphysics to American society and culture as a whole. His dialectical approach to the American experience was especially evident in the 1950 manuscript *American Civilization*. Unfortunately, this work never attained the form that its author envisioned for it, in part because by the late 1940s James was already embroiled in the legal conflict which eventually led to his internment on Ellis Island and subsequent deportation. Its completion was further complicated by the fact that Constance and C. L. R. had a son, C. L. R. James, Jr. ("Nobby"), in April 1949, a happy event which nevertheless "exacerbated his longstanding financial anxieties . . ."[53]

American Civilization constituted something of a departure from the usual polemical intercession in left-wing debates. Like *The Black Jacobins* (but unlike, say, *State Capitalism and World Revolution*), the project was intended for the widest possible audience. The book's key terms were words like *personality, universality, civilization,* and *happiness*. References were made not to leftist tracts but to magazines like *Colliers, Fortune,* and *Life*; to middlebrow pundits like Peter Drucker, Robert Hutchins, and Walter Lippman; and to larger-than-life figures like Daniel Webster, Mark Twain, Frederick Douglass, and Ernest

Hemingway. While James had revealed something of the depth of his interest in American history and literature in private correspondence, *American Civilization* reflected a different, more "culturalist" side of its author's personality than the one disclosed in the Johnson-Forest tendency's formidable documents and pamphlets.

The book's central argument was that America's distinctive and expansive contribution to world civilization was the high value that her people placed on the individual and his or her quest for happiness. Where European political discourse emphasized such abstract ideals as liberty and equality, American society valorized and legitimated the pursuit of personal happiness. In this context, "happiness" refers to the integration of the individual with the society in such a way that would allow the individual to express his or her distinctive personality. That the pursuit of happiness was socially legitimate did not in and of itself guarantee satisfaction, of course, any more than egalitarian rhetoric guaranteed fairness. But for James, the democratic idealism that served as a cornerstone of the American political landscape made that landscape quite promising from a revolutionary vantage point. Furthermore, America could only be understood on its own terms:

> Any attempt to show what America is today which does not scrupulously define and delineate the unique origins of the country and the creation of the special ideas and ideals which distinguish it, any book on America which does not do these things, is doomed to failure. Liberty, freedom, pursuit of happiness, free individuality had an actuality and a meaning in America which they had nowhere else. The Europeans wrote and theorized about freedom in superb writings. Americans lived it. That tradition is the most vital tradition in the country today. Any idea that it is merely a tradition, used by unscrupulous July Fourth politicians to deceive the people, destroys any possibility of understanding the crisis in America today.[54]

The New World had initially held out great promise for common laborers of European ancestry, but during the nineteenth century the "heroic individualism" of immigrants, farmers, and slaves clashed with the relentless march of "Northern capital" and with "the individual industrialists and financiers who organized the vast industries of the West . . ."[55] By 1900, "the system of mass production had spawned social conditions deeply inimical to the country's original ideals."[56] The struggle for happiness—a struggle that had been sanctioned by the nation's constitutive ideology—had become thwarted by a pernicious combination of the bottom line and the assembly line. This, then, was the crisis of American civilization. The contradiction between liberal values and socioeconomic realities was gnawing at the society's foundations, and collective self-activity—where Americans "can express their national genius for organization . . . their national characteristic to roll up the sleeves and get to work"[57]—represented the only hope for turning things around. But James made no promises as to when the masses would achieve victory in their struggle for freedom. What he did stress was that across the country people were striving to create "a totally integrated human existence."[58] Their effort would challenge the very basis of capitalism, pointing humanity toward the new society. "The present writer advocates nothing," James wrote:

> This is an objective analysis. But this much can be said. There will be no peace, no cessation of crisis, there is no haven ahead. *It will be many, many years before the whole world is reorganized*, and whoever believes or claims to believe that there is some possibility of emerging from the crisis on a world scale without blood, suffering, wearisome struggles, on a national and international scale, whoever says this is a charlatan or a fool, most probably the former.[59]

One of the more striking aspects of *American Civilization* is its dismissive treatment of twentieth-century intellectuals. Modern American intellectuals were viewed as fundamentally alienated, both from the masses and from themselves. Fads such as existentialism, psychoanalysis, and Catholic humanism were described as different expressions of the same misdirected sense of discontent. American intellectuals "drift along, knocking from pillar to post and finding themselves in the strangest places."[60] Blinded by their narcissism, intellectuals "have nothing to say that is new. They will make no special contribution to the future of American society, they formulate no doctrine, reactionary, progressive or otherwise . . ."[61] American intellectuals could no longer depend on a "passive subordinate mass" to remain deferential or grateful to those with advanced degrees. As a social category they would become irrelevant once individual creativity and intellect were nurtured across the society. In the "new society," "[i]ntellect will play a high role, higher than ever, but it will be

the intellectual activities of millions of men, dealing with realities."
James went on to explain that intellectuals "will be of use to the
extent that they recognize the new forces but as a class they will recognize it only when they see and feel the new force."[62]

American Civilization devotes considerable attention to the
realms of art, entertainment, and culture. Prior to the modern epoch,
the inner thoughts and feelings of the American people were
expressed through the stories, poems, and novels of writers such as
Whitman, Melville, and Twain. With the advent of movies, radio, and
other popular art forms, literary intellectuals had much less of a role
to play in conveying the popular mood. Even novels like Richard
Wright's *Native Son* or Norman Mailer's *The Naked and the Dead* could
hardly compete with Hollywood's glossy output. James's thesis was
admirably straightforward:

> The modern popular film, the modern newspaper (the *Daily News*,
> not the *Times*), the comic strip, the evolution of jazz, a popular peri-
> odical like *Life*, these mirror from year to year the deep social
> responses and evolution of the American people in relation to the
> fate which has overtaken the original concepts of freedom, free
> individuality, free association, etc.[63]

The point was that popular culture offers a wealth of insight into the
public's consciousness:

> To put it more harshly still, it is in the serious study of, above all,
> Charles Chaplin, Dick Tracy, Gasoline Alley, James Cagney,
> Edward G. Robinson, Rita Hayworth, Humphrey Bogart, genuinely
> popular novels like those of Frank Yerby (*Foxes of Harrow*, *The
> Golden Hawk*, *The Vixen*, *Pride's Castle*), men like David Selsnick,
> Cecil deMille, and Henry Luce, that you find the clearest ideological
> expression of the sentiments and deepest feelings of the American
> people and a great window into the future of America and the mod-
> ern world.[64]

One of James's specific observations concerned the way in which
popular culture underwent a major transformation during the early
1930s, with 1929 marking a break between the illusions of the earlier
period and current stark realities. After 1929, the new cinematic
heroes were gangsters and private detectives. These archetypes had a

lot in common, as the detective "is in reality the same character as the gangster. He uses what methods he can, he is as ready with his gun-butt or a bullet as the gangster. *Both have a similar scorn for the police as the representative of official society.*"[65] The Depression ushered in an era of unparalleled savagery in the popular arts. For the first time, the "funnies" (comic strips) depicted acts of depravity and murder. Mass anxieties mounted in the 1930s, and then pushed even deeper into the collective unconscious after 1945. "The bitterness, the violence, the brutality, the sadism simmering in the population, the desire to revenge themselves with their own hands, to get some release for what society had done to them since 1929"[66]—all connoting the crisis of American civilization, the gap between the desire for meaningful individualism versus the drudgery and manipulation of everyday life. This "desire . . . to get some release" could only temporarily be assuaged through the consumption of cultural objects. Art may have "assumed a very intimate relation to the daily lives of the great masses of the people,"[67] but it was a poor substitute for collective action. Indeed, there was the danger that such innovations as the detective genre and the idolatry of the movie-star system could fuel ominous trends in American society. "The possibility of totalitarian power arises," James warned,

> only when the suppressed hatreds, antagonisms, frustrations, burst irrepressibly into the open . . . The necessity to suppress unrealized instinctive needs for a new way of living, but the actual demands, wishes, deep hopes of a new universality for the individual, this can be done only by violence, brutality, terror and sadism which must correspond in depth to the hopes aroused and now in the open.[68]

While the text eschewed socialist rhetoric, *American Civilization* nevertheless fell within the parameters of a heterodox Marxism. It was, for instance, informed by a sort of Hegelian dialectic, emphasizing social-structural contradictions and the movement of world history toward the "actualization of the universal."[69] Furthermore, the chapter on industrial workers echoed the Johnson-Forest tendency's "worker-centric" politics: "forgetting for the moment such terms as free enterprise, socialism, communism, etc. the industrial workers and their future are the basis of the whole edifice."[70] A repetition of the upsurge of industrial unionism and militancy of the 1930s was predicted, but on a grander scale, with "forces . . . gathering below the surface, and if we can judge at all by the past, forces of a power of which we have had so far only indications."[71] So far, so Marxist. But the stress on industrial conflict was matched by an emphasis on what later became known as "new social movements" based among blacks and women, if not homosexuals.[72] The discussion concerning the lowly status of women in modern America—despite certain material and cultural advances—was particularly acute:

> A modern man has grown up in an environment of a man-dominated civilization, education, books, movies, his parents, even the experience of his very early infancy (Margaret Mead has written on this). These have gone to make him what he is. He has as a rule little except the most abstract sense of equality. He and his wife may both work, but almost inevitably the responsibilities of the home fall upon the woman, not only in the material sense of cooking and cleaning but in the sense that except in rare cases, the responsibility for adjustments to differences of personality fall automatically upon her.[73]

Tackling the roots of women's oppression required a drastic overhaul of household relations:

> Men and women will be equal when from the very start, cooking, washing and other household duties, child care, personal adornment, games, sports, etc. are taught to children by a world which makes no distinction at all between the sexes. The age of chivalry must go and go finally and irrevocably . . . Only when men by upbringing not so much in words but by social practice can turn their hands to every single social and domestic necessity in the home and not feel it a disruption of the personality pattern to do so, will there be any possibility of equality. Under these circumstances, even a baby in the home does not become automatically the woman's sphere, except for a very few months at least.[74]

Passages like these began to map the contours of the "new society," where the transformation of work and politics would be accompanied by dramatic changes in the sphere of intimate social relations. But James also warned that, in the absence of a second American revolution, authoritarianism (on the right and on the "left") would gain momentum, and that the status of women and blacks would deteriorate.

Herman Melville's name crops up throughout *American Civiliza-tion*, and the nineteenth-century novelist occupied a special place in James's critical pantheon. James saw Melville as a masterful interpreter of America's transition to capitalist modernity, creating distinctive characters and realistic workplace settings that encapsulated all of the tensions and contradictions inherent in American society and culture. In James's view, Melville's fiction became more relevant, and therefore valuable, as time went by. His affection for Melville's work was made plain in *Mariners, Renegades and Castaways*, which appropriated and distilled many of the literary and historical arguments advanced in *American Civilization*. This short work of literary criticism offered an unconventional yet thoughtful reading of Melville's novels, concen-trating in particular on *Moby Dick*. Like *American Civilization*, it was intended as an appreciative study of the people with whom its author had spent nearly fifteen years.

Although James would have preferred to remain in the country indefinitely, this option was closed once he was apprehended by the immigration authorities for "passport violations" in the spring of 1952. His arrest and subsequent internment came at the height of America's fearful response to the Cold War rivalry with the Soviet Union, and was part of a wider government crackdown on illegal aliens identified with radical causes. He served out a six-month internment on Ellis Island waiting to hear if his application for U.S. citizenship had been accepted.[75] When the application was rejected, he was given a few weeks to leave the country. In the fall of 1953 he departed for England.

While James had lectured to a variety of audiences on the topic of Melville, *Mariners, Renegades and Castaways* was completed dur-ing the author's arduous confinement on Ellis Island, and it was intended to bolster his case for U.S. citizenship. As part of this pro-cess, the book's final chapter recounts his experiences as an internee facing expulsion from his adopted homeland. In one passage, he describes his arrival on the Island, where he was placed in a small cell with five Communists, who immediately recognized the notorious anti-Stalinist:

> [F]or a day or two, the Communists were somewhat uncertain as to what should be their attitude toward me . . . I could see them whis-pering and consulting together. Finally, however, they seemed to come to the conclusion that they would treat me as a fellow-pris-

oner. And this they did with that thoroughness and scrupulousness
which characterizes them in any line that they are for the moment
following.[76]

The assistance of his determined cell mates proved critical as James
lobbied the prison authorities for adequate food and milk for the
treatment of his stomach condition. Diagnosed as having a duodenal
ulcer in 1937, James had recurrent health problems throughout his
stay in the United States. In 1942, he collapsed on the street and was
hospitalized as a result of his perforated stomach. Despite the help
provided by his cell mates, prison life did not in any way modify
James's negative assessment of Communism. He did, however,
become more sympathetic to the civil libertarian strain of American
liberal thought, after receiving firm support from civil libertarians for
his appeal for citizenship. "In years past I have smiled indulgently at
the grandiloquent statements and illusions of these old liberals," he
admits, "but recently in the light of modern events I have been re-
reading some of them and the conditions against which they struggled to establish the principles by which only a few years ago we
thought we lived."[77] It is indicative of James's whole approach to his
confinement that he found solace in that quintessentially American
phenomenon, the principled liberal. Ellis Island simultaneously symbolized the callous nature of the state and brought its prisoner into
contact with the country's finest traditions.

At the heart of *Mariners, Renegades and Castaways* is an analysis
of the characters and moral subtext of *Moby Dick*. Ahab in particular
is singled out as signifying the essentially totalitarian impulse concealed behind capitalism's relentless pursuit of conquest and expansion. In his mad hunt for the white whale, Ahab loses his humanity.
A power-hungry renegade from civilization, he lords over his subor-
dinates just as he seeks to dominate technology and nature. The
invention of Ahab is, for James, a momentous event in the development of American literature. He is an original character, the "embodiment of the totalitarian type."[78] Ahab's officers, Starbuck, Stubb, and
Flask, on the other hand, are well-drawn but essentially familiar
types. They find themselves prostrate before the totalitarian personality, fretting over the ship's mission, but offering no alternative.
Trained to obey orders, they are the *Pequod*'s white-collar strata,
unable to function outside of the bureaucratic routine. The ship's
crew, in contrast to both the officers and the captain, enjoy the dignity

and autonomy that accompanies meaningful labor. Unlike Ahab, they live by no plan. James effusively praises "the warmth, the humor, the sanity, the anonymous but unfailing humanity of the renegades and castaways and savages of the *Pequod*, rooted in the whole historical past of man, doing what they have to do, facing what they have to face."[79]

There is a sense in which, for James, the whaling ships of New England were some of the earliest factories in American history. In writing about the *Pequod*, Melville was thus able to dissect the contradictions of wage labor under conditions of mounting tyranny, just as Marx and Engels had written about industrial capitalism in light of the forced urbanization of the English countryside. Like Marx, Melville had a keen eye for the structuration of social conflict through processes of production, and a discernible sympathy for those at the bottom of the totem pole.

Ishmael, the narrator, is an intermediate character, whose introspection and self-absorption is viewed as representative of the ideological plight of the educated middle class. Although Ishmael works alongside the mariners, he cannot focus clearly on the task before him. Always dreaming, he is the ship's intellectual, and is manifestly unable to either formulate a coherent strategy (like Ahab), or simply "be" (like the crew). Not surprisingly, James is less than effusive in his depiction of Ishmael's character:

> Just look at the names of the famous books which will be handed to future generations as a picture of our times: *The Waste Land, Journey to the End of the Night, Darkness at Noon, Farewell to Arms, The Counterfeiters, In Remembrance of Things Past*—a catalogue of misery or self-centered hopelessness. These are the books that Ishmael and Pierre [another Melville character] would write if they wrote novels . . . Melville describes the same world in which they live, and Ishmael and Pierre are sick to the heart with the modern sickness.[80]

With its thirty-some crewmen, the ship's social partitions and troubled voyage were described as anticipating contemporary dilemmas over such issues as class stratification, the abuse of technology, the alienation of the intellectual, and, above all, the malignancy of totalitarianism. Thus, in a sense, *Moby Dick* should be of greater relevance to readers of, say, *Labor Action*, or the *Saturday Evening Post*, than to Melville's contemporaries. James claims that in Melville's

"great book the division and antagonisms and madnesses of an out-
worn civilization are mercilessly dissected and cast aside."[81] The
interaction of the officers, crew, captain, and Ishmael (with each
other, with technology, and with the natural order) drives the plot
forward. Tragedy looms as Ahab's compulsive need for domination
over man and nature threatens the ship itself. In the same way that
Ahab draws closer and closer to Moby Dick, modern totalitarianism
pushes society in the direction of barbarism. James emphasizes in
particular the threat that Ahab poses to the natural world. One of the
book's many stirring passages argues that man is ultimately dependent on nature, and should respect its sovereignty:

> Nature is not a background to men's activity or something to be
> conquered and used. It is a part of man, at every turn physically,
> intellectually and emotionally, and man is a part of it. And if man
> does not integrate his daily life with his natural surroundings and
> his technical achievements, they will turn on him and destroy
> him.[82]

Mariners, Renegades and Castaways called on Americans to reformu-
late their country's relationship to the natural and social world. From
the pen of an obscure Ellis Island subversive came a curiously sympathetic but terribly angry cry. As Darrell E. Levi has suggested, while
the book "seems to have had little, if any, impact on subsequent
Melville scholarship," it nevertheless "can still lead readers to a wider
and more enlightened reading of Melville."[83]

After James's banishment, the Correspondence group undertook
the task of privately publishing and circulating *Mariners, Renegades
and Castaways*. It proved to be an expensive proposition, since 20,000
copies were printed whereas "actual sales amounted to less than 2,000
copies."[84] Resentment over the inevitable financial burden helped to
fuel the fight between the Dunayevskaya camp and the group loyal to
James's legacy. Some years later, James reflected on Correspondence's
assorted problems. "The movement which we started," he wrote, "has
been broken up almost to bits."[85] In a different letter James described
the personal toll involved in observing the group's decline:

> Even now when I think of it, of the work that I used to do, I feel
> distressed. It is perhaps the only thing in my life which I look back
> not so much with bitterness, but with regret, with recognition of

the fact that I wasted my strength, my time and my physical health on something that was absolutely useless.[86]

Attempting to build a group like Correspondence during the economically buoyant and—despite certain expectations—politically somnolent Eisenhower years must have invoked intense frustrations and difficulties. It would be surprising if a few of the group's key players did not feel at least a little bitter over the course of events.

Paul Buhle has suggested that the "fifteen-year sojourn in the U.S. represents in many ways the most curious and personally obscure part of James's life."[87] It is evident that James combined revolutionary activism, philosophical study, and an enthusiasm for popular culture in an energetic and iconoclastic fashion. Yet if the period is now a little less "personally obscure" than before (on account of the biographical efforts of Buhle, Cudjoe, Grimshaw, McLemee, and others) there is still perhaps something curious about the way in which C. L. R. James approached American politics and history as a leftist and as a cultural critic. The connection between his unorthodox Trotskyism, and *American Civilization* and *Mariners, Renegades and Castaways*, may require some elucidation.

American Civilization in particular represents both an affirmation of and a departure from its author's work in the Trotskyist movement and in the Johnson-Forest tendency. It was an affirmation in the sense that its emphasis on self-emancipation and collective action was rooted in classical Marxism and in the tendency's own political program. Furthermore, the rejection of elitist solutions along social democratic or vanguard party lines was entirely compatible with the radically democratic inclinations of the Johnson-Forest tendency. It should come as no surprise that at the core of *American Civilization* was the argument that American society faced a crisis that could only be resolved through the development of a mass revolutionary movement. It is also not so astonishing that the book expressed a marked confidence in the capacity of Americans to reorganize their society on a participatory and egalitarian basis—after all, as we have seen, the Johnson-Forest tendency was distinguished not only by its program (the autonomy of social movements, Soviet "state capitalism," the rejection of the vanguard party), but also by its optimistic and almost romantic conception of revolutionary possibilities under advanced capitalism.

At the same time that the book articulated certain themes that were characteristic of the Johnson-Forest tendency, *American Civilization* also went beyond the essentially political and economic problematic of such intellectuals as Dunayevskaya and Grace Lee by highlighting cultural and social questions. The crisis facing American society was seen as being reproduced across a multitude of cultural and social sites—popular fiction, Hollywood movies, and family relations—as well as in industry and on the shop floor. At the same time, the resolution of this crisis seemed to require the mobilization of cultural as well as political energies. The book's conceptualization of revolutionary politics seemed broader and more eclectic than that of the tendency's political pamphlets, which were of course written for a specific and possibly narrower audience.

It may also be argued that both *American Civilization* and *Mariners, Renegades and Castaways* displayed a much greater sensitivity to American traditions and conditions than many of the Johnson-Forest tendency's documents. As was the case in the writings on black politics, these books represented a serious attempt to truly "Americanize Bolshevism" without doing an injustice to either Marxist fundamentals or American realities. The key was the way in which James was able to encompass cultural as well as political and economic issues in his work on black struggles, the crisis of American civilization, and the literary contribution of Herman Melville. By emphasizing the totality of American life, he was able to bring into focus the social contradictions of the American Century. The prophetic aspect of his work was expressed in his understanding that contradictions in the early postwar order would eventually produce dramatic changes in the spheres of race relations, family relations, culture, and left-wing politics.

It seems likely that, with the composition of *Notes on Dialectics* and *State Capitalism and World Revolution*, James had taken the Johnson-Forest tendency problematic just about as far as it could go. Of course, the founding of the Correspondence group offered new possibilities for radical interventions. But the theoretical issues that had seemed desperately urgent in the early 1940s had been largely worked through by the end of the decade. With *American Civilization* and *Mariners, Renegades and Castaways* James seemed to be saying that he was ready to incorporate the theoretical and political lessons of his years as a Trotskyist and as a Johnsonite in a way that would allow him to move on to a whole new array of concerns. The collaborations that had characterized his life in the 1940s were interesting and provocative, but they also provided an intellectual foundation for what I would argue to be an ultimately more consequential set of explorations of the politics of art, society, and culture that opened with *American Civilization* and reached their apex with *Beyond a Boundary*. However, instead of making a clean break with the Johnsonite past, James devoted considerable attention to the Correspondence group while resident in Britain.

CHAPTER FIVE

—

Facing Reality

LONDON IN THE 1950s was a less glamorous, less dynamic, and in many respects more provincial city than its New World counterpart. Yet, as far as its treatment of political exiles was concerned, the English capital felt more tolerant than New York City. Although James was hardly feted by London's cliquish literary community on his arrival in 1953, he renewed several old friendships and quickly settled into a book-filled domestic arrangement centered around the typewriter, revolutionary politics, and the companionship of Selma Weinstein James, who joined him in London several months after his banishment from the United States, to become his third wife in 1956.[1] Selma James was a self-assured Brooklynite who made a big impression within the Johnson-Forest tendency. Her areas of interest included the labor movement and the black movement, and she was one of the most outstanding of the organization's younger generation. From the outset of her political activity, Selma James had always been particularly interested in the condition of women. In London, she worked hard to provide them both with a supportive context within which to carry out their individual and mutual political work.

The relationship with Selma was not without its difficulties. Although they never obtained a formal divorce, C. L. R. and Selma began a painful process of separation by the mid-1960s. For over a decade they had a productive but stressful marriage, which almost certainly lacked the emotional intensity of James's relationship with Constance Webb. As Selma was almost thirty years younger than her husband, it was in certain respects an unequal partnership, and she chaffed at being relegated to the role of the "leader's wife" in a small organization.

The novelist George Lamming purportedly drew on their relationship for his frank portrait of a troubled marriage in *Natives of My Person* (1972). At one point Lamming has the character "Surgeon" ruminating on the difficult circumstances of his marriage:

> He had married her because he needed her support, but the marriage had gradually withered away. Circumstances had reversed their roles. She who was so zealous for his success had become an obstacle to his progress. He had made no attempt to disguise this feeling. Every stratagem that would advance his reputation was later threatened by the irrelevance of their association. She was in the way, and he had told her so.[2]

Toward the end of the book, "Surgeon's Wife" complains to friends about her exclusion from her husband's circle:

> It was such a noble sight. Men of learning collaborating on a plan. And my husband at the center of their attention. He was always like that. It was his natural place. At the center of their attention. I would serve them food and drink. But I could not partake of their analysis. Their talk was always above my understanding, although I was the substance of their concern. I and all who might be victims of any sickness in the Kingdom. To hear them predict the future that could come if circumstances allowed their plans to operate, it was like waiting for heaven.[3]

Lamming takes artistic license to absurd lengths with this depiction of Selma, who was more than capable of holding her own among her husband's circle. But the portrait of C. L. R. as a rather aloof companion, more concerned with politics than personal intimacy, is quite recognizable.

The breakdown of their relationship was several years off, however, and in this period both of them labored to create an effective partnership. As before, money remained a major problem, and James's letters from this period are filled with anxious references to their pecuniary difficulties. The household received sporadic funds from one or two supporters on the other side of the Atlantic, and writings and lectures may have generated the occasional remittance. It was in this period that he began to write on cricket once more, earning small fees as a newspaper correspondent. In addition, Selma James managed their household budget and held outside jobs as a typist. She also did a prodigious amount of typing for C. L. R., as had Constance Webb before her. He was utterly dependent on her contribution. His letters make it clear that, despite whatever monies were coming in, their day-to-day existence was cramped, hand to mouth, and sometimes desperate. The situation constrained their individual writing projects and perhaps also their marriage. It may have been an especially disheartening state of affairs for C. L. R., who was by this time well into middle age.

One of the people James looked up was his boyhood friend and fellow Pan-Africanist, George Padmore. The two had remained in touch in the 1940s, even as Padmore moved in the direction of neutralism, African socialism, and cultural nationalism.[4] On several occasions after James's return to London they consulted each other about the progress Kwame Nkrumah's Convention People's Party was making in bringing about independence for the west African nation Gold Coast (present-day Ghana). James also corresponded with a range of literary and political figures in Britain and elsewhere—such as the writer Neville Cardus, the Labour parliamentarian Michael Foot, the art critic John Berger, and his old anarchist friend Daniel Guerin—and spent a productive afternoon with Dr. Martin Luther King and Coretta Scott King when the famous civil rights leaders visited London in the spring of 1957.[5]

The connection with Kwame Nkrumah was particularly important to James. He had first met Nkrumah in 1943 when the latter was a student at Lincoln College in Pennsylvania, and they met on several occasions during the war to talk politics and go over issues of political strategy. Nkrumah was later to write that it was through C. L. R. "that I learned how an underground movement worked."[6] Toward the end of the war James penned a letter of introduction for Nkrumah to take to George Padmore in London. This put him in touch with the best-connected household in the entire Pan-African community. Padmore and Nkrumah later served together as political secretaries to the fifth Pan-African Congress, and Padmore acted in an informal capacity as the Convention People's Party representative in London in the mid-1950s.[7] In James's view, Nkrumah was perhaps the most promising African leader to emerge out of the political diaspora associated with the work of the International African Service Bureau.

Despite his extensive international contacts, James was fairly isolated in this period. As Padmore well knew, British politics had moved on in James's absence. Concerns associated with the Depression—Labour Party betrayals, the Popular Front, working-class privation—had receded to the background, while issues like the welfare state, NATO, and the breakup of the Empire were uppermost in the minds of progressive activists. Furthermore, things had changed in James's old corner of the left. Although there were still Trotskyists burrowed inside the Labour Party, the Marxist Group was long forgotten. Even Pan-Africanism, while enjoying great success in the African diaspora, no longer represented the fresh force that it had in the 1930s. For a distinguished visitor returning after an absence of less than two decades, the cultural and political differences must have seemed profound.[8]

How much had James's own personality evolved in the intervening period? In fundamental respects he remained unchanged. He was still charming, good natured, unsentimental, reserved, cerebral, and militant in outlook. While he had added some weight, he continued to carry himself like a former athlete, with an unequivocal physical grace and personal confidence. At the same time, he was in all probability more melancholy than he had been twenty years earlier; in particular, the breakup with Constance Webb and the fact that he was physically separated from C. L. R. James, Jr., must have weighed heavily on his mind. As before, he shielded his feelings from all but the closest of friends and continued to put political and literary work above psychological introspection.[9]

The depth of James's commitment to organized political activity was suggested by the fact that he maintained an intimate relationship with the Correspondence group throughout the decade. Through lengthy letters, and discussions with the occasional visitor, he took every opportunity to influence Correspondence's development. In return for these labors, the membership helped to subsidize James's activities and household expenses, as well as the mother of his child. Despite the fact that the new organization's prospects were at best uncertain, Selma and C. L. R. were committed to sponsoring from abroad a new type of revolutionary organization. Yet their "interference" may have been one of the underlying factors behind the 1955 split that so severely undermined the organized expression of Johnsonism.

Apart from prodding the Correspondence group into shape, James devoted his energies to writing on aesthetics, the visual arts, cinema, and literature. This second, less overtly "political" project involved building on the Marxian cultural theoretic advanced in *American Civilization* and *Mariners, Renegades and Castaways*. While some of this work made its way toward a public audience (the Correspondence group issued his pamphlet on democracy in ancient Greece, *Every Cook Can Govern*, for example), the bulk of it remained unfinished or unpublished. The archives in England hold numerous documents and letters written in this period.[10] They also house nearly thirty children's stories ("the Nobby stories") written for C. L. R. James, Jr. between 1953 and 1957. Children's fiction was the major medium through which he attempted to speak to his son and provide him with some form of moral inspiration.

Most of the stories revolve around the adventures of two young boys, Bad Boo Boo Loo and Good Boongko, who, as Anna Grimshaw notes, "often got themselves into scrapes." The two boys were members of a Club, a kind of friendly discussion circle where members of the local community reflect on issues of the day. In addition to Bad Boo Boo Loo and Good Boongko, the Club included such interesting-sounding characters as "Moby Dick, General Sharkenhower, Lizzie the Lizard, Filbert and Flibbert the Fleas, Storky the Stork, Leo the Lion, Big Bruno, Peter the Painter and Nicholas the Worker."[11] Through a metafictional device, Nobby himself belonged to the Club, under the name Choongko. Several of the stories refer either to actual historical personages, such as Michelangelo, or to ancient mythology, such as the tale of Troy and the Trojan horse. In one story, Bad Boo Boo Loo forces himself to learn how to read, in order to participate in a "competition by which everybody would tell some stories about the struggle for independence." The fable Bad Boo Boo Loo tells is that of William Tell, "one of those who helped Switzerland to gain its independence." When he finishes telling the story of the arrow, the boy, and the apple, Big Bruno says that "I think we can say that today we have seen Bad Boo Boo Loo win his own independence." Given that Nobby's father was writing on the eve of his second visit to Africa's Gold Coast, to participate in the founding of the "new independent state Ghana,"[12] the story contained an added, allegorical dimension.

Toward the end of the decade, James began to refocus his efforts. While remaining in close touch with individual Correspondence members (as well as Constance and their son Nobby), his interest in West Indian affairs was reawakened by the news that national independence was finally on the political horizon. In 1958, he returned to Trinidad and Tobago for the first time in twenty-five years. As we shall find, this shift in focus accompanied a more general, if incomplete, reorientation toward Third World issues. The late 1950s was also a period when he began to review his life's course. *Beyond a Boundary*, published in 1963 but largely written in Europe during the mid- to late 1950s, connected its author's rediscovery of Caribbean themes with autobiographical material. Its lucid and affecting prose style confirmed James's renewed commitment to the occupation of writing. I discuss his Caribbean sojourn in the next chapter.

The main threads of James's life in the 1950s and early 1960s—revolutionary instigator from abroad, literary intellectual, and anticolonial activist—did not mesh in the way that his diverse interests had during the 1930s. Instead, he gradually drifted from one activity to the next. A sense of frustration would have been natural given the difficulties associated with building a revolutionary tendency at the height of the Cold War. Indeed, the space for radical intervention throughout the industrial world (with exceptions such as Italy) had shrunk considerably between the 1930s and the 1950s. Consequently, James effectively abandoned the project of trying to devise an appropriate strategy for American radicalism. Correspondence's publications rehearsed themes and values that anticipated the early New Left, and we shall have ample reason to pursue the trajectory of the Johnson-Forest tendency in this period. But ideas failed to translate into numbers or power. James turned his hopes and attention to other forces in the New World, forces concentrated not in midwestern American factories but Caribbean villages and West African cities.

Emboldened by the sheer novelty of its project, Correspondence attempted to make good on its promise to go beyond Trotskyist and vanguard politics by promoting the creative self-activity of the masses. It sought to create a democratic form of organization that would encourage the active participation of all members and "prefigure" social relations in the "new society." From its inception, the group's leaders attempted to give working-class members a powerful voice in the organization's decision-making process. This was done in part by formally dividing the group into three tiers, or "layers." An anonymous, clearly embittered former Correspondence activist later described the group's internal organization to the writer Ivar Oxaal:

> The real proletarians were put in the first layer, people of mixed status, like housewives, in the second, and the intellectuals were put in the third. Our meetings consisted of the now highly prestigeful first layer spouting off, usually in a random, inarticulate way, about what they thought about everything under the sun. The rest of us, especially we intellectuals in the third layer, were told to listen.[13]

The group's worker-centric politics were reflected in other ways. Within months of its formation, Correspondence had published not one, but two "thick descriptions"[14] of work and politics in the auto plant. One of these, Charles Denby's autobiographical *Indignant Heart: A Black Worker's Journal*, recounted one militant's journey from the deep south to a Michigan auto plant, offering a vivid and ultimately hopeful portrait of black-white relations in the context of plantation and factory labor in midcentury America.[15] *Punching Out*, a terse yet entertaining pamphlet written by Martin Glaberman, chided the United Auto Workers for siding with management against the rank and file. Characterizing the UAW as a "source of strength," Glaberman nevertheless claimed:

> The working class today recognizes the labor bureaucracy as an enemy, as an administrator of capital. They look to the union as a ... means of keeping the gains they have made over the past years. But they do not look to the union for the next steps to be taken. They resent and oppose the domination and interference of the union bureaucracy.[16]

This theme of class resistance to the "domination and interference of the union bureaucracy" was more than a little reminiscent of the critique of capitalist society generated by the Parisian-based *Socialisme ou Barbarie*. Formed in 1949, *Socialisme ou Barbarie* was led by two former Trotskyists, Cornelius Castoriadis and Claude Lefort, and offered an alternative to French Communism and the Marxist existentialism propounded by Jean-Paul Sartre and the circle around *Les*

Temps Modernes. Although the group disbanded in 1966 after a series of schisms and faction fights, *Socialisme ou Barbarie* was later credited with inspiring many of the key demands identified with the May Events in France. As Lefort later recalled, *Socialisme ou Barbarie* and Correspondence enjoyed fraternal relations throughout the 1950s.[17] Lefort and Castoriadis were particularly taken by the Romano/Lee pamphlet *The American Worker*, which they reprinted in the first eight issues of their journal. (German and Italian translations were to follow.) For these European Marxists, the pamphlet documented the capacity of the American working class to theorize its own condition and to resist the ideological trappings of the consumer society. As one member of the organization, Jean-Francois Lyotard, later wrote, the pamphlet advanced "a class point of view without blinders . . . it stressed the incommensurability of the 'same' experiences, depending on whether they are spoken in the idiom of the owner or the foreman or in that of the workers; and it did so without concern as to whether one side or the other spoke or did not speak 'Marxist'."[18] Lyotard affectionately terms the pamphlet a "provocation."

Lefort and Castoriadis drew on material featured in the newspaper *Correspondence*, which was launched in October 1953 (after a two-year trial run of mimeographed issues[19]) and published twice monthly until April 1955. A memorable inaugural issue opened with a column written in the first person by Charles Denby, entitled "Worker's Journal." The front page also featured a sympathetic discussion of Lucille Ball's appearance in front of the House Un-American Activities Committee as a friendly witness ("In those days," Ms. Ball claimed, referring to the 1930s, "it was almost as bad to be a Republican" as a Communist) and a long statement by the paper's first editor, Johnny Zupan (a Detroit autoworker and shop steward who had drifted out of the organization by 1955). Inside *Correspondence* were articles on conditions at Detroit's Ford Rouge plant, a report from the coal fields, a couple of cartoons, editorial comment on the Kinsey Report, a review of the movie *From Here to Eternity,* and columns on "How We Beat the Boss," "Young Guys and Gals," and "In this Corner"—about sports. Later issues examined baseball, the Western movie *Shane*, race relations, the United Auto Workers, the 1954 Supreme Court ruling on desegregation, and a section on "Why Workers Don't Read." As its unusual combination of interests made clear, the paper was very much absorbed in the fabric of everyday life.

Indeed, the paper's concern with popular culture and daily life was years ahead of its time. Unlike other leftist papers produced in the heyday of Fordism, *Correspondence* openly discussed issues like human sexuality, male chauvinism, blue-collar discontent, and high school alienation. *A Woman's Place* (1952), one of the group's best-selling pamphlets, was written by Selma James and Filomena Daddario. *Artie Cuts Out* (1953), by "Arthur Bauman," tells the "story of a Brooklyn youth and his relations, with his school, parents, police and the student strike of 1950."[20] Both the pamphlets and the newspaper itself relied heavily on what Dunayevskaya termed the "full fountain pen" method of writing. This involved having members of the group interview workers and then allowing these workers to edit their comments for publication. The center pages of *Correspondence* became filled with readers' comments on a wide array of topics, not a few of which had been collected through the use of the full fountain pen. And many of the paper's articles were written in the first person—not only columns, but news stories as well—so as to generate a close rapport with its readership.

The cartoons of *Correspondence* deserve special mention. In a series promising to explore the positive side of unemployment, sharply etched drawings highlighted captions reading: "It gives you free time for that Bermuda trip," "The best things in life are free," and "You learn to live with your human relations." One recurrent character was "Egghead," who said things like "Our committeeman is real conscientious. He's been working on my grievance for almost a year," and "I can't see why the fellers criticize the contract. Why it's so complicated they can't even understand half of it." Another regular was "The Needle," a box-headed prankster who sent his shop steward pointed valentine cards: "To Joe the Steward: Roses are Red/Violets are Blue/The Contract Stinks/And so do you." After Fidel Castro's ascension to power in 1959, the Needle was seen marching around an assembly line sporting a bushy beard and a cigar. No doubt the Needle sent chills down the spine of UAW representatives and middle management alike.

Despite the paper's engaging style and wry sense of humor, getting it into the hands of new readers was an uphill battle. Since *Correspondence*—along with numerous other radical periodicals—had been characterized by the U.S. Attorney General as a "subversive" publication, many readers were wary of adding their names to the newspaper's mailing list. Glaberman later recalled that approximately

5,000 copies of *Correspondence* were regularly printed per issue. Even though an annual subscription cost only two dollars and fifty cents, "I don't think we ever reached very much more than a hundred in terms of subscriptions," Glaberman estimated.[21] According to one document, the paper generated a monthly deficit of two thousand dollars.[22] Because of its supposedly treasonous content, the United States Postal Service denied *Correspondence* second-class mailing rights. The July 24, 1954 issue was deemed "unmailable" because, by expressing sympathy with shop-floor rebellion, the newspaper "tended to incite to murder and assassination."[23]

Peripheral members drifted away, and a membership that had never been larger than one hundred slowly dropped past half of that. As the U.S. economy expanded and the broad ranks of the left shrank, the audience for unorthodox Marxist politics became smaller. Inevitably, tensions within the group mounted. James's letters to the American comrades returned again and again to the group's troubled internal dynamics, and the need for political clarity and intragroup solidarity. These letters—which ran as long as twenty pages, single spaced, and which were generated on a weekly and even daily basis—exhorted members to turn outward and leave introspection to the doleful Trotskyists. At the same time, the letters voiced James's assumption that a mass radical upsurge was still imminent, which helped breed a slightly passive orientation toward the outside world. It was not enough to print stimulating articles on everyday life; the paper had to circulate as widely as possible, and this effort (already handicapped by the historical context) was perhaps limited by a somewhat rosy or complacent reading of the political tea leaves. James addressed this issue in somewhat different terms in a private letter, remarking: "In the past our great weakness has been that we produced the documents with energy and devotion but were conspicuously deficient in circulating them. That was because I daresay we were over-concerned with the production of other documents."[24]

In early 1955, the impending break with Dunayevskaya and her followers became a reality. The unavoidable tensions and conflicts that arise within small political groups operating under unpromising circumstances had escalated into a full-blown factional schism. The split also reflected the failure of James and his supporters to formulate a persuasive model of proautonomy, "post-Leninist" political practice. In emphasizing the need for a disciplined cadre organization (one that nevertheless eschewed the Leninist notion of a vanguard

THE NEEDLE   by Frank

Hello . . . hello . . . International? It looks like we're
in for trouble.

EGGHEAD

That's shrewd, making
big demands when contract
negotiations start. That
way we won't lose too
much of what we've got.

THESE UNITED STATES   By Frank

EGGHEAD

I can't see why the fel-
lers criticize the contract.
Why it's so complicated
they can't even understand
half of it.

Selected cartoons from *Correspondence*—1953–1961
Permission: Martin Glaberman

party), Dunayevskaya reassured those who sought a more conventional approach to politics. Dunayevskaya envisioned a *Correspondence* that was more explicitly "political," less chatty and informal. She wanted the group to place more of a priority on recruitment, arguing that new members would reinvigorate the faltering movement. In addition, James's bid to direct the organization from London caused a certain amount of resentment. Clearly, the difficult work of maintaining the organization in the context of the postwar boom and anti-Communist fervor aggravated whatever latent personality clashes already existed.

By late March, the grouping around Dunayevskaya bolted. Acting on the principle that since they constituted a majority of the membership, their faction was entitled to Correspondence's property, Dunayevskaya's group took much of the organization's physical belongings with them. A member of the minority, Freddy Paine, reported that the organization's office

> had been cleaned out of everything in it. Literature; desks; file cabinets; chairs; and the refrigerator—all were gone. Even the display board with the different books [*Indignant Heart* and *Mariners, Renegades and Castaways*] was gone. The only stuff left was the piles of back issues of the paper.[25]

The remaining Johnsonites claimed that in forming her own organization, Dunayevskaya was returning to her neo-Trotskyist roots. "The last thing," she said in response, "anybody ever talked about in the other group is *building* the organization. You would think that just because we broke with the concept of a party to lead and thirst for no such thing, that therefore there is no reason for our being."[26] Paper selling and organization building became central foci of Correspondence's new rival, the Detroit-based News and Letters organization. The group continues to champion "Marxist-Humanism" and the teachings and writings of its founder and theoretical guru, Raya Dunayevskaya.[27]

It was a significantly weakened Correspondence (numbering perhaps twenty-five people) that continued to receive letters from London. The group faced competition not only from News and Letters, but from more established groups on the left, such as the Socialist Workers Party (where Cannon was still a dominant presence) and Shachtman's Independent Socialist League.[28] As the SWP and the

Johnsonites had gleefully predicted, the Shachtmanites were moving away from democratic centralism in favor of an independent, anti-Communist, democratic socialist stance. Glaberman and other Correspondence members tended to dismiss the notion that these groups had anything in common with their approach. But for anyone who was looking to become active in leftist politics, the proliferation of anti-Stalinist formations in such an unpromising period would have made the situation baffling and perhaps a little disorienting.

With the consent of the London household, James Boggs was named editor of a *Correspondence* that retained the overall style of the 1953–1955 bimonthly, but with a somewhat narrower range of articles.[29] Grace Lee, Martin Glaberman, and Freddy Paine were among those who played an active role in the organization. James contributed pieces as "our European" and "our West Indian" correspondent; private letters were occasionally excerpted under the title "letter from abroad."[30] The group also issued a couple of pamphlets, both reprints from the newspaper, during the second half of the 1950s. The first was Glaberman's *Union Committeemen and Wildcat Strikes* (1955). Like *Punching Out*, this pamphlet contrasted "bureaucrats and ranks" and provided plenty of examples of working-class resistance to management tactics inside auto plants. Glaberman concluded:

> If all that was needed was a new program and a better plan to challenge the bureaucrats, *Correspondence* would never have been started. The futility of such an undertaking is adequately provided in the pitiful lives of the radical sects . . . [T]he only reason that *Correspondence* has for its existence is to provide a place and a means for the expression of the hostility to all forms of bureaucracy that exists in every section of society.[31]

Next came James's *Every Cook Can Govern: A Study of Democracy in Ancient Greece*, one fragment of the humanistic project that James had been working on since the late 1940s. Drawing on the author's extensive knowledge of classical Greek texts, as well as his ongoing examination of the historically conditioned role of art in mediating the relationship between the individual and society, it provided a stirring account of the institutionalization of direct democracy in the city-states of antiquity and took issue with those who castigated Greek society because of slavery and male domination of the public sphere. Although he acknowledged the existence of coerced labor and women's oppression in ancient Greece, James maintained that the city-state in its highest form represented a breakthrough in terms of the quality of its political relationships and institutions. For James, the crucial point was that Greek democracy rested on institutions of direct popular power, including juries that interpreted the law, selection by lot for the Athenian executive council of five hundred, a minimum of permanent functionaries, participatory religious commissions, and popular judgement at the annual theatrical festival of Dionysus.[32]

Subsequent historical research has qualified some of the broad generalizations drawn in *Every Cook Can Govern*. In particular, scholars are now more liable to point to the uneven and episodic character of democracy in ancient Greece. Nevertheless, the pamphlet advances an appealing portrait of direct democracy in action, arguing that a politics based around participatory civic institutions could be (a la *The Invading Socialist Society*) revived in modern society. In later documents, James would suggest that the city-state model was applicable to the independent nation-states of the Caribbean.[33] The close-knit communities of the West Indies could, he would argue, replicate the face-to-face political relationships of the Greek *agora*. Through financial support and, more importantly, through encouragement and civic promotion, West Indian politicians could stimulate the kind of cultural dynamism that characterized the city-states of antiquity. Periclean Athens could serve as a model for Third World cities such as Port of Spain, where the astonishing productivity of twentieth-century technologies could be substituted for the slave labor of antiquity.

As we have seen, *Every Cook Can Govern* was part of a larger project dealing with cultural themes from a broadly historical materialist perspective. Much of this work took the form of personal correspondence with individuals he knew from the radical movement, but some of it also went to a tiny circle of professional critics whose writings he respected. Three surviving "letters to critics" are reprinted in *The C. L. R. James Reader*, and they offer a marvelous point of entry into James's reflections on art, literature, and society.[34]

Written on the eve of his impending expulsion, all three letters reprise the themes of *American Civilization* and *Mariners, Renegades and Castaways*. A letter to Melville critic Jay Leyda offers a spirited defense of the author's depiction of *Moby Dick* as exploring the contradictions of modern capitalism (particularly through the character of Ahab, who represents the totalitarian personality). "I have put forward," James tells Leyda, "a theory of *characters in great fiction*."[35] (He could also have called it "a theory of *great* characters in great fiction.") This theory traces the "social roots" of characters like Ahab or Hamlet, who emerge out of the creative process but whose distinctive personalities reflect the deepest impulses of specific epochs. Thus the Promethean Ahab struggles to assert his mastery over the ship and over nature herself, even as the Age of Industry marks the transformation and degradation of labor. Like the New Critics whose meticulous movement thrived in the 1950s, James advises Leyda to pay attention above all to the text itself, rather than the biographical trajectory or stated political opinions of any given writer. It is the writer's language that discloses the true dimensions of the "great characters" and allows their congealed social natures to work themselves out in the context of an invented reality. The writers in whom James was interested (Melville, Shakespeare, Aeschylus, etc.) did not consciously set about to capture the underlying reality of their social environments—and if they had, they would have failed in their efforts. Instead, their genius lies in their ability to create characters whose personalities rest along the fault lines of a society.

James advances a complex notion of the relationship between literary innovation and literary tradition. In a determinedly dialectical fashion, each epoch generates new characters who are nevertheless connected to earlier literary movements. This is because the best writers are deeply concerned with both the past *and* the present, "bringing as they do imaginative conceptions of history which they boldly place in the contemporary world." For example, Melville's Ahab draws on Dante's Satan, but he is also utterly unfamiliar and modern. "Each historic rebel, rebels against something very specific and it takes a specific literary form, precisely because of its specific social character."[36] The critic's job is to make meaningful distinctions between characters and stories produced under different historical conditions and, at the same time, point out underlying similarities. These similarities, James suggests, are a reflection not only of the conversation that individual authors seek to hold with their predecessors, but also of the fact that certain social contradictions (such as the alienation of the intellectual, or the confrontation with the Other) reappear in various guises, to be approached in fundamentally different ways.

The letters make extensive reference to the plays of Shakespeare, whose tragic characters (Hamlet, Macbeth, Othello, and Lear) are seen as internally conflicted as a consequence of the transformation of Elizabethan society and the emergence of a way of life which offers an "assault upon the ordered conception of the medieval world."[37] "Hamlet," he suggests, "is an intellectual, the first of the moderns, in drama what Descartes, Hobbes, and Locke are in philosophy. His virtue (and his vice) is his love of intellectual speculation, and that in a world where his special business is to think primarily of his social responsibilities."[38] Once again, the emphasis is on the central characters, their struggles, feelings, and mental processes. But James adds a new dimension to his character-centered analyses in his discussion of Shakespeare's tragedies. That dimension is the public audience. On the dramatic stage, the "social roots" of the individual personality are laid bare for all to see. For the ticket-buying audience of Elizabethan London, the agonies of a Hamlet or a Macbeth were the stuff of daily life. "How much did his audiences see?" James asks. "I believe that they saw, or rather felt, as much as we—and perhaps more, though in a different way."[39] It was the mass audience that nourished the Bard's work, and it is this audience that is missing from contemporary criticism. Even as James reasserts the centrality of individual characters, he places their overall development in the context of repeated public performances. "Poor Melville," he sighs, "he had no audience. His real audience were the mariners, renegades and castaways; but they could not read."[40]

The crucial clause in the quote above is "or rather felt"; Shakespeare's contemporaries may not have thought much about literary theory, but they had direct access to the experiences that acted upon the author himself. As James aptly puts it, the "elements from which Hamlet and Lear came were all around them, existing in themselves—a very concrete reality, enabling them to follow emotionally the speculative ranging of Shakespeare in a way that we cannot."[41] In his 1982 letter to Professor Kermode, James advances a number of suggestions about how King Lear could be staged for a modern audience—and again, his interest is in allowing the characters to express their inner selves and to connect their passions with the needs and expectations of the contemporary audience. The English actress Vanessa Redgrave, he says, would make an exemplary Edgar, "the embodiment of a man not born but shaped by a society out of joint, to be able to set it right."[42] Even those living several centuries apart from the author of *King Lear* could sympathize with Lear's "impaired ravings" and Edgar's painful accommodation with a "world of unrestrained struggle for power." The real question is whether any director would have the courage to place Shakespeare's essentially political concerns at the center of a modern theatrical production.

As the letters suggest, James's sympathy for the contemporary audience remained undiminished; and its ability to recognize and respond to its own situation was only limited by the material structures that perpetuated class society. His 1953 letter to Daniel Bell nicely captures the extent of his confidence in his contemporaries and his appreciation for the role of popular culture could play in fostering self-awareness among the masses. Revisiting *American Civilization*'s central theses, he describes the routine "which I followed about four or five nights a week for months." Waking around 9:00 A.M. after a fitful sleep, he would listen to a radio soap opera, "carelessly at first, but with a fascination that never ceased to grow." The soap's convoluted plot revolved around a wounded American soldier living in France, his wife at home who had gone into business, and his sister-in-law who "fell in with gangsters and was saved in the nick of time." He describes how, when a holiday came, the characters and the listeners celebrated the "national holiday together":

> This is what struck me. Every day for fifteen minutes, there was being reproduced an approximation of what was the living experience of millions of American soldiers and their families split apart by the war. *Every day*. I can imagine that millions listened in as I did, every day, and saw themselves and their families and their friends in a form of artistic representation. As "art" it was good or bad—I do not care; and some of it, I thought, was very good. But it was new, this daily attempt to chart the emotional and artistic needs of a vast population. It is new, and it is here to stay.[43]

As he wrote elsewhere in the same letter, "newness distinguishes the soap opera, the comic strip and jazz music because of the peculiar conditions of the twentieth century—the impact of the mass audience on the one hand and the fact that some artists set out to fill the needs of this vast population."[44] He seemed enthralled by modernity's "peculiar" combination of "organization and personality," that is, the way the culture industry reproduces the inner feelings of literally millions of people. Shakespeare's audience had a hand in inventing humanistic traditions; the potential was there for the modern audience to remake global society.

Building on the 1950 and 1953 manuscripts and on private correspondence, two of the more significant longer pieces produced in this period—significant both in terms of their discernment and what they disclosed about James's intellectual development—were "Popular Art and the Cultural Tradition," and *A Preface to Criticism*. The former was a talk delivered at a forum on "mass culture" sponsored by the Congress of Cultural Freedom held in Paris in March, 1954. The latter was a lengthy, unpublished essay written in 1955–1956 on the contemporary relevance of Aristotle's *Poetics*. In tandem with the private letters, these texts provide the foundation for a distinctively Jamesian approach to the relationship between aesthetics and politics.

"Popular Art and the Cultural Tradition" exemplifies James's Marxian cultural theoretic at its most inventive. Proposing to relate "artistic creation in the great tradition of Aeschylus and Shakespeare," and "films by D. W. Griffith, Charlie Chaplin, and Eisenstein,"[45] the paper makes a number of interesting points about the capacity of individual artists to simultaneously divulge and mold the innermost feelings and aspirations of the mass audience. James opens with the observation that modern film reflects "the extended interests, awareness, needs and sensibilities of modern men." A world of "constantly increasing multiplicity" engenders "techniques of *flash-back, cross-cutting* and a camera of extreme mobility." Modern cinema's "panoramic view" is accompanied by an awareness of "the depths and complexities of the individual personality . . . This finds its most plastic representation in the *close-up*."[46]

Modern aesthetics, James insists, must draw "upon modern popular art and above all, the modern film,"[47] because film allows the artist to form a complex bond with the mass audience. The "modern director," he writes,

> moves his camera always with a view to whether he wishes the audience to be directly involved in the middle of the action or for some artistic reason to be removed from it. Never before has the audience been so directly a constituent of the process of artistic creation.[48]

In principle, then, the modern artist can go further in illuminating social relations than in any previous epoch. But James is hardly complacent.[49] Revisiting *American Civilization*'s analysis, James contrasted modernity's recognition of "the inviolability of the single human personality" with "the immense accumulation of institutions and organized social forces which move with an apparently irresistible automatism."[50] It is precisely that oppressive sense of "automatism" that is absent in the work of Shakespeare and Aeschylus. James does not attempt to determine who is the better artist, Aeschylus or Eisenstein, Shakespeare or Chaplin. He merely points out that the moderns work under extraordinary pressure. "The solution of that," he writes, "is not an aesthetic question. It is a question of politics."[51]

If anything, *A Preface to Criticism* is even more audacious in terms of its central thesis, which is that "any integration of contemporary literary criticism must begin with Aristotle, the first and still the greatest of literary critics."[52] Modern criticism, for James, is characterized by a lack of unity or consistency. By way of contrast, Aristotle starts with an integrated conception of the role of the artist in society. James's argument is stated boldly at the outset:

> Never before have scholars piled up such mountains of information necessary for criticism or discovered such a variety of technical instruments as during the last quarter of a century; yet never before has criticism been so incapable of integrating it into any coherent system or method.[53]

With its emphasis on the role of the audience in responding to and shaping the theatrical experience, Aristotle's *Poetics* offers an "integrated" or holistic perspective on the study—and, more importantly, practice—of drama. In this respect (as in others), Aristotle's approach contrasts favorably with the then-hegemonic school of New Criticism, which James dismisses as "the textualists, the metaphoricals, the cultists of ambiguity and the whole formalist school . . ."[54] With Aristotle (and arguably Shakespeare), the focus is not so much on the script but on the overall theatrical experience. The theater, in this view, represents an ensemble of social relations, where the text, author, audience, and actors constitute or create a cultural and aesthetic totality. Aristotle famously argues that to be successful any given play must be divided into clear and distinct sections, with a beginning, middle, and end, so that the audience feels that some sort

of resolution is offered to the problem or crisis identified at the outset. An effective playwright must also give serious consideration to
what Aristotle terms the "plot." In this context, the plot refers more
to the underlying logic of the action than to the story line as such.

Much of *A Preface to Criticism* is taken up with Shakespeare's tragedies and their appeal to an Elizabethan audience. As we have seen,
the specific composition of the audience is of particular concern for
James, and a good deal of interesting material is presented concerning
the sociological makeup of this audience, its popular and democratic
character, how it felt a need for new kinds of stories. The central
point that James has to make is that—as in ancient Athens—Shakespeare's audience was a "national" audience, one that was more inclusive than any particular sectional interest. "It was the stage on which
this audience saw and marked out its destiny," he writes.[55] In passing,
he suggests that the company that produced and performed Shakespeare's plays were representative of the earliest modern intellectuals—and that their audience responded to the broad theme of individual responsibility and autonomy. The conclusion to be drawn
from this analysis is that the theater (especially modern drama) will
only recapture or reconstitute the national audience when it can pose
solutions to the crisis of individual autonomy in modern society—or
at the very least specify the nature of this crisis. The text ends on the
following note:

> On the morning after the first performance of *Hamlet, all* who had
> seen it would be talking about the soliloquies. They form a clear
> and connected sequence. They tell us of a representative Elizabe-
> than, who terribly wanted as all Elizabethans wanted, to perform
> great actions, who was eminently fitted to do so, a man conscious
> of great powers but fatally handicapped by the diseases from which
> in that generation all of them suffered—disbelief in the old stan-
> dards of social life visibly crumbling around them and a desperate
> search for new ones.[56]

What is most striking about these essays—apart from the erudition—is their resolute classicism. Although the political implications
of these essays are modernist and radical in intent, many of the references are to works that his teachers at Queens Royal College would
have used in the classroom. At no point does he attempt to denigrate,
simplify, or relativize the ideas of Plato, Aristotle, Aeschylus, or

Shakespeare. The essays convey an almost Victorian insistence on the transcendent and enduring quality of these authors' writings. They manifest a strong concern for the autonomy of culture and aesthetics, and the centrality of supposedly "super-structural" epiphenomena for issues of social and individual identity, with a corresponding resistance to the notion that everything can be reduced to politics, sociology, or political economy. This is not to suggest that James is oblivious to the political dimension of the ideas he presents. Indeed, all of his writings from this period were animated by an interest in deepening the political awareness of his readers. But at the same time there is the clear sense that, although the relationship between the two realms of human action is rich and complex, aesthetic and political judgements should never be conflated.

Every Cook Can Govern, "Popular Art and the Cultural Tradition," and *A Preface to Criticism* were produced at a time when their author felt increasingly burdened by the onerous task of keeping Correspondence afloat. Perhaps James too was a "man conscious of great powers" who was beginning to lose faith in the "old standards of social life" and was searching for new standards. He complained in a letter:

> This household has been kicked around for two years and at present, it has had just about enough. Every aspect of life, from social life to the most intimate personal relations are bogged down and inhibited and frustrated by the weight of the U.S. work. And yet I know very well that it has to be done. I know that better than all of you. Therefore it will be done. But we must come to an understanding that at the upcoming [Correspondence] convention, it comes to an end.[57]

Not surprisingly, the convention changed nothing, and C. L. R. and Selma continued to supply political and tactical advice, journalism, and commentary. Although the political climate in the U.S. was slowly unthawing, with McCarthyite paranoia giving way to a bland consumer culture, the Correspondence group enjoyed only a modest success in drawing new supporters into its ranks. Some members looked abroad for inspiration. James himself believed that as a result of certain dramatic developments in Eastern Europe, international politics was poised on the brink of a decisive transformation. The

Trotskyists were not the only tendency that hoped that the telos of history would ultimately justify or redeem their political program.

In October of 1956 Hungarian society erupted in open revolt against Communist rule. Taking advantage of a schism in the ranks of the party elite, industrial workers in the larger factories formed a network of rank-and-file organizations, and a delegation of these groups called on the government to abolish factory norms and quotas, raise wages, and transfer decision-making powers over issues of health and safety to the ad hoc network. The new reform-minded Communist head of state, Imre Nagy, opened negotiations with workers' groups partly because of the economic power they wielded and partly as a result of the enormous public sympathy these groups had generated. Within days, this policy of limited cooperation had provoked an armed Soviet intervention which efficiently crushed the rebellion. Some Hungarians responded with strike activity. "For seven weeks the strikes continued, sometimes dwindling into a partial paralysis of a few branches of industry, then enlarging again into a universal work stoppage," wrote two Hungarian intellectuals.[58] Industrial militancy proved no match for Soviet tanks. Yet in June, 1956, Polish workers in Pozan demanded that a new plan be implemented by the Polish state which ceded control to democratically constituted workers' groups over the production process. An "October Crisis," precipitated by the collapse of party authority in Poland, brought Soviet soldiers into Warsaw on October 19, 1956.

Coming only three years after strikes in East Berlin had rocked the newly partitioned East German state, the Hungarian uprising neatly subverted Soviet and Communist claims to political legitimacy in Eastern Europe. By using troops to smash autonomous workers' councils in a nominally sovereign country, the Soviets had reaffirmed the imperial character of the Stalinist regime. In addition, the Hungarian and Polish protests demonstrated the potent force of democratic forms of mass mobilization. By challenging Soviet power in the Eastern bloc and by establishing a political system based on workers' power—however short-lived—the Hungarians had, in the words of Irving Howe and Lewis Coser, "vindicated man in the twentieth century."[59] At the same time, the failure of the United States and its allies to provide meaningful backing to the Hungarian rebels highlighted the limitations and shortcomings of the Western alliance. As James and others had argued, there was indeed a sphere of independent political action that existed outside the realm of the superpowers and their military blocs. It was this sphere, in fact, that the Shachtmanites knew as the "third camp." The Hungarian uprising was perhaps the most dramatic manifestation of the relevance of third camp politics in the entire postwar era.

While the events in Europe seemed to leap out of the pages of *Correspondence*—and, for that matter, *Labor Action*—they had little impact on the fortunes of the embattled Johnsonite movement. But the group's London-based leaders found their spirits rekindled overnight. C. L. R. and Selma were not especially interested in the details surrounding the rise and fall of the Nagy government, nor did they care about the reform program offered by the Polish regime. Instead, they found solace and inspiration in the emergence of working-class self-organization. For the Jameses, events in Eastern Europe confirmed the original Johnson-Forest perspective on the struggle against state capitalism and the democratic potential of the proletariat. Workers themselves, electing their own leaders, were willing to assume the responsibility of reorganizing production. Without the "benefit" of a revolutionary party, Hungarian workers had advanced a proletarian form of direct democracy, and Polish workers had demonstrated that they were willing to follow the Hungarian lead. It boded well for the future. As James wrote to his U.S. comrades:

> I don't think you all recognize what the Hungarian Revolution means. *Since 1917 nothing has so shaken the world.* Europe is on fire with it. So is Asia. It may hit the U.S. with full force later—I don't know. But everybody *knows* that 1945–1956 is finished, and they *feel* that perhaps probably, the future is with the revolution after all. Go to meet it.[60]

But what did it mean to say that Asia and Europe were "on fire"? James's imagery evoked more than it explained. Certainly Communist parties and governments across the globe were challenged by events in Hungary and Poland. American leftists of all stripes were taken aback by signs of rebellion within the Communist bloc. But if it was James himself who was on fire, he did not make it very clear what it meant to "go to meet" workers' upsurges in Eastern Europe. What could the tiny Correspondence group do?

Facing Reality, a book-length discussion of the "New Society . . . Where to look for it, How to bring it closer," was designed to answer this question. Written by Grace Lee and C. L. R. James, the cover

proclaimed *Socialisme ou Barbarie* leader Cornelius Castoriadis to be
a coauthor. Although Castoriadis contributed a chapter on "The
Marxist Organization Today," he did not see the manuscript before it
went to press.[61] The book generalized from the Hungarian case to
argue that modern society was moving toward a series of confronta-
tions between workers' councils and bureaucratic institutions. Dis-
counting the specific factors that stimulated working-class resistance
in Polish and Hungarian factories (national oppression, Communist
manipulation, accelerated industrial development, and so on), *Facing Reality* provided a provocative defense of the revolutionary internationalism of the Correspondence group. It also attempted to spell
out ways in which the Johnsonite perspective could be implemented. The chief task of Correspondence-style Marxists was to
connect the emergence of workers' councils in Eastern Europe to the
daily resistance against the labor process that was said to be taking
place in factories and other work sites. Newspapers like *Correspondence* could help educate readers about the fundamental reality of
the "new society," as exemplified by the "mutual help and solidarity,
of organization, which already anticipate socialist relations . . ."[62]
The authors cited the advice Trotsky gave to the Socialist Workers
Party on how a radical newspaper must reflect the existential reality
of lived experience:

> Each of them [the paper's journalists] speak for the workers (and
> speaks very well) but nobody will hear the workers. In spite of its
> literary brilliance, to a certain degree the paper becomes a victim of
> journalistic routine. You do not hear at all how the workers live,
> fight, clash with the police or drink whiskey.[63]

The book also called attention to the considerable potential
embodied in anticolonial movements. Particular emphasis was laid
on the "Gold Coast Revolution," the nationalist movement that was
in the process of securing independence for the African nation of
Ghana. According to the authors of *Facing Reality*, Kwame Nkrumah,
the chief strategist and political leader of the Ghanaian national independence movement, "singlehandedly outlined a program, based on
the ideas of Marx, Lenin and Gandhi, for expelling British imperialism from the Gold Coast."[64] It was suggested that the people of the
Gold Coast/Ghana could help to initiate and inspire radical movements elsewhere. "[T]o the extent that they envisage their own future

as part of a new world-order," they wrote, "every step that they take
to solve their own needs can at the same time serve as inspiration and
example to the advanced proletarians hacking their way through the
jungle of official society."[65] At the same time, the authors wanted to
emphasize that Nkrumah's supporters (and by implication other
mass movements in Third World settings) "cannot solve their problems except in a global context." This stress on the intervention of the
proletariat went far beyond calls for foreign aid or even Pan-African
solidarity, and effectively echoed Fourth Internationalist doctrine.

Facing Reality was received in silence by "official society," but it
later circulated among anarchistic elements in the New Left and civil
rights movements.[66] Not everyone warmed to the book's euphoric
workerism, however; Raya Dunayevskaya in particular had a number
of pertinent criticisms to make of the definitive Johnsonite tract. Her
main charge was that the book was pervaded by an atmosphere of unre-
ality. "The man who can write 'It is agreed that the Socialist society
exists'," she argued, "need never face reality . . ."[67] As Dunayevskaya
points out, James and his coauthors had reached the conclusion that
the "invading socialist society" of which Engels had written was fast
becoming reality in the capitalist West. It was almost as if a situation
of "dual power," the unstable coexistence of two competing systems
of sovereign authority, actually prevailed in the 1950s. Cornelius Castoriadis made a similar point when he argued that James tended to
emphasize "unilateral, and hence absurd, positions" and erect them
"into an absolute." It is "not too difficult to understand," wrote Castoriadis, that "if socialist society already existed, people would probably have noticed it . . ."[68]

Dunayevskaya also took exception to the book's opening sen-
tence: "The whole world today lives in the shadow of the state
power." This seemed to allow "state power" a full measure of autonomy from the economic order. She writes, "now statism has become
the evil—not state capitalism . . ."[69] Marxists had typically analyzed
the state in terms of its connection to class relations and the institutionalization of class-based conflicts and coalitions. Facing Reality
seemed to divorce the modern state from socioeconomic processes
that had been viewed as determinate by Marxists, without much in
the way of theoretical justification. The notion of "statism," of course,
could in theory coexist with any number of social systems or modes
of production, and Dunayevskaya was keen to announce the Jame-
sians' apparent break with the Marxian paradigm. At the same time,

the growth of enormous public institutions had indeed become a defining aspect of modern society. Any critical assessment the balance of class or progressive forces would have to recognize the complex, and, in certain respects, autonomous role of states and the state system in mediating, reinscribing, and displacing conflict at the societal and international level.

Dunayevskaya's third objection was that the authors of *Facing Reality* placed too much faith in the progressive character of movements like Nkrumah's and, thereby, obscured a critical distinction between Third World nationalism and internationalist class politics. Granted, anticolonial movements could, as the book's authors maintained, inspire and instruct the struggles of the metropolitan industrial working class. But she sharply opposed their claim that underdevelopment had ensured that colonial peoples were free of the "accumulated rubbish" of capitalist ideology. James and Lee—unlike Dunayevskaya—had inched closer to an identification with the radicalism of postwar Third World nationalism. Yet James at least combined this identification with an explicit worker-centrism. As events soon made clear, Grace Lee's position was less fixed.

A centerpiece of the group's political work, the Detroit-based Correspondence group heavily promoted *Facing Reality* at its public forums on Hungary and Ghana. But neither nationalist ferment in Ghana nor the extraordinary example of working-class mobilization in Hungary enabled the group to recruit new members. Indeed, the Correspondence group split apart in the late winter of 1962, just as leftist ideas were gaining currency in the wider culture. A gang of four—James Boggs and Grace Lee, Lyman and Freddy Paine—broke with C. L. R. and Martin Glaberman to launch *Correspondence* under new management. Their magazine called for the revival of public morality and civic virtue in modern America and ardently backed the movement for black civil rights in the South. They took the notion of "Americanizing" Marxism one or two steps further than the Johnson-Forest tendency, placing an even greater value on the importance of speaking in the American vernacular and on integrating socialist themes with indigenous traditions.

In retrospect, it seems evident that at some point during the late 1950s Lee and the other members of her circle had lost their faith in Marxism's social-scientific explanatory power. They now sought to discard Marxian concepts of "class," "party," and "struggle" in favor of somewhat looser notions of "community," "freedom," and "justice." They still maintained a commitment to socialist principles, broadly defined, and their overall analysis certainly drew on Johnsonite themes. At the same time, their vision of humanity's future was less centered on the state of working-class consciousness and mobilization than James's (or Marx's). Substituting a quasi-New Age conception of the development of the whole person for the worker centrism that they had once embraced, they later said that they had been seeking to "advance beyond the idea that all radicals have held—that in order to advance socialism, you must first smash capitalism. We have to advance towards the new society by projecting an entirely different way to live and by building new social ties."[70]

After the 1962 split, the circle around Martin Glaberman changed the group's name to Facing Reality. This late reconstitution of Johnsonite forces was more successful at producing pamphlets than recruiting new members.[71] At the same time, the circle around Glaberman was able to enjoy a real impact on radical politics in Detroit and beyond. There was a great deal of contact and intellectual exchange, for example, between Glaberman and a new generation of black militants at Wayne State University and in the auto plants.[72] Detroit's self-described "black community newspaper," the *Inner City Voice*, ran articles by James, James Boggs, and others in the late 1960s. In addition, George Rawick described an afternoon he and Glaberman spent in Ann Arbor in the early 1960s, lecturing to a political science class taught by Bob Ross on radical alternatives. Out of the sixteen students who showed up, twelve were signers of the *Port Huron Statement* (1962), including Tom Hayden. But no one around the early Students for a Democratic Society (SDS) expressed any interest in joining the Johnsonites, even though there were discernable similarities between the constitutive SDS document and the radical, small "d" democratic politics of Facing Reality.

James reflected on the decline of the Correspondence tendency in a letter to Glaberman penned in 1962. "The movement which we started," he wrote, "has been broken up almost to bits." He then sketched the personalities of Dunayevskaya and Lee, the formidable women who had led the 1955 and 1962 splits from Correspondence respectively:

> There was Rae [Raya], an old Bolshevik, very highly trained and very dedicated . . . Next on the list is Grace, a very highly capable person. All that Rae gave us to use in experience and knowledge of

Bolshevism Grace gave us in philosophy and a general high level of education. I cannot forget not only what the movement but what I personally owed to both of these girls [sic]. We as an organization could not forget it either. If we forget it or ignore it or pass superficial remarks about it, it means that we don't know what we had and therefore we don't know what we are now without.[73]

One final note on Correspondence's decline. Irving Howe, in his noteworthy autobiography, *A Margin of Hope*, described what it is like to belong to an organization (in his case, the Workers Party) that is on its last legs. He writes:

> Its decomposition takes on a life of its own. You feel as if you have been invaded by some mysterious sickness, a Hardyesque fatality. Leaders lose their power to persuade; the bonds of fraternity crack; the very aroma of the movement—the air in the office, the mood at a meeting—turns bad. It's no longer a pleasure to go down to the party headquarters, to kibitz and gossip with comrades. At meetings everyone seems to be counting the house. For the few to whom it matters, this decline can be agonizing, like a secret, nagging pain.[74]

Yet few Johnsonites succumbed to Howe's "mysterious sickness." In different and sometimes opposing contexts, each of the group's leading activists sought to reach the campus radicals of the 1960s, producing reflective books and essays filled with interesting ideas. From the outside, removed by the passage of time, we can hardly comprehend what it must have felt like to have been an American radical at the height of the Cold War. James was quite right. Passing superficial remarks would only mean not knowing "what we are now without."

Our attention moves from the United States southward. When the James household moved to Trinidad in 1958, C. L. R. was still somewhat preoccupied by Correspondence. He was writing for their paper, and sending them lengthy letters. But we are finished with that part. We will follow him to the Caribbean and then back to Britain, where *Beyond a Boundary* was published and his reemergence as a literary figure seemingly assured.

PART THREE

Only after I had chosen my themes did I recognize that I had completed a circle. I discovered that I had not arbitrarily or by accident worshipped at the shrine of John Bunyan and Aunt Judith, of W. G. Grace and Matthew Bondman, of *The Throne of the House of David* and *Vanity Fair*. They were a trinity, three in one and one in three, the Gospel according to St. Matthew, Matthew being the son of Thomas, otherwise called Arnold of Rugby.

—C. L. R. James, *Beyond a Boundary* (1963)

___

CHAPTER SIX

Parties and Politics
in the West Indies

THE YEAR 1958 REPRESENTS the first time James had set foot on native soil in twenty-six years. Although he had a young son, he was fast approaching old age. The occasion of his return was an arranged invitation from the British-appointed Governor General of the West Indies to take part in the opening ceremonies of the transitional Federal Parliament. This provided the pretext for the return home. He and Selma were met at the airport by two island notables—the librarian Carleton Comma and his younger brother Eric James, who had made a name for himself both as general manager of the Trinidad Government Railway and as secretary of the Trinidad Football Association. Eric and Olive received their older brother with open arms, even though C. L. R. had been an uneven correspondent after relocating to Europe. If asked, the siblings allowed that they were proud of their brother's accomplishments but refrained from offering any specific opinion about his political proclivities.

Initially, C. L. R. only intended to stay in Trinidad for a few months. But within hours of his arrival he was entertaining offers from friends in the nationalist movement to put his voice and expertise at the service of the national cause. Eric Williams in particular was keen on having James work for the up-and-coming People's National Movement, a new political party. James could work in an advisory capacity perhaps, or as an editor, pamphleteer, and journalist. As evidence of his firm commitment to this obviously controversial figure, Williams helped arrange James's appointment as Secretary of the West Indian Federal Labour Party, a formal alliance of progressive nationalist forces in the region. Yet it soon became clear that the two men could never really work together on the same political stage and that the radical idealism of the nation's most infamous expatriate was incompatible with the cautious realism of parliamentary politics in the West Indies. In fact, the Jameses quietly left the country in 1962 to return to Britain, just days before Trinidad and Tobago's full independence was officially declared and celebrated.

It may be wondered what James hoped to achieve through his participation in the nationalist movement. He had little interest in building a Caribbean workers' party, nor was he inclined to restrict himself to primarily literary matters, as he had done in the 1920s. Yet some aspects of the past were, clearly, a source of inspiration. For example, his efforts in this period were informed by the sort of Pan-Africanism he had embraced in the 1930s. His call for a political and economic federation of the new nations of the West Indies had a Pan-African flavor and was designed, in part, to inspire similar initiatives in Africa and elsewhere. In addition, he wrote on Afrocentric themes and movements in articles published in Trinidadian newspapers, and took a well-publicized trip to West Africa in 1960 to revisit the former Gold Coast, where his old comrade Kwame Nkrumah had led the Convention People's Party to power three years earlier. As one might expect, James took a "macro" perspective on these events. His involvement in West Indian affairs was at least partly animated by his concern for the contribution that the region could make to the wider struggle for Pan-African/Third World emancipation.

In a series of articles and speeches—several of which were reprinted in *Party Politics in the West Indies* (1962)—James tentatively raised the question of what sort of steps should be taken by forward-looking Caribbeans in the postcolonial period. As an anti-Stalinist and a Marxist, he dismissed the possibility of "socialism in one country"; and he did not foreground the transition to a pan-Caribbean or global socialism in his political propaganda. There was a sense that his ideas concerning the future of the West Indies had a decidedly modest character. If his conception of independence was at all ambitious or radical, it was in the way James saw social and cultural matters as integral to the construction of a viable model of postcolonial development. For James, the creative act could become the very essence of the nationalist project. Novelists, poets, musicians, and

Eric James, left, and Carleton Comma, right, meet C. L. R. James
at the airport in 1958.
Permission: Trinidad Guardian

other artists had a critical role to play in advancing the national and democratic agenda.

If there was one overriding mission adopted by James in this period, then, it was to help articulate a specifically West Indian identity. This was a task of some complexity. The people of the West Indies represented an agglomeration of several distinct yet overlapping histories and cultures, and their relationship to British and more generally Western traditions was both longstanding and problematic. On the island of Trinidad itself there were a variety of ethnic groups, with Afro-Caribbeans and Indo-Caribbeans in particular divided along religious, cultural, geographic, and often economic lines. Although the People's National Movement sometimes billed itself as an all-peoples' organization, it manifested a definite tilt toward the Afro-Caribbean population. Despite a certain amount of universalist rhetoric, the coming of Independence only increased the saliency of race, ethnicity, and other social cleavages. The scene was further complicated by the fact that Tobago, the smaller island that the British affixed to Trinidad to form a single administrative unit, was predominately rural, whereas many aspects of Trinidadian society and culture were more or less urbanized. Elements of the urban sector were linked, sometimes through ethnic ties, to European elites, while much larger numbers retained familial and emotional ties to the rural areas. As far as the region as a whole was concerned, there was "no common mint of origin" between the people, and so whatever bonds were forged would have to be based on a "common mint of relations."[1]

As we shall find, James was inclined to emphasize the independent contribution that West Indians could make to world civilization as a whole. At the same time, he liked to stress the lasting value of classical Greek and modern European influences in the spheres of art, politics, culture, and morality, and he could be quite scornful of purely Afrocentric conceptions of West Indian identity.[2] *Modern Politics*, a collection of lectures delivered in 1960, reaffirmed James's belief in the relevance of classical and Western traditions for a New World audience. I summarize the book's analysis toward the end of the chapter, after examining the author's experiences as an impassioned and later somewhat embittered observer/participant in the transformation of West Indian politics at the close of the colonial era.

Postwar economic growth and the decline of the British Empire provided the essential backdrop for the emergence of independence movements that could reasonably expect to inherit the reins of power in the West Indies as a matter of course. In Trinidad, the organizational expression of cross-class nationalism was the People's Nationalist Movement, or PNM. The PNM's founding conference, held on January 15, 1956, aimed to both inspire the grass roots and reassure the British authorities. The demands that came out of that conference—public investment in the private sector, extensive social services, and "immediate self-government"[3]—hit just the right populist-yet-responsible note. The same can be said of its early motto: "Together We Aspire, Together We Achieve." Having attracted favorable notice for his work as a development economist, Dr. Eric Williams was quietly approached to serve as the leader of the PNM. As an Oxford-educated academic (who received a "first" in Economics) with ten years' experience as a professional staff member at the

Anglo-American Caribbean Commission, Eric Williams turned out to have the appropriate blend of qualities needed at the time. Williams was widely deemed bright, hard working, and sober minded. He could deliver tightly argued speeches that nevertheless gave voice to popular concerns, and he was exceedingly gifted in the area of organization and political tactics.

Williams had come to the attention of the nationalist community as a result of his public denunciation of the Caribbean Commission, "with which he had been associated for over a decade."[4] While he could sometimes indulge in militant and even racialist rhetoric, Williams eschewed the socialist label and jealously guarded and conserved his political power. Like James, Eric Williams was a graduate of QRC. They had known each other since the 1920s, and both men had profited from a friendship that survived despite their obvious differences, which were both political and stylistic. James's complicated and problematic relationship with the younger PNM leader proved to be the brittle linchpin of his involvement in the nationalist movement. As the personal connection fractured the wider relationship was undermined. Once frozen out of the PNM, James found it difficult to situate himself as an effective actor in Trinidadian politics.

In its early years, the PNM carefully negotiated a middle ground between its mass Afro-Caribbean following and middle-class base. In mediating these divergent group interests, the party often shifted politically and tactically from one position to another. A pugnacious Albert Gomes complained that "Dr. Williams and his Party have been zig-zagging along the political road since 1956, alternately driving to the Left and to the Right . . ."[5] As it zig-zagged along, the PNM secured seats on the British Colonial Office's Legislative Council and launched several projects aimed at consolidating popular support for the nationalist cause. Among the most successful of these was the so-called University of Woodford Square, where Williams and other party leaders spoke to assembled crowds of many thousands.[6] A delighted George Lamming was able to report that the "middle classes have actually taken to mixing with the peasants and longshoremen who attend the lectures in the University of Woodford Square."[7] The administrative center of public authority in Port of Spain, Woodford Square became a symbol-laden site for the Movement as it staked its claim to political legitimacy.[8] As a result of its black-centered, urban-based anticolonialism, and through its ability to seize the political initiative, the PNM quickly eclipsed an older generation of political figures and captured the nationalist high ground.

It was into this "nationalist whirlwind"[9] that an astonished James entered in April 1958. According to one eyewitness, James told Williams that "with a movement like this, you can do anything."[10] Williams returned the compliment (for it was a compliment, as well as an observation) by inviting his friend to stay and work for the People's National Movement in an official capacity. With George Padmore, they had already discussed the PNM strategy during Williams's visit to London in 1956. But Williams's offer entailed a much larger role than the occasional consultation. It was inspired by Williams's affection for a capable old friend, as well as by a calculated appreciation for the way in which the polished intellectual's presence could protect Williams's left flank and provide the PNM with a useful patina of unorthodoxy. On James's part, the decision to stay was at least partly motivated by the sense that West Indian society was in motion and that something new and interesting could emerge as a result. The unpleasant part was that he would have to shed his independent Marxist identity, at least temporarily. In the interests of party unity, James promised Williams he would curb his political rhetoric and antileadership tendencies.[11]

The PNM did in fact shift leftwards, in part as a result of James's influence. From all appearances, Williams placed great value on the older man's political judgment, and some younger nationalists were attracted to James's eclectic blend of revolutionary commitment and Victorian decorum.[12] Others thought that the legendary activist carried excessive ideological baggage. "For over a year Nello was number two in the party," worried one party leader. "In fact, there were times when we thought he might be number one."[13] Kamaluddin Mohammed, Gerard Montano, and other PNM figures were concerned that James would seek to inject Trotskyist or Communist doctrines into the party's political program. The American Consulate General was sufficiently riled up to send his superiors in Washington, D.C. a rather ominous report:

> Although the Consulate General has no evidence, there is always the possibility that James is under international communist discipline, and continues to use his Trotskyite identification as a cloak. It is rumored locally that James has access to communist money.[14]

Fueling these concerns about the possibility of "communist infiltration," the People's National Movement took a populist turn during the winter of 1958–1959. Evidence for this turn could be found in the document "Perspectives for Our Party," prepared in October 1958 for the PNM's third convention. Officially penned by Williams, several passages bore the imprint of the chieftain's controversial new advisor.

In one passage, Williams's ghost writer asserted that in "Trinidad and Tobago and in the West Indies a conception of the new society [has developed] to the point where the old situation will never again prevail." The passage went on to claim that "[t]his is not merely a theory, in practice the PNM has tackled the big boys."[15] Both the "new society" and "big boys" phraseology is unmistakably Jamesian, as was the call to "build our party organization from the bottom up," and "reorganize our system of education so that, through the party, it penetrates into the deepest masses of the people."[16] In this document Williams/James proposed that the party initiate a program of political education, extend contact with progressive nationalist forces abroad, erect a party headquarters, and generally overhaul the party's internal apparatus and public profile. The overall point was that the PNM could become a special kind of political organization, a campaigning party rather than an electoral machine. While the document's proposals were not couched in explicitly socialist terms, traces of James's experiences in a variety of radical movements are evident.

Moving on from drafting party documents, James was offered the job of editing the PNM's newspaper. His political enemies could not have been pleased. Relaunched in December 1958, *The Nation* was the party's premiere recruiting tool and political journal. Boasting a print run of several thousand, C. L. R. James, Selma James, and a sizable technical and editorial staff created a brash, argumentative news weekly that walked a thin line between promoting PNM policies and pushing the mass movement forward. Selma James worked tirelessly on the paper, as did their friend Walter Annamunthodo, a Guyanese-born activist and pamphleteer who served as the paper's subeditor.[17]

Early on, Williams described *The Nation* as "the established spearhead of the party militant, the textbook of independence."[18] The PNM's chief organ of political propaganda featured an unusual mix of historical essays, short news items, cultural commentary, sports journalism, and columns by Dr. Williams and others. The idea was to produce a paper that was as entertaining as it was informative and accessible to the widest possible range of readers. According to one

promotional advertisement, the paper offered a "vital" alternative to
the established press. "So dishonest are our daily newspapers that *The
Nation*, a weekly, constantly has to report vital news that the people
otherwise would never know. Support *The Nation*. IT IS A NATIONAL
DUTY."[19]

The overworked editors felt no hesitation in running C. L. R.'s
own pieces in the paper. In addition to writing the lead editorial,
James often provided the front page news story and a regular column
that appeared under the title "Without Malice." Longer essays were
also featured; a couple of these were reprinted as PNM pamphlets.
One such pamphlet, "Our Upper Classes," sought to reassure nervous Europeans that the "PNM is not some monstrous misfortune
which has overtaken the unfortunate upper class in Trinidad and
Tobago. Something like the PNM was due in Trinidad sooner or later.
It is one of the features of modern society."[20] In certain respects *The
Nation* was modeled on the Detroit *Correspondence*. Both papers were
aimed at a mass audience, both featured articles on cultural and social
questions, and both encouraged feedback from readers. Like *Correspondence*, *The Nation* strived to transpose broadly socialist themes
into a native idiom. In their effort to go beyond social democratic or
liberal-nationalist rhetoric, the Jameses were able to draw upon a
more relevant model than Cannon's *Militant*, or Lenin's *Iskra*.

The growing impact of *The Nation* matched the political success
of the People's National Movement as a whole. Whereas the party
secured nearly 40 percent of the popular vote in elections held in
1956, it obtained an impressive 57 percent of the vote in 1961. Yet the
party—like its newspaper—was primarily rooted in the Afro-Caribbean section of the population, and its ties among "West Indians of
East Indian descent" were weak at best.[21]

From the outset, the PNM vacilated over whether it was a universalist party or whether it should build on its special relationship to
the black community. Some Indians charged Williams with a propen-
sity to "play the race card" when he deemed it advantageous.[22] Not
surprisingly, Williams' main electoral challenge came from a party
that enjoyed far stronger links to Indo-Caribbeans, both Hindu and
Muslim, as well as the Catholic hierarchy. Led by Bhadase Maraj and
Dr. Rudranath Capildeo, the Democratic Labour Party (DLP), formed
in 1958, came to offer a perennial, quasisectionalist-based challenge
to the PNM. It was eventually succeeded by the National Alliance for

Reconstruction, which achieved power under the austerity program of A. N. R. Robinson in the mid-1980s.

Under James's brief tenure, *The Nation* kept cross-party or intra-ethnic sniping to a minimum, but he nevertheless was to come under heavy fire for associating with a "racialist" party. One DLP supporter, Trinidadian Indian Hindu H. P. Singh, strongly attacked James for deigning to lecture Indians about politics. "It is really amusing," he writes, "that you, Mr. James, who spent almost all your time or life away from Trinidad, should appeal to Indians here to make their Trinidad into something! This is unadulterated jingoism." Singh accused James of having a perverse interest in breaking up the Indian family through liberal sexual values and miscegenation: "Negro intellectualism, judging from Mr. James' reasoning, seems to be interested more in sexual union between Indians and Negroes than in unity of minds between the two races."[23] As befitting his status as a national figure, Williams was more often the target of this kind of acrimonious attention than James, however.

The paper's finest hour may have arrived during the winter of 1960, when it intervened vigorously in the arena of international sports by advocating the appointment of Frank Worrell as captain of the West Indies cricket team. Worrell was a black man, and the West Indian team had always been led by a European. As James wrote in his column:

> It is the constant, vigilant, bold and shameless manipulation of players to exclude black captains that has so demoralized West Indian teams and exasperated the people . . . The more brilliantly the black men played, the more it would emphasize to millions of English people: "Yes, they are fine players, but, funny, isn't it, they cannot be responsible for themselves—they must always have a white man to lead them."[24]

James vowed to "clean up this captaincy mess once and for all." After several solid weeks of journalistic agitation, which stirred up popular resentment against the implicit whites-only policy, Frank Worrell was appointed captain of the West Indies team, "the first black captain in the history of representative cricket."[25]

Other campaigns proved less successful. For many months the paper advocated West Indian federation. The topic of federation had been of enduring interest to the middle class in the Caribbean. Its appeal gathered strength once politicians and intellectuals came into contact with each other through the aegis of regional institutions such as the University of the West Indies, which opened in 1948. Given the geographic and economic constraints facing the region, a federation of Jamaica, Trinidad, the Windward and Leeward islands, and British Guiana (now Guyana) was seen by many as the only solid basis on which a sustainable independence could be constructed. As the Colonial Office admitted in 1945, "it has become more difficult for very small units whatever their outward political form may be, to maintain full and complete independence in all respects of government."[26]

The cause of federation gained considerable momentum in the late 1940s, in part as a result of a 1945 U.S. speaking tour that allowed two West Indian politicians, Grantley Adams from Barbados and Norman Manley from Jamaica, to create a network of profederation sympathizers. One of their allies was Eric Williams, who was teaching at Howard University at the time. Through the work of the Caribbean Labour Congress, Adams and Manley further expanded their network and put pressure on the British authorities to pursue decolonization in such a way as to facilitate the emergence of a postcolonial federation. Their efforts provided an important backdrop to the decision taken in the early 1950s to open up negotiations between the Colonial Office and West Indian political parties regarding the transition to a federated West Indies. It was agreed that a loosely structured Federation (with its own parliament) would be formed in 1958, and that subsequent negotiations would establish the precise configuration of a potential political and economic union.

James was strongly committed to the ideal of federation, which he saw as essential to the development of black unity and as the only plausible solution to the problem of underdevelopment in the East Caribbean. This was a problem that had both political and economic aspects. Speaking in his capacity as editor of *The Nation* and as secretary of the West Indian Federal Labour Party, he told an audience in Demerara, British Guiana, that:

> Federation is the means, and the only means, whereby the West Indies and British Guiana can accomplish the transition from colonialism to national independence, can create the basis for a new nation; and by reorganizing the economic system and the national life give us our place in the modern community of nations.[27]

A year later he insisted at a public lecture in Kingston that Jamaica's economic difficulties could only be attacked through the creation of federal-level planning mechanisms. "I believe," he stated, "that the time has come for the State Plan. So far we have been clearing up the imperialist mess. The activity of the last years has been to prepare the ground for a new stage of the economy, and that is the economy of the State Plan."[28] What James actually meant by this rather centralist phraseology is somewhat murky, although he referts in passing to the need for the government to "decide on a programme, aiming by stages to try to raise the general level, to satisfy the urgent needs of the people and . . . to make an impatient people understand that some serious, tremendous, new and sustained effort is being made to satisfy the demands which are increasing every day."[29]

Just what precise mix of private enterprise, planning, welfare provision, and other forms of public intervention would emerge as a result of this "programme" was not clearly specified. While it seems evident that James was rather loosely trying to map out a postcolonial "third way" between free market capitalism and state capitalism, the actual set of proposals he wanted to use seems rather incomplete. There is a voluntarist dimension to his conception of the political economy of underdevelopment, with the spontaneous initiatives of the masses sufficient to smooth over any gaps in the economic logic.

The link between this statist economic program, and his overall commitment to socialism-from-below, also seems somewhat tenuous. The West Indian scholar Paget Henry finds it striking that James's model of economic transformation "is not constructed from inside the dynamics of the regional labor process." Instead, "the stress is on the more careful planning of an externally initiated, capital-led process of industrial development." "It is not," as one might expect, "a worker-led strategy of development based upon an assessment of the organizational forms and capabilities that regional workers have produced or demonstrated in the course of the major insurrectionary activities."[30] One must simply assume that, for James, federation was a means of stimulating a mass movement as well as a transitional mode of governance on the road to a more participatory society.

Toward this end, The Nation tried to keep its readers fully apprised of the progress of the high-level negotiations for federation. The largest obstacle to the creation of this para-state appeared to be the unwillingness of certain forces to cede, in the words of the PNM, "common allegiance to a Central government."[31] In particular, the Jamaicans seemed reluctant to share their sovereignty with other West Indians. Although Norman Manley had long backed the concept of federation, influential members of his party feared that the drift toward federation was premature and that any likely arrangement would be inequitable from a Jamaican point of view. As one of the larger and oldest of the former British colonies in the West Indies, Jamaica's participation was seen as crucial to the success of the project.[32] Manley sought to resolve his domestic dilemma by calling for a nationwide referendum on the issue of federation. This produced an antifederation vote (54 percent against) in September 1961. In the aftermath of the Jamaican referendum, the provisional Federation was dissolved and negotiations called off. James later blamed the region's leaders for failing to mobilize popular support around the project. He promised that West Indians would return to the project of building a federation, arguing that there was finally no other way forward. But more than a few politicians grew to appreciate the relative autonomy furnished by the status quo.

Both the campaign for Frank Worrell and the controversy over federation added to tensions between James, with his reputation for unpredictability, and the more conservative clique around Williams. The stage-managed resolution of the so-called Chaguaramas Affair had an even greater adverse impact on James's position within the Movement. Chaguaramas, a district of northwest Trinidad, had been used by the U.S. military as a naval base after the British had "leased territory on some of the West Indian colonies to the United States in exchange for military equipment" during World War II.[33] The U.S. was the beneficiary of several similar arrangements in other parts of the world, which came about largely as an unanticipated consequence of the British debt, and the Americans used their new access to British sites to adopt and reinforce a Cold War posture.

Advocates of political reform had come to resent this arrangement on the grounds that it symbolized the lack of input that West Indians had into their own affairs. Although the PNM raised the issue of Chaguaramas's peculiar constitutional status in part to safeguard its position at the head of the nationalist movement, the campaign was clearly rooted in popular feelings. The issue seemed to resonate particularly among Afro-Caribbeans, and Williams may have used Chaguaramas to highlight the contrast between his party's own resolutely nationalist base and that of its "traitorous" political opponents. Hoyos simply reports that Williams "drew his strength from the support of the mass of the people," and that "the campaign captured the imagination of Trinidad and other territories of the Caribbean."[34]

Williams called on the United States and the British to sit down in three-way negotiation with the PNM to arrive at a more equitable arrangement, one that recognized the legitimate aspirations of the West Indian people. A 1960 demonstration intended to bring the U.S. authorities to the bargaining table (known as the "March in the Rain") proved, in retrospect, to have been "the militant high point of Trinidad nationalism."[35] Negotiations opened in Port of Spain in June 1960 and were attended by the British Conservative prime minister Harold Macmillan. In September 1960 it was announced that the U.S. would release 21,000 acres, keep the rest for seventeen years, and provide $30 million in international development money to be spent on road construction and education. The bargaining process was no doubt smoothed by Williams's declaration in May 1960 that Trinidad was "west" of the "Iron Curtain." During the negotiations, Williams began to disassociate himself from James. "Williams was turning away from close personal contact with his old mentor," according to Oxaal.[36] "There is a strong suspicion that the Americans demanded James's 'scalp' as part of the Chaguaramas settlement," writes another historian.[37]

Seemingly unaware of these machinations, James took note of Williams's tactical shift and went so far as to say that he too would now modulate his public rhetoric.[38] More was at stake, however, than a question of tonality. James's entire intellectual and political style had always been viewed by party insiders as a liability to the PNM, and with the compromise of Chaguaramas and the failure of the PNM to capitalize on its popularity among the people, James experienced sharp feelings of alienation from the party. On March 26, 1960, prior to traveling to Ghana, James wrote to Eric Williams, asking to be "relieved from my post at The Nation . . . Too many people," he said, "seemed to have forgotten or never knew that I am a person with definite political principles and attitudes. I have subordinated myself to the PNM completely. I can do so no longer."[39] In July, he sent Williams a final letter, stating that "I am not going to work at The Nation any more . . . I couldn't carry on there if I wanted to."[40]

Judging from the contents of The Nation, the party's apparatus had engineered a relatively trouble-free transition during the period between March and July 1960, where James's articles were run but editorial control was being shifted elsewhere. The party gave the appearance of being Janus-faced regarding the paper's ousted editor in chief. On the one hand, at the party's fifth convention delegates asked—apparently with official sanction—that James return to his editorial post. A convention resolution commented on the fact that "the absence of Mr. James at *The Nation* as Editor has already diminished substantially the effectiveness of the paper as a vital sinew of the party . . ."[41] On the other hand, at the same convention party leaders circulated an internal document that charged James with "mismanagement": "Given a free hand, he appeared to use it freely without regard for his own or the Company's responsibilities."[42] These charges were used to justify James's expulsion from the PNM in October 1960. Thus his first, and penultimate, encounter with the responsibilities of electoralism ended abruptly and with remarkably little fuss. Having spent several decades in the socialist trenches, James was unsuited for the rather different demands and constraints of electoral politics.

After being ejected from the PNM, James was freer to advance his own view of West Indian development and identity. The book *Party Politics in the West Indies* offers a particularly useful point of entry into his thinking in this period. The first half of the book had been circulated inside the People's National Movement during the winter of 1960, under the title "PNM Go Forward." *Party Politics* coupled this pamphlet with a collection of essays addressing West Indian sociology and culture. The underlying logic of the book was that an invigorated PNM should go beyond the confines of a routinized electoralism and try and engage the masses. This would require finding some way to link up with artistic and cultural currents that were, by their very nature, unlikely to gravitate toward purely political or instrumental forms of activity.

"PNM Go Forward" is marked by a rather embattled, almost self-involved tone. Written in something of a hurry, the document seeks to justify the author's position vis-a-vis the PNM in the aftermath of the Chaguaramas compromise and the clandestine battle over *The Nation*. It documents a series of occasions when the author was betrayed or rebuffed and offers a critique of the PNM's drift to the right. Three criticisms are of particular note. The first was that the party had failed to provide the party newspaper with sufficient resources or to use it to build a loyal following among the people.

James strongly believed that the paper should have come out as often as twice a week. "I am dissatisfied," he wrote, "with a *Nation* which needs the concentrated attention of an Editor and more than ever with a prospective twice-a-week."[43] Indeed, he suggested that the paper should have appeared on a daily basis, a proposal that would have required an extraordinary commitment of the party's resources.

The second criticism was that the PNM had become dominated by one man—Dr. Williams—who aggregated power unilaterally. Williams, it was said, was loath to relinquish authority or permit independent centers of power to emerge inside the party. "It is common knowledge that only committees on which the Premier is active carry out any activity at all," he noted.[44] Up to the point of his expulsion, James had publicly deferred to "the Doctor's" wishes and had affected the air of a loyal PNM member. All that was now forgotten. Under the pressure of events, the personal rapport that had made the 1958 document "Perspectives For Our Party" possible had dissipated, just as that document's ambitious organizational agenda had been disregarded and ignored.

Finally, as a direct consequence of Williams's apparent unwillingness to allow for the consolidation of independent perspectives and tendencies within the PNM, James charged that the party's institutional apparatus was being undermined and neglected. "The organization of the Party, the organization of the Convention, is very defective," he claimed.[45] What was needed was an emergency convention to find ways to strengthen the party's internal functioning and organization so that a process of democratization could be facilitated. But where James saw organizational atrophy, the circle around Williams saw progress and development. The party had attracted a loyal mass base, and there was every expectation that the PNM would be asked by the Colonial Office to form a transitional government as part of preparations for independence. Every indication suggested that an orderly transition, such as the one promised by Williams, would maintain the measurable economic growth and prosperity that Trinidad and Tobago had achieved by this time.[46] Drafted at a time when the party was enjoying measurable success as a mainstream nationalist formation, "PNM Go Forward" failed to resonate beyond a handful of friends and sympathizers.[47]

The second, more compelling half of *Party Politics* consisted of eight essays on cultural and social themes. The thrust of these pieces was that independence and political democracy had to serve some "social purpose." As he argued in the context of a discussion of the West Indian middle classes:

> The middle classes point to parliamentary democracy, trade unions, party politics and all the elements of democracy. But these are not things in themselves. They must serve a social purpose and here the middle classes are near the end of their tether. Some of them are preparing for troubles, trouble with the masses. Come what may, they are going to keep them in order. Some are hoping for help from the Americans, from the Organization of American States.[48]

The parochialism and passivity of the West Indian middle classes posed a serious obstacle to the creation of this sense of a collective purpose. Aspiring merely to protect their jobs and salaries, the white-collar strata had little notion of what "kind of society they hope to build . . ."[49] The dyed-in-the-wool revolutionary expressed a certain degree of frustration as he interrogated the class into which he was born:

> Where does personality, literature, art, the drama stand today in relation to a national development? What is the relationship between claims of individuality and the claims of the state? What does education aim at? To make citizens capable of raising the productivity of labor, or to give them a conception of life? West Indian intellectuals who are interested in or move around politics avoid these questions as if they were the plague.[50]

By "social purpose," James clearly had in mind something grander than an aspiration for material wealth or even national sovereignty. Prosperity and independence were of course necessary, but they were at the same time insufficient. What James was calling for was nothing less than the formation of a coherent national identity, what he referred to in a speech delivered at the University of the West Indies in Mona, Jamaica, as a "long and deeply rooted national tradition . . ."[51] Only through the development of a "national consciousness" could the West Indian people transcend "this matter of shallow roots," as James so delicately put it.[52] "We can console ourselves," he added, by pointing out that "[s]ize has nothing to do with it. Look at Ibsen and Kierkegaard, and the Greek city-state."[53]

It was a matter of developing a national will, a sense of mutual purpose and endeavor. It is little wonder that *The Nation* became so preoccupied with the negotiations over federation, with the status of the Chaguaramas territory, and with the campaign for Frank Worrell. All of these issues had the potential of arousing in the West Indian population a national sensibility. Each invoked, to one extent or another, a process of demarcating the sociocultural boundaries of the East Caribbean nation.

There was one artist whom James felt had already made a special contribution to the creation of a specifically West Indian character: the calypso singer Francisco Slinger, "otherwise known as The Mighty Sparrow."[54] There is a venerable tradition of calypso singers/songwriters using their music to offer satirical commentary on sports, politics, marriage, and other topical subjects. Calypso music, of course, is a central attraction of the annual Carnival, a two-day festival of song, dance, and costume that is held on the Monday and Tuesday preceding Ash Wednesday. A great deal of planning and preparation goes into each Carnival, which nevertheless retains the feel of a spontaneous event, with spectators "jumping up" to the music.[55] The Mighty Sparrow remains one of the best-known and most highly regarded of these Carnival performers. James was struck not only by The Mighty Sparrow's appreciation for the social dimension of political independence,[56] but also with the unusually close bond that the singer/songwriter enjoyed with an embryonic national audience. James wrote:

> His talents were shaped by a West Indian medium; through this medium he expanded his capacities and the medium itself. He is financially maintained by the West Indian people who buy his records. The mass of people give him all the encouragement that an artist needs. Although the calypso is Trinidadian, Sparrow is hailed in all the islands and spontaneously acknowledged as a representative West Indian. Thus he is in every way a genuinely West Indian artist, the first and only one that I know. He is a living proof that there is a West Indian nation.[57]

Given his political sympathies, it is perhaps not too surprising that a class-conscious figure like The Mighty Sparrow comes off better than members of the elite. The book's preface offered a familiar restatement of the author's "from-the-bottom-up" message:

[A]ny government that is not conscious of the power of the people is bound to be a bad government, that is to say, it will fool you, cheat you, and if need be reduce you to hewers of wood and drawers of water, and without mercy keep you in what it considers to be your place. That is the last hill which the people of the West Indies will have to climb. It is hardest of all. When you climb it you will have arrived at a height from which you will never fall.[58]

Thus there were grounds for optimism. Yet one can detect a certain amount of misgiving about the political culture of the West Indies. "I have never known," he wrote at one point, "a population claiming to be democratic where so many people (both Negroes and Indians) live in such fear of the whole apparatus of government . . ."[59] At another juncture he states:

I have repudiated in unambiguous terms the false and dangerous conception that we have been so educated by the British that the instinct for democracy is established among us. I want no misunderstanding here. I see every sign that the tendency to naked power and brutality, the result of West Indian historical development, is here all around us . . . Has democracy sunk ineradicable roots in us? I say that I see no sign of it and many signs to the contrary.[60]

Despite his anticolonialism, James nevertheless saw the merit of many aspects of the "Western tradition." He did not suppose that West Indian politicians and civil servants would be necessarily better than their British counterparts, nor did he counterpose the achievements and limitations of European civilization to the virtues of Minty Alley. If West Indians were to move beyond the colonial mentality, they would have to appropriate and transform, rather than reject wholesale, the political and cultural traditions they had inherited. It is difficult to see how he could have been more explicit on this point:

We have to master a medium, whatever it is, that has developed in a foreign territory and on that basis seek and find out what is native, and build on that. It is obvious that our present race of politicians are too far gone ever to learn that. But there are signs that this truth is penetrating younger people. It is the West Indian truth that matters above all. Perhaps Sparrow will make a calypso on it.[61]

A cruder form of nationalism, one that failed to excite the deepest aspirations of the people, would only exacerbate the tendency toward "naked power and brutality" that was colonialism's unfortunate legacy. From James's perspective, there was the danger that Williams's politics could move in this direction, crudely adopting the linguistic and rhetorical style of the working class, but refusing to lay the foundation for a higher purpose.

Achieving the proper balance between forging a distinctive West Indian identity and learning from the West was a key problematic animating the six lectures on "modern politics" that James gave under the auspices of the Trinidad Public Library's Adult Education Program in 1960. His central theme concerned the historical, intellectual, and cultural contributions of classical, Renaissance, and liberal thought to humanity and their contemporary relevance for a West Indian audience. Each lecture attracted an audience of several hundred, serving to underscore James's point that cultural and social progress would depend on the involvement of large numbers of people. The fact that James had only just relinquished his editorship of *The Nation* may have added to the sense of anticipation that the series generated. Some in the audience may have perceived that a break was imminent between the peripatetic dignitary and the PNM leadership over the nature and future of Trinidad's independence. As if to confirm this rupture in relations, Williams ordered that the printed compendium of the 1960 lectures be suppressed.[62]

The project's ambitious scope was clearly reflected in the range of material covered in the series. The first lecture introduces the concept of direct democracy, as practiced in Athens and other Greek city-states, favorably contrasting it with liberal representative government. The second traces classical Marxism's roots in French and German philosophy, emphasizing the democratic character of Marx's thought. The third and fourth lectures cover a wide array of topics related to contemporary history, such as the emergence of a world market, the threat of fascism, the "failure of the nation-state," and the promise of a better way of life as symbolized by the Hungarian workers' revolt of 1956. The final two lectures concern leading artistic figures of the twentieth century and their complex relationship to "crises in intimate relations" which originate in "a dislocation of society"[63] under modern capitalism. The thesis tying these variegated topics together was that only a sweeping reconstruction of public and industrial life could avert the disintegration of modern society.

As in any standard survey of Western civilization, *Modern Politics* opens with the Greeks. In this particular investigation the city-state's virtues—particularly its capacity to integrate individual wills—is a recurrent theme. One reason for this emphasis on classical civilization is that James believed that small nations with meager economic resources could achieve grand results in the spheres of politics and culture. A more fundamental justification, however, had to do with the intrinsic value of classical Greek culture and the "remarkable" character of Athenian civilization. The ancient city-states

> formed, in my opinion, the most remarkable of all the various civilizations of which we have record in history, including our own . . . And it is not only that we today rest upon their achievements. It is far more wonderful than that. If today you want to study politics, it is not because Aristotle and Plato began the great discussion, not at all; in order to tackle politics today, fundamentally, you have to read them for the questions that they pose and the way that they pose them; they are not superseded at all.[64]

Building on a long-standing interest in the foundations of political theory, James ascribed the exceptional character of social life in ancient Greece to two main factors: mass participation in the institutions of the city-state and the dense emotional and political bonds harmonizing the individual with the wider community. Since male citizens (but not, of course, slaves, females, or foreigners) had an authentic voice in the polity, they felt an intense attachment to the city-state. This attachment itself constituted "the basis of a good life."[65] In appreciating the need to reconcile communitarianism and free individual expression, Athens attained a more or less rational balance between the "individual citizen and the City-State . . ."[66] Despite two thousand years of scientific and technological progress, humanity never recaptured the organic equilibrium of the city-state. It is with a considerable sense of melancholy that James announced that *"people have lost the habit of looking at government and one another in that way."*[67]

In the domains of art, politics, and philosophy, the citizens of the ancient city-state created the foundations for a meaningful life for the enfranchised minority. But recapturing the spirit of the ancient city-state's communal solidarity—and extending its benefits to all members of society—involved something more complicated than simply harking back to the past. Above all, it required an international movement toward the realization of a democratic, noncapitalist order where the alienation of modern individuals from the public sphere, and from the tyranny of political economy, could be meaningfully addressed. This in turn necessitated an engagement with the question of capitalism versus socialism. Here James called attention to the contribution of Marxism, believing that this tradition represented the most fully developed analysis of capitalism and the struggle for its transcendence. Drawing on classical Marxist precepts, the lectures stressed the capacity of ordinary workers to effectively intervene in revolutionary situations and otherwise defend their autonomous interests. The Marxist conception of the social power of workers is memorably expressed in the following passage:

> When ten thousand school teachers, bookkeepers, the writers and talkers like myself, and editors and so forth, vote, that is ten thousand votes; and they can have one thousand extra and have eleven thousand votes and defeat ten thousand workers, in votes. But the moment a revolutionary struggle is on, the workers—this group takes the railway, the other one the waterfront, the other one turns off the electricity, and the other one stops the transport; the teachers, etc., can only make some noise but they cannot do anything; they can send the children back home or bring them back or something. In all struggles of this kind it is the proletariat that is master of the situation.[68]

This mastery of the revolutionary conjuncture reflects the structural power of the working class as constituted in the sphere of production. The working class was not only a powerful social group, however; it was, for James, a vital component in the creation of a new order based on an enlightened form of workplace and community-based councils. History's forward march clearly points toward the possibility and desirability of reorganizing society along democratic and participatory lines: "There has been a development; the development is along the lines that I have tried to show. Man is ready for great strides forward today."[69]

James saw in Trinidad's movement toward independence the opportunity for challenging the logic of capital through popular mobilization and education, for creating a new type of society that nevertheless shared certain features in common with the ancient city-

state. That a connection is drawn between the new West Indian society and the ancient city-state is surely not accidental. In his biography
Paul Buhle writes that in *Modern Politics* "world history assumes a
spiral upward which recapitulates the original in many ways, albeit at
ever higher stages."[70] Patrick Gomes argues that James's philosophy
of history had distinctly evolutionary and optimistic overtones:
"Rather than Marx, the influence of [English historian Arnold] Toyn-
bee is clearly evident and an accumulative tradition enriches the
development of human civilization."[71] At the same time, the fear that
the future could prove profoundly retrogressive is barely concealed.
"The world will choose between hydrogen bombs and guided mis-
siles, and some form of Workers Councils. In 1960, the Marxist doctrine: either socialism or barbarism, seems to me truer than ever
before."[72]

In *Modern Politics*, the movement for Caribbean self-determination has the potential for playing a critical role in the development of
a new order. By setting out along the path of self-organization laid out
by the city-state, West Indians could break with the colonial past and
instigate regional rebellion. But the revolutionary capacity of the
West's industrial proletariat to avert the collapse of world civilization
is emphasized as well. "The passing of colonialism," he wrote,

> is a sign of the weakness of the capitalist bourgeois state and at the
> same time it provides ammunition for the breakdown of these
> imperialist states which dominated them before. Nevertheless there
> is no question about it: the basic opposition to imperialism must
> come from the proletariat of the advanced countries.[73]

As sympathetic as he was to the cause of national liberation, James
clearly remained committed to Trotsky's theory of permanent revolution. Thus, as paradoxical as it might have seemed to some members
of the audience, Trinidad's most famous Marxist and Pan-Africanist
maintained an abiding commitment to the prospect of First World
working-class insurrection coming to the aid of Third World nationalist forces. As we have seen, this was a commitment he combined
with a profound respect for classical and Western intellectual traditions.

Lecturing on modern politics in Port of Spain was perhaps
James's finest hour during this strange and compressed episode. The
contribution that he had to make was in the realm of theory, not prac-

tice. In retrospect, it is clear that his ability to alter the course of events had from the outset been limited by a number of external factors. These included Williams's considerable organizational talents and political instincts, the region's reasonably solid economic prospects, and perhaps, as some authors have suggested, the backstage role of the United States authorities. His impact was also, perhaps, limited by his decision not to build an independent political vehicle and by the fact that James's island roots had withered over time. In addition, a brutal 1962 road accident in Jamaica had an adverse effect on his already delicate health.[74] He had to apologize to a group of West Indian students in Edinburgh, Scotland for sitting down to lecture there in 1964.[75] He told them:

> Much to the disappointment of some of my friends, my mental facilities were not affected by the accident. They began assiduously to spread the news around that James's brain was not what it was. I am not able to stand as much as I used to; but my brain, for what it is worth, is what it always was.[76]

He then added: "I am much better educated in the ways of West Indians after spending five years among them." It was a melancholy remark. His time in Trinidad did not go nearly as well as he had originally hoped.

◆◆◆

This Trinidadian episode has a bittersweet coda. James returned to Trinidad in March 1965 to cover the English and West Indies test match cricket for the *London Times* and the Sunday *Observer*. Within twenty-four hours of his arrival, he was placed under house arrest.[77] Coincidently, the government's powers of detainment had been strengthened under the 1965 state of emergency, declared "during an outbreak of periodic unrest in the sugar belt."[78] Despite protests from the *Trinidad Guardian* and other respected sources, the house arrest lasted six weeks, coming to an end only once the labor dispute had been resolved. For Williams, James's return raised the spector of "subversion" and helped spark calls for a Commission of Enquiry into Subversive Activities. The name of Williams's old tutor featured prominently in the resultant report.[79]

Seeking to mobilize public opinion against an increasingly autocratic PNM, James returned to Trinidad in the summer of 1965 to join forces with two well-known figures: George Weekes, president of the Oilfield Workers Trade Union (OWTU), which had been founded in 1939, and former Democratic Labour Party politician Stephen Maharaj. Maharaj had previously served as deputy to oil worker leader Uriah Butler and had been a prominent member of the DLP's prolabor wing before being edged out of the party. Although Weekes was widely seen as a capable and popular trade union leader, some criticized him for attempting to import Marxist ideas into the labor movement.[80] In collaboration with a number of associates, Maharaj, Weekes, and James proudly launched the Workers and Farmers Party (WFP) on August 8, 1965. They used their new four-page newspaper, *We, The People*, which James edited, to criticize the government and build support for their populist venture. As the editor wrote in one article, "there is nothing that you wish to teach them which they [the people] cannot learn. We, therefore, propose to teach them how actually to practice democracy."[81]

Their high-profile organization vowed to run a full slate of candidates against the PNM in the 1966 election and to provide a radical and yet responsible alternative to the policies of "instability and repression" that was said to characterize Trinidad and Tobago under Dr. Williams.[82] The party's program called for a "repudiation" of the historic tensions between Afro-Caribbeans, Indo-Caribbeans, and other Trinidadians; for a defense of such "basic democratic rights" as freedom of speech and assembly; for "vigilance" against governmental corruption; and for the "development of a nationally based economy" through encouraging small-holder agriculture, greater public supervision of the nation's financial and economic resources, and a dynamic industrial base.[83] The overall thrust of the program was nationalist, neo-Keynesian, and social democratic. Williams and his supporters responded to this unanticipated challenge on its left flank by claiming that the Workers and Farmers Party was led by pederasts[84] and Castroites.[85] During the election the government had James's movements closely monitored by the security forces.[86]

Despite its democratic and progressive program for change, the party failed to mobilize the kind of popular support it needed to mount a serious electoral challenge to Williams's rule. The party's rallies never rivalled those of the PNM. Walton Look Lai asserts that the WFP "never managed to develop truly organic links with either ethnic section of the Trinidad working class."[87] He goes on to argue that "James's own image was somewhat damaged by this hurried venture into left politics . . ."[88] Sharp questions were raised about the basis on which the leadership of the party had come together, and even sympathetic critics saw the leadership of the WFP as "an unlikely triumvirate."[89] In an 1987 interview, the West Indian author George Lamming said that it was a "mistake" for James to enter into a "battle of political rivalry with Williams." This brief flirtation with an electoral strategy was "fundamentally in contradiction to James's position that what was more important was the building of movements, not getting parties ready for election . . ." Lamming went on to say that "[w]hen the gladiatorial show was over, the next move was departure."[90]

While the Workers and Farmers Party ran a spirited campaign,[91] the final result was more than a little disappointing. In fact, the party did very badly in the election, "failing not only to win a single seat with just about 3% of the popular vote, but actually losing all their candidates' deposits in the process. This included James himself, who managed to win just 2.8% of the votes cast in his home constituency of Tunapuna . . ."[92] The PNM, on the other hand, secured 68 of the 100 available seats, with the bulk of the rest going to the Democratic Labour Party. James packed his bags for London a few weeks after the results were announced. He always maintained, however, that the WFP had run a principled campaign and had raised many important issues. As he later recalled: "The program we had was a more powerful program than any of the revolutionaries have had up to now. They are ready to overthrow, but the problem is that they can't say what they want instead."[93]

C. L..R. JAMES author, historian, politician
Drawing from Queen's Royal College 75th Commemorative Album.
Permission: Queen's Royal College.

CHAPTER SEVEN

At the Rendezvous

The images and memories of C. L. R. James held by most people who knew him or who saw him speak, date from the publication of *Beyond a Boundary* or later. From this point on, James was a de facto living historical figure, with an accumulated record and reputation that gave him an entree into certain discussions, but that was also something of an incomplete caricature. Linked to the great causes of the receding past, James carried with him the burden of self-presentation in this period as never before. It was in the 1960s and 1970s that he struggled to find a way of transmitting his ideas and writings to a new kind of audience. This task was both assisted and complicated by his historical presence and historical self-consciousness. His exciting personal story exuded a special kind of revolutionist glamour that made it more and more difficult to locate the complex individual personality housed inside the impressive historical trajectory.

This question of the tension between James's heart and his historical reputation lies at the center of V. S. Naipaul's painful dissection of the C. L. R. James story. In his recent, quasiautobiographical book *A Way in the World* (1994), Naipaul presents us with a character named Lebrun, "the Trinidadian-Panamanian communist of the 1930s" who later assumed the role as "the black spokesman of our century."[1] Although Lebrun bears a certain resemblance to C. L. R. James, they are not the same person. Unlike Lebrun, James did not work with the oil worker leader Uriah Butler, he did not have family ties to Panama, and he never spoke at the University of Woodford Square. Yet the similiarities are too striking to be overlooked: Lebrun is a reknowned leftist and Pan-Africanist who built a small radical organization in the United States during a long period of exile. Some of the character's features may have been intended as a slam at James's politics—Lebrun foments political mischief in West Africa, for example, and his book *The Second Struggle: Speeches and Writings 1962–1972* is printed in East Germany—by a writer and QRC graduate who initially valued James's support but who decisively broke with all forms of leftist politics during the 1960s.

In some respects Naipaul's characterizations are keenly observant. His depiction of a dinner party in London, for example, where C. L. R. and Selma entertain a young, unnamed Indo-Caribbean writer, is classic:

> It was all immensely intelligent and gripping. He talked about music and the influence on composers of the instruments of their time. He talked about military matters. I had met no one like that from our region, no one who had given so much time to reading and thought, no one who had organized so much information in this appetizing way . . . It was rhetoric, of course. And, of course, it was loaded in his favour. He couldn't be interrupted, like royalty, he raised all the topics; and he would have been a master of the topics he raised.[2]

In Naipaul's story, the young writer becomes partially seduced by Lebrun and his circle, to the point where "I couldn't help noticing that I was being regarded as part of Lebrun's revolution." For a brief moment, he finds this thought rather appealing. "I could sense that I was being invited to shed my racial or cultural burdens and to be part of their brotherhood . . . it would have been marvellous, it would have been less trouble, if I could have pretended to be a convert."[3] But he ultimately resists losing his Indian identity and takes objection to the "communist" terminology of Lebrun's "hack work" essays dating back to the anticolonial movement. "Did he believe in those articles?" he asks quizzically. "Or were they written by a man who knew that such articles only filled space in official magazines?"[4]

Naipaul's portrait is both recognizable and troubling, because of its didactic conflation of James's radicalism and Soviet propaganda. While he evinces some sympathy for the man, Naipaul has no time for the man's politics. He dismisses his fictionalized character as "an impresario of revolution" and contrasts the "complicated ideas of Lebrun and the simple politics he encouraged."[5] With great sensitivity, he admits his failure to come to terms with Lebrun's dense subjectivity, asking "How could one enter the emotions of a black man as old as the century?" But he quickly turns around and jabs Lebrun for pandering to sycophants and for the "hysteria" of his speech.[6] Where Naipaul really veers off is in his notion that the hardships of the past distorted Lebrun's personality. In an unconvincing concluding passage, Naipaul writes,

> They had no means of understanding or assessing a man who had been born early in the century into a very hard world, whose intellectual growth had at every stage been accompanied by *a growing rawness of sensibility*, and whose political resolutions, *expressing the wish not to go mad*, had been in the nature of spiritual struggles, occurring in the depth of his being.[7] (My emphasizes.)

What Naipaul describes as raw sensibility, James knew as a cool maturity that expressed itself primarily through irony and measured historical observation. James simply wasn't as torn up inside as Naipaul's account would suggest. Furthermore, to the degree that Lebrun is intended to represent James, the idea that he actively repressed an underlying madness is completely at odds with all other portrayals of a proud and dignified rhetorician. A closer approximation of the truth would be to say that James—"in the depth of his being"—had a pacific temperament, coated by a pride in achievement and aptitude. *Pace* Naipaul, James was never a Stalinist hack, nor was he in "anguish." James did not "become a child again . . . looking only for peace" in his old age.[8] Instead, he remained a sane old man, waiting to be liberated from a sick body, committed to basic socialist principles.

A very different version of these years was offered by George Rawick, a young historian who had been active in the Socialist Party. Rawick traveled to England in 1963 and stayed with C. L. R. and Selma James for several months in their home in north London. He later described their household as cluttered with books and papers, its occupants strapped for cash but nevertheless busily receiving visitors from all corners of the globe. Rawick also recalled the strong impression that con-

versations with James left on him: "We spent a lot of time talking about
politics, history, literature and art . . . Living with him was like an
apprenticeship. Writing history, which I had been doing, is nice but
it isn't revolutionary politics. I learned by watching him speak, listening to him speak. I lecture like him—never using notes."[9] Rawick, who
had known Martin Glaberman in Detroit, had been won over to the
socialism-from-below perspective of the Facing Reality group by the
late 1950s, and was impressed by the purity of its state capitalist analysis of the Soviet Union. One point he remembered in particular was
James's habit of purchasing multiple copies of books, magazines, and
picture postcards to pass on to friends and acquaintances. "James was
always broke," Rawick said, "because he was always giving away books
and never getting them back. He wanted people to read."[10]

Of course, going as far back as the early 1920s, James had exchanged books, manuscripts, and ideas with acquaintances and
friends.[11] As Rawick's anecdote suggests, James had a generous
nature, as well as perhaps a careless attitude toward money. As he
entered old age his personal style mellowed even as his politics
remained firm. He combined a number of different and in certain
respects contradictory elements: a cool revolutionary ardor, a seriousness about ideas, a wry sense of humor, a friendly disposition, and
a deeply internalized code of honor. Although these elements had
been present from the very beginning, the particular way they were
combined and integrated was distinctive to this period of his life.
Anyone who had known him as a 1940s Johnsonite and then talked
to him in London in the 1960s would have appreciated this evolution, how he had shed the aroma of revolutionary conspiracy and
adopted a dignified, older-gentlemanly persona in its stead. Yet he
retained the crisp reserve that had always made him stand out in the
Trotskyist milieu.

George Rawick returned to London in 1967 for more collaborations, joining James, Glaberman, and another former Johnsonite, William Gorman, to work on a sequel to Facing Reality entitled The Gathering Forces. Marking the fiftieth anniversary of the Russian
Revolution, the document was intended as a response to the new political realities of the mid-1960s. It was the most sustained, most ambitious, and perhaps the most disappointing of the various attempts that
C. L. R. and his associates made to reach out to black and New Left
movements in the Age of Aquarius. They clearly hoped that the Johnsonite perspective could win converts among the young and the newly

radicalized. Yet the impact of their views was felt more on the under-growth of the New Left, rather than on its public manifestations. Part of the explanation for this had to do with their ingrained worker-centrism, and also because James's polemics were framed in terms that rendered them inaccessible to a nonsocialist audience. C. L. R.'s avowed sympathy for aspects of American history and culture may also have puzzled some activists. Yet connections were made: by the late 1960s, James was well received on many college campuses, and he prodded a number of individuals in an independent-Marxist direction.[12]

The New Left was only one of several disparate audiences that James and his old comrades sought to address in the heady 1960s and enigmatic 1970s. Another potential constituency was generated by the late-'60s revival of Pan-Africanism across the African diaspora. The black studies movement in the United States, the Black Power marches in the West Indies, and the attempt to concoct an authentic "African socialism" were all signs that a "third-wave" (Garveyism and the IASB standing for the first two waves) Pan-Africanism had finally arrived. While close observers may have judged particular expressions of this third wave to be hopelessly compromised by one or more individual personalities, the underlying, welcome pulse of a (re)emergent Afrocentrism was unmistakable. Few individuals were in a better position to both comprehend and speak to the internationalist dynamic of this resurgent Pan-Africanism than C. L. R. James. But somehow the transition from celebrated-representative-of-an-earlier-generation to tactician-for-today's-movement never quite arrived.

In addition to Pan-Africanism, the world of literature and criticism was one that James responded to. With the publication of *Beyond a Boundary*, James was in a position to reinvent himself as a person of letters in the Anglophone world. Despite all of the caveats and disclaimers, there was no denying the powerful appeal of English literary life and manners. His nickname for the *Times Literary Supplement*—Old Solemnity—betrayed a deep affection for a publication that had a formative influence on his whole outlook.[13] Besides, he had always felt that he was as good a writer as any that the London scene had to offer. And by contributing occasional pieces to such quintessentially English publications as the *New Society*, *Encounter*, and *The Cricketer*, he played a part-time role in the literary agenda setting of the metropolitan intelligentsia.

Although his public reputation never quite gelled—except perhaps in the West Indies—he seemed unperturbed by his relative anonymity in the United States, which he was able to visit from 1967 onwards, once he had been granted permission to return by the appropriate authorities. As had always been the case, the influence he enjoyed was mainly through personal contacts and chance encounters that scattered readers and listeners had with his books, essays, and speeches. Everywhere the story was the same: some people knew his work intimately, and had been forever challenged by it, but most of those who could have benefitted the most never had the opportunity to hear of the man or of his ideas.

Largely completed before the author's return to Trinidad in 1958,[14] *Beyond a Boundary* remains a classic of Caribbean literature. Two small extracts published in the late 1950s neatly illustrated the major themes that the book so artfully combined: West Indian autobiography and the organic connection between cricket and artistic and social practices. In "Dr. W. G. Grace and English History," published in *The Nation* (Trinidad), James describes the elegant batting style and personal accomplishments of the Victorian cricket batsman W. G. Grace. The article argues for the centrality of major sporting figures such as Grace in the cultural development of the West Indies. James acknowledges the degree to which Grace's career inspired and instructed him in the ways of the English gentleman. In the article "Nationalist Strain," which appeared in the *New Statesman*, another key formative influence—his maternal grandfather, Josh Rudder, the first black engine driver on the Trinidad Government Railway—was woven into the Jamesian tableau. Rudder was a "great favorite with everyone," particularly his grandson. Responsible for the run between San Fernando and the hamlet of Princes Town, where he lived, Rudder's story is used to embody the triumph of the individual personality.

The trainman had one special day of glory. "One Sunday afternoon near the end of the century," Rudder was asked by the manager of a nearby sugar estate to look at a broken-down engine which was causing delays in shipping. All of the foremen had tried to restart the engine, with no success:

Now on the way to the factory, Josh may have dug up from his tenacious memory some half-forgotten incident of an engine which would not go, or he may have come to the conclusion that if all of these highly trained and practised engineers were unable to discover what was wrong, the probability was that they were overlooking some very simple matter that was under their very noses.[15]

When Rudder arrived at the estate, he insisted on working on the engine alone. The manager agreed, albeit with reservations. "No one will ever know exactly what Josh did in there," but the engine quickly sputtered to life. The key aspect of the story is that Rudder refused to tell anyone how the job was done. "The obstinate man wouldn't even tell me," James later remembered. But as his grandson was preparing to leave for Nelson, England in 1932, the eighty-year-old grandfather explained himself: "They were white men with all their MICE and RICE [engineering certificates] and all their degrees, and it was their business to fix it. I had to fix it for them. Why should I tell them?"[16]

Returning to what I have termed his "anthropological" intellectual roots, James found a way to weave his family story into an allegorical reading of West Indian history. While the book's themes—the author's childhood, cricket, art, and politics—are complexly interconnected, each may be viewed in its own terms. *Beyond a Boundary* opens on an autobiographical note, with "a small boy of six" discovering that by "standing on a chair" he "could watch practice every afternoon and matches on Saturday . . ."[17] The book introduces us to such memorable characters as the truant Matthew Bondman and the author's own family, led by a strong-willed mother and stern father. As we have seen, the family lived in a close-knit social environment that James left behind in the 1920s and 1930s. In different ways, cricket and literature represented two paths pointing beyond Tunapuna and North Trace, and yet they reinforced the sense of discipline, fair play, and the reward of effort that was drilled into his brain at home and at school. Their power for good is lovingly described in the book: literature represents enlightenment; cricket exemplifies the dialectic of individual freedom and collective organization.

The autobiographical sections of *Beyond a Boundary* persuasively attribute a powerful sense of enchantment to the Trinidad of the not-so-distant past. This aspect of the book appealed to several generations of readers who might have been expected to be unimpressed by the author's revolutionary ideology. In addition, the book advances a provocative argument about cricket's central role in shaping Anglo-phone Caribbean culture and identity. As Neil Lazarus rightly notes, James "identifies cricket as a privileged site for the playing out and imaginary resolution of social antagonisms in the colonial and post-colonial West Indies."[18] The most provocative aspect of *Beyond a Boundary*, however, concerns the argument that cricket is effectively an art form. The author defends cricket not merely as an instrument of identity formation but as an expression of the artistic impulse. In a chapter entitled "What is Art?" he claims that cricket is unique in offering a ritualized performance piece that connotes complex human relations rather than mere competitive entertainment. Cricket's elaborate rules and patterns of play, in James's view, address deep aesthetic longings that arise out of our collective need to give a coherent shape to the social world. The game, he argues,

> is so organized that at all times it is compelled to reproduce the central action which characterizes all good drama from the days of the Greeks to our own: two individuals are pitted against each other in a conflict that is strictly personal but no less strictly representative of a social group. One individual batsman faces one individual bowler. But each represents his side.[19]

In cricket, the audience's attention is divided between the batter and the bowler, two dramatic figures harmonically joined in a circle of sport. The conflict between the two is constant and, at the same time, it is dynamic, in motion, and ever changing.

For James, cricket is a kind of dramatic art because the repetition appeals to the human need for "collective sensations." These sensations are "the stuff of human life. It is of this stuff that the drama of cricket is composed."[20] The individual cricketer displays all of the "immense variety of physical motion" suggested in figurative oil portraits and ballet. "The batsman can shape to hit practically around the points of the compass."[21] The chapter records the different strokes that a batter can choose, at all angles. Cricket thus differs from other organized sports in the way that it combines the artistry of pure motion with the theater of the batter versus the bowler. Despite its low social (and historiographical) status, cricket allows the audience to perform a special kind of role, as it is the audience, James insists, that ultimately decides what constitutes good cricket—on, and off, the playing field.

The very ambition of James's discussion is impressive, and the historical and anthropological analysis of the impact of cricket on West Indian identity (which I have only alluded to here) is highly plausible.[22] Furthermore, one cannot help but be moved by the democratic thrust of the central argument—that humble and unlettered individuals can produce their own masterpieces, in collaboration with the mass audience. Yet while it is important to recognize the aesthetic dimensions of athletics, there may be obstacles in categorizing cricket as another subject of the humanities. Unlike drama, music, or literature, cricket as a specific practice has limited potential as a reproducible object. As engaging as the evolving patterns of play may be, they are unlikely to sustain our interest if the performance is repeated (say, with the aid of a video recorder). In addition, the distinction between cricket and other sports is perhaps not as firm as James's analysis would suggest. International cricket takes place in a determinedly capitalistic environment,[23] and even at the local level it is played as a competitive sport, with losers, winners, and score keepers. Like other sports, it contains artistic aspects, and it may generate or satisfy specific artistic aspirations. However—and at the risk of confirming E. P. Thompson's wry observation that "American theorists will not understand this, but the clue to everything lies in his proper appreciation of the game of cricket"[24]—it seems to me that as a material social practice cricket is only problematically described as the epitome of high art.[25]

Having lifted cricket above the realm of entertainment, James uses his particular conception of sports to address the question "What Do Men Live By?" The answer is clear: not by politics alone. Taking issue with Trotsky's bald assertion that "workers are deflected from politics by sports," James writes that "With my past I simply could not accept that."[26] It was no accident, he argues, that nineteenth-century movements for universal male suffrage and a new popular passion for organized games emerged at the same historical moment: "this same public that wanted sports and games so eagerly wanted popular democracy too . . ." He goes on to find significance in the fact that "[o]ver the second half of the nineteenth century, sparking the great international movement [for the democratic franchise], drawing all eyes to it, startling millions who otherwise would have taken no notice, creating the myth and legend, there began to loom the gigantic black-bearded figure of W. G. Grace."[27] The conjunction of democratic movements and popular enthusiasm for games in the nineteenth century paralleled the union of the Olympic games and participatory democracy in ancient Greece. "They who laid the intellectual foundations of the Western world," he says, "were the most fanatical players and organizers of games that the world has ever known."[28] By comparison, Trotsky's position looks somewhat unimaginative and philistine. "Men" live by that which truly animates them—and sports play a positive role in mobilizing, inspiring, and instructing the masses, despite Trotsky's dismissive stance.

Beyond a Boundary returns again and again to cricket's potential as a social, cultural, and historical force. Posing the question "What do they know of cricket who only cricket know?" (the book's original title), *Beyond a Boundary* also offers a dense mixture of technical information concerning various aspects of the game. Here the author recounts the performance of his old friend Learie Constantine on the pitch in 1928: "Hammond bowled a ball pitching a foot or so outside of the off-stump, breaking in. Constantine advanced his foot halfway to meet the ball and saw the break crowd in on him. Doubling himself almost into two, to give himself space, he cut the ball a little to the left of point for a four which no one in the world, not even himself, could have stopped."[29] A succession of passages movingly describe incidents that occurred on some long-forgotten pitch. The effect is so charming that the book, in the words of one English newspaper columnist, made cricket "safe for the left."[30] In providing so much rich detail and by investing it with such great affection, the book effectively does for cricket what Melville's *Moby Dick* did for whaling. Both books swamp the reader with thickets of seemingly extraneous material and yet somehow manage to transcend the realm of mere description.

Upon publication, V. S. Naipaul said that the book "gives base and solidity to West Indian literary endeavor."[31] Even the British Communist newspaper, the *Daily Worker*, gave the ex-Trotskyist a friendly notice. Yet American publishers shied away from the book for some two decades, perhaps fearing it would attract the sort of backhanded compliment that was paid by a reviewer in the Boston *Globe* in the mid-1980s: "Unless you are in some way a part of the diseased Empire or admirer thereof, you probably wouldn't care to read it, but you would be missing something rare and strange."[32]

Rare and strange as it may have been, *Beyond a Boundary* took several years to become a classic. After an initial burst of favorable reviews, James's life settled back into the old routines. On the surface, a parallel may be drawn between James's activities in London during the 1930s and during the 1960s. Both decades were marked by rising social unrest and left-wing political mobilization. International issues—Vietnam, Spain—played an important role in demarcating political boundaries in the 1960s as well as the 1930s. More specifically, James struck Marxist and Pan-African chords in both periods, promising to import a kind of Marxian strategic acuity into Pan-Africanism and a more or less Pan-African grasp of the social integration of the world system into Marxism. In both decades, moreover, the possibility of identifying and stimulating a revolutionary breakthrough was uppermost in his mind.

An important difference, however, between his efforts in the 1930s and in the 1960s was that he had less success arriving at the sort of intellectual and political synthesis in the latter period that had been achieved in *The Black Jacobins*. Nothing that he wrote in the 1960s came close to bringing together the two political movements in such a provocative and intellectually satisfying form. Indeed, only a certain percentage of what he wrote in the aftermath of his return from Trinidad exhibited the same sort of flair or acumen as his best work from the 1930s. For reasons having to do with changes both in the society and in himself, he was unable to forge the same sorts of nourishing ties to small groups of talented individuals as he had in the 1930s and 1940s. As a result, it appeared during this later period that he switched from one enthusiasm to another, failing to connect each activity with the others in a way that illuminated the whole. Yet it can be argued that by the late 1970s or early 1980s he had managed to concentrate once again on the fundamentals of his politics, imparting a belief in the creative power of the masses through conversations and formal interviews held in his small flat in London's Brixton area.

Three documents in particular may be seen as emblematic of James's failure to go beyond what he had achieved in the area of Marxist theory in the wartime and early postwar period. The first, "Marxism 1963," is the transcription of a speech delivered at a meeting of Solidarity, the British counterpart to the French organization *Socialisme ou Barbarie*. By the early 1960s, both groups were backing away from the independent Marxism these groups had advanced in the 1950s. Guided by the writings of Cornelius Castoriadis, they maintained that Marx's historical materialism could no longer explain the central dynamics of really existing capitalism. For Soli-

darity, Marxists had underestimated the power and autonomy of
state bureaucracy and were wedded to an outdated conception of
politics which valorized class struggle over and above the needs of
society as a whole. In addition, Solidarity members feared that Marxism was hopelessly compromised by the experience of Stalinism in
the Soviet Union. Castoriadis himself had come to believe that the
Marxist conception of economics was tainted by a theoretically
unsustainable account of value and crisis, and argued that "neopa-
leo-Marxists" had lost sight of the decisive developments taking
place in the postwar period.[33]

In "Marxism 1963," James sought to show that Marxism was
indeed capable of theoretical renewal and development, that Marx's
writings could still be used to illuminate the central features of a
world that was, admittedly, very different from that of a century past.
The key, for James, was that Marx was committed to a genuinely revolutionary politics. Marx understood that capitalism was in a constant process of transformation, but also saw that the abolition of
oppression and exploitation would require a thoroughgoing overhaul
of modern practices and institutions. James asserted that the major
Marxist theorists were continually occupied by the problem of theoretical renewal. He pointed to Lenin's last writings, dating from 1922
and 1923, when the Bolshevik leader had taken up such ideas as
reforming government bureaucracy, weakening the powers of the
security apparatus, and revamping the country's agricultural policy.[34]
The thrust of these writings concerned the need to educate the peasantry and to somehow inhibit the bureaucratization of the state.
Lenin's final, seemingly revisionist documents suggested, for James,
the truly critical and subversive foundations of Lenin's method. "Col-
lectivization? Mechanization? Improvement of this or that? Lenin
naturally wrote often about these things but they were not his main
concern."[35]

In order to renew Marxism, James told his audience that contemporary radicals had to do "for 1963 what Marx did in the 'Historical
Tendency of Capitalist Accumulation' and what Lenin did in *State and
Revolution* . . ." This meant going back to political fundamentals and
attempting to "draw the necessary conclusions for the advancement
of the socialist conception in the world in which we live."[36] *Facing
Reality*, and the 1967 document *The Gathering Forces*, were indicative
of the kinds of analyses James had in mind. However, what if—as
Castoriadis would have insisted—these "necessary conclusions"

invalidated Marxism's core theoretical propositions? To what extent were the categories themselves open to transformation and repudiation? Toward the end of the talk, James made it clear why he was so certain that Marxism could be renewed through revolutionary praxis: because, as the Johnson-Forest tendency had insisted, the concentration of capital spontaneously generated working-class rebellion and solidarity. Despite the material bounty of the postwar boom, the Invading Socialist Society still threatened to seep through the interstices of a moribund world system.

"Existentialism and Marxism," a talk delivered in London in 1966, represented another defense of Marxism mounted before an audience of young radicals. He had dismissed existentialism as a "fad" in *American Civilization*, even as he had sympathetically discussed Kierkegaard with his friend Richard Wright.[37] By the mid-1960s, existentialism was more fashionable than ever, and in this talk James tried to meet the hot Continental import half way. He defined existentialism as an analysis that understands man "not as a single individual," but as a "being-in-the-world." This was similar, but not identical, to Marx's notion of man as an ensemble of social relations. To their credit, existentialists recognized that large-scale modern institutions fostered an "inauthentic" form of existence. Only by first acknowledging the inauthenticity of modern life and then by "setting his pattern toward something that is peculiar to himself,"[38] could the individual hope to achieve something approaching an "authentic" existence.

This reading of existential doctrine drew not only on Jean-Paul Sartre's writings but on those of Martin Heidegger, a more austere and less politically sympathetic figure. Finding agreement in Heidegger's notion of alienation-as-inauthenticity, James said that an "inauthentic temporality and spatiality confine a whole society and the individuals in it to the everyday experience of 'falling into the world.'"[39] He suggested that this evocative metaphor could be used to help explain Marx's conception of the development of working-class consciousness. The capitalist mode of production itself forces workers to undergo this existential experience of "falling into the world." Only under a revolutionary democracy, where workers had secured control over the conditions and products of their labor, could the working class hope to achieve a real sense of actuality and authenticity and thereby determine or stabilize their collective relationship to the social world. James knew that Heidegger believed that the dictator-

ship of the proletariat would in all likelihood obliterate the individual, reconstructing impersonal institutions that would once again cut
off the individual from his or her autonomous will. But James also
believed that Heidegger's philosophy nicely captured certain aspects
of individual alienation under capitalism.

Like "Marxism 1963" and "Existentialism and Marxism," *The
Gathering Forces* was aimed at young radicals of the early New Left.
What is particularly striking about this document is its pronounced
Third Worldism. *The Gathering Forces* announced in no uncertain
terms the centrality of the peasantry to the socialist project:

> Fifty years ago, the October revolution made mankind aware of the
> task placed in the hands of the proletariat: destroying the accepted,
> constantly increasing evils of capitalist society. Today there has
> emerged a new force to join the proletariat, comprising of hundreds
> of millions. This force is engaged in the struggle to rid contempo-
> rary society of the incubus which weighs upon it and which threat-
> ens to destroy mankind itself by fratricidal struggles for power. This
> force is the people of the Third World, whose liberation is possible
> only by the destruction of the economic and cultural domination of
> imperialism. For us who celebrate the fiftieth anniversary of the
> October revolution this political emergence of the Third World is a
> culmination of what emerged from theory into reality in October
> 1917.[40]

Rawick later reported that the four men had argued about how much
strategic weight to place on the peasantry as an autonomous revolutionary agent.[41] The final version, at any rate, insists that it is "reactionary prejudice" to assume that "supposedly backward masses"
cannot achieve popular sovereignty. Johnsonism never sounded more
Maoist than when Glaberman, Gorman, James, and Rawick wrote:
"within fifteen or twenty years we can have a totally different world
society."[42]

Clearly, postcolonial nationalism, such as that practiced by Williams's People's National Movement, would be insufficient from a radical standpoint. "Political independence," they argued, is only a "first
step . . . Now must come the working out of the difficult internal
problems, the work relations, the connections between town and
country, the utilization of popular resourcefulness."[43] Yet not all
nationalists in the underdeveloped world favored "ever-centralizing

bureaucrats" over the "resourcefulness of local initiative."[44] In the final section, entitled "What is Socialism?" the authors declared that Castro's regime had made impressive gains:

> The Cuban Revolution indicates the road to this realm of freedom. The Cuban Revolution does so in the fact that it begins to do away with commodity production. It is pulverizing the myths about how the fate of peoples presumed to be backward must wait for their salvation upon the graciousness of the great capitalist states.[45]

Some have argued that James was inconsistent in applying his perspective.[46] For the time being, the authors had set aside the notion of permanent revolution that had guided James's writings from *The Black Jacobins* to *Modern Politics*. Having only recently stressed the role of class struggle at the point of production, the quartet now described socialism as a matter of synthesizing distinct traditions:

> What is chosen from Europe is the signal heritage of the Hungarian revolution, workers' councils, direct democracy. What is selected from the Cuban Revolution is national self-assertion and now a vision of the socialist future of mankind. What is selected from the European heritage as a whole is the notion of human activity, economic, political and social, the work of Marx, the vision of humanistic societies.[47]

In retrospect, the period from around 1967 to 1976 was a dramatic high point for the international Left. And although *The Gathering Forces'* Janus-faced combination of command economy Third Worldism and First World Marxian-humanism may have fundamentally breached the founding principles of American Johnsonism, it nevertheless seemed in tune with the anarchic and contradictory political temper of the times. The late sixties and early to mid-seventies were the years from the Tet Offensive in South Vietnam and the May Events in France, to the "Revolution of the Carnations" in Portugal and the rising tide of citizens' action movements in Germany. This was the period in which New Left and environmental parties were able to affix themselves onto the political landscape in a number of European countries. In the West Indies, leftist study groups and independent radicals, some of them attached to social democratic formations (such as the Jamaican People's National Party), managed to influence political discourse and even public policy. Other Third World liberation movements—from Angola to the Philippines and from Nicaragua to Tanzania—exploited political openings of one kind or another to launch bold military offenses and to sometimes launch "antiimperialist" regimes. Even in the United States, a culture of tolerant individualism and mass opposition to the Vietnam War spawned a revived leftist discourse and "countercultural" institutions. One of the less appealing aspects of this period, however, was the resurgence of a virulent sectarianism that divided black Marxist-Leninists from cultural Pan-Africanists, anarchists from neo-Marxists, and liberal feminists from socialist feminists (and from radical feminists).

The student-worker uprising in France in May to June 1968 was perhaps the most explosive movement of all. The May Events were set off by protests centered in urban centers over the poor conditions and prospects French students faced as a social group. Thousands of students participated in marches and other public demonstrations demanding an overhaul of the nation's system of higher education. Radicalized by the heavy-handed response of the French authorities and police, student demonstrators helped ignite a national, factory-based general strike involving over ten million workers. Even though Socialist and Communist leaders feared the subversive and "irrational" aspects of the student movement, their working-class constituents were inspired to raise "irresponsible" demands for shorter work weeks, better working conditions, and, in some cases, *autogestion*—the democratization of industry. In a few regions, students and workers collaborated on individual projects while in other areas, trade unionists refused to even talk to outsiders, who were regarded as middle class and "unserious." The general strike lost steam as the French President Charles De Gaulle moved to reestablish authority by promising social reforms and new elections. Traditional parties on the Left hoped that their cause would gain power at the ballot box, but De Gaulle was reelected president, which cemented the return to "normalcy."

Commenting on these tumultuous events through a series of letters published in Facing Reality's newsletter, *Speak Out*, James claimed that the lesson of May '68 was that socialism was once more on the political agenda. He insisted that the "national state must be destroyed and the only way that can be done is the break-up of all bourgeois institutions and their replacement by socialist institutions."[48] The French people had demonstrated that they were "ready

to take over society and to form new institutions." Dramatically over-
stating the potential for radical change, James argued that the "World
Revolution in 1968 has entered in what could be a decisive and final
stage. De Gaulle is an episode as were the Tsar and Kerensky. Judge
the seriousness and understanding of a babbler [pundit] by what he
makes of this: De Gaulle is Nicholas, Kerensky and Kornilov all in
one."[49] In a letter written a few months later, James described what
he found when he visited Paris in December 1968 (some thirty years
after his library work on San Domingo). The impression he gained
was that the masses were highly charged by the concept of *autogestion*. However, he backed away from some of his earlier predictions,
noting that the "creation of new institutions must seem even in the
minds of the working class a task which is beyond the immediate possibility."[50] Yet he insisted that the restoration of social consensus was
a temporary affair. Whatever their public rhetoric, union leaders and
politicians in France recognized that their world could quite easily
come undone again. When society was ready, it would seize the day.
As he had written earlier, "We do not make the revolution to achieve
the socialist society. The socialist society makes the revolution."[51]

Revolutionary rhetoric filled the meeting halls of black radicals as
well as student Marxists. James's stature as a historian of slave revolution and as a leading 1930s Pan-Africanist gave him a certain
amount of credibility in North America and Africa. The *New York
Times* sought out his opinion on the Marxist/nationalist rift that the
newspaper described as "the chief development in black thought
since the civil rights movement culminated in black power."[52] Black
nationalists were said to downplay the importance of class conflict
and capitalist economics, while one African-American Marxist characterized the nationalists as being obsessed with "how many kings we
had in Africa."[53] A cultural nationalist, writing in the pages of *Black
Scholar*, asserted that for some black intellectuals their "turn towards
Marxism has represented a way out, a way to take off their African
clothes, change back their names, refry their hair, pick up white
friends again."[54] With each side claiming to be anticapitalist and critical of the Soviet Union, however, certain common assumptions
linked the two camps.

James told the reporter from the *Times* that too much emphasis
was being placed on symbolic issues. He pointed out that in the
1930s London-based black activists had been able to set aside their
differences to work together in the International African Service

Bureau and other organizations.[55] The first five Pan-African Congresses, he noted, were models of united action. It was the inspiration of the fifth Pan-African Congress, held in Manchester in 1945, that James had in mind when he helped issue *The Call* for a sixth Congress in 1973 in association with H. Rap Brown, Shirley Graham DuBois, Amy Jacques Garvey, and others. Their document urged that the Congress address three specific themes: economic independence, scientific and technical cooperation, and the liberation of South Africa. James suggested that the Congress focus in particular on the concept of "self-reliance." By this he referred to the idea that "the future of Africa must depend upon the Africans relying on themselves and using what they have and seeking what they want with their own conception."[56] A variety of individuals and organizations agreed that a new Congress would be useful, and in the fall of 1974, Dr. Julius Nyerere, the head of state of Tanzania, hosted the Congress in Dar es Salaam, with attendance exceeding three thousand people. The actual Congress was a disappointment, however. No single theme provided the meeting with a coherent focus, and many sessions were marred by sectarian in-fighting between nationalists and Marxists.

Two weeks before its scheduled opening, James was informed that organizations from the Caribbean that were not officially sanctioned by their governments (such as the New Jewel Movement of Grenada and Trinidad's National Joint Action Committee) could not attend. This effectively excluded dissidents from a number of countries and lent the authority of the Pan-African movement to regimes that had arguably betrayed the aspirations of the West Indian peoples. Adamantly opposed to this administrative fiat, James refused to lend his name to a meeting he had canvassed for so energetically:

> I went to Nigeria, I went to Ghana, I went somewhere else in Africa—I can't remember. I went to the Caribbean twice, I went to Guyana, I went to Trinidad, I went to Jamaica twice. I travelled all over the United States. I went to the West Coast. I would have eight or ten meetings over a weekend between Sacramento, Los Angeles, and San Francisco . . . [But] I know those Caribbean governments as well as anybody else. And I was not going to be a representative of any one of them![57]

"Because he believed that solidarity between Africans and people in the diaspora must be forged among mass-based revolutionary groups rather than among governments," writes Consuelo Lopez, "James called on all delegates to boycott the conference." She notes that Nyerere phoned James at his hotel in Washington, D.C., in a futile effort to change his mind.[58] Soon after the Sixth Congress had taken place, James dusted off a proposal that he had batted around a decade earlier and called for a seventh Pan-African congress that could promote the idea of federation—not only in the East Caribbean but also in West Africa. He argued that the state was too fragile to cope with the pressures of underdevelopment. Federal arrangements could encourage Pan-African unity and cultural autonomy and find ways to promote sustainable economic development. Yet although this theme had been broached at Dar es Salaam, it failed to rally the participants or to convince politicians to abandon their commitment to the nation-state.

It was in his capacity as a Pan-Africanist that James was asked to speak on the subject of black studies in 1969, at Federal City College (now the University of the District of Columbia), where he obtained a teaching position. The talk was one of many he gave throughout the late 1960s and 1970s, and it exemplified his virtues both as an orator and as an independent Marxist. It also revisited the distinctive position he had articulated a decade earlier in the context of debates in the West Indies. "Black Studies and the Contemporary Student" opened on a quintessentially Jamesian note:

> I have to make certain things clear from the beginning. I do not recognize any distinctive nature of black studies—not today, 1969. However, the history of the United States being what it has been and what it still is, there is a serious struggle going on between the advocates of one lot of black studies and the advocates of another lot. And, therefore, I am compelled for the time being to take sides . . . [59]

There were, on the one hand, advocates of an autonomous, "nation-building" black studies movement (which James was critical of) and advocates of a sort of pacification strategy where black studies would play the same role in the universities that Nixon's "black capitalism" program was designed to play in the community. James was an opponent of the latter, which he summarized as saying "what you really need to do is to get the kind of education which will fit you for your 11 percent of the top jobs and your 11 percent of the middle jobs,

C. L. R. James speaking on Pan-Africanism
Washington, DC, 1981
Photo: Kent Worcester

too."[60] While his overall position was neither black nationalist nor liberal accomodationist, James clearly felt for tactical reasons that he had to side with the nationalists. As he stated toward the beginning of the talk:

> A man like Rap Brown says things that I can't imagine my saying. But if anybody wants to criticize him, especially people in England, I tell them, "You shut up and leave him alone. What he says and what risks he chooses to run, that is his business, comes from his past and his experience of the people around him."[61]

Militants like Rap Brown voiced the concerns of many urban African-Americans and, however critical one might be of certain manifestations of black nationalism, one had to accept that it was a social movement with a history, logic, and appeal all its own. As James had argued in his seminal document "The Revolutionary Answer to the Negro Problem in the USA," there was an intrinsically radical dynamic to black nationalist movements, one that Marxists should learn to appreciate and even accommodate on its own terms. Furthermore, the black studies movement was correct in insisting on the relevance of the black experience to the history of the West. As he argued in his lecture, "to talk to me about black studies as if it's something that concerned black people is an utter denial. This is the history of Western Civilization. I can't see it otherwise."[62] If it took a nationalist perspective to challenge moribund conceptions of history, then so be it.

This is not to suggest, however, that James's position was one of passively accepting whatever demands were raised by a given social movement. For one thing, the impassioned discourse of 1960s-style Black Power movements was not exactly to his taste. "I am not boasting about black is beautiful," he emphasized. "Please, I don't go in for that. If other people want to, that's their affair, if they say 'Black is beautiful,' 'Black is ugly,' black is whatever they like. I am concerned with historical facts."[63] The phrase "historical facts" was the critical one. James's interest was in interrogating and opening up the study of Western societies—in strengthening and deepening our collective understanding and appreciation of history as a totality—and not in Western Civ-bashing. An interesting light on his perspective is cast in a section when he discusses his conversations with West Indian graduate students in London:

I am in London and I see some of the students and I ask one of
them, "What are you doing?" He says, "I am doing a study of T. S.
Eliot." I say, "Fine." I ask another West Indian student, "What are
you doing?" He says, "I am working for the Ph.D." I say, "What are
you doing?" He says, "I am studying D. H. Lawrence." I say, "Very
nice." The most fantastic of them all is another fellow who tells me
he is doing Joseph Conrad. Conrad is a Pole who wrote in the
English language and wrote very well indeed.[64]

At this point the listener might have supposed that James advised
these students to probe, say, the history of the Haitian slave revolution or the life of Marcus Garvey. But his advice went in a rather different direction:

But why should these West Indian students be doing D. H.
Lawrence, Joseph Conrad and T. S. Eliot when a man like Alexandre Dumas, the father, is there? . . . I want to tell you what those
novels [e.g., Dumas's *The Count of Monte Cristo*, *The Three Muske-
teers*] did. After the French revolution, Europe and the rest of the
world broke out into what was known as the romantic period
which meant a tremendous expansion of the individual personality
of the ordinary man. Previous to the French revolution, men lived
according to a certain discipline, a certain order. The French revolution broke with that and people began to live more individual,
more experimental, more romantic lives—Personality. Among the
forces which contributed to that were the romantic poets and novelists of the day. And not one of them stands higher in the popular
field, in the expectation and understanding of the people of those
days, than Alexandre Dumas . . . What I am saying is, not only did
the black people contribute, not only did they fight in the ranks, but
in forging the kind of lives which people lived afterwards, one of
the foremost men is a man from the Caribbean. How do I make that
into black studies? I can't. No! I can understand some university
saying, "We are going to study the lives and works of black men
who have not been done before." That I understand, but to make it
black studies![65]

An instructive passage. As far as one could tell, its author had no
special interest in the works of Alexandre Dumas. But he called attention to the Romantic's West Indian roots to highlight the intersection

and interdependence of Western traditions and the African diaspora. This passage is also instructive for what it says about how James could upset listeners' expectations, be they nationalist or "Eurocentric." There is something pointed about the suggestion that Dumas' romantic individualism could be of significance to the black studies movement.[66] Finally, the passage reasserted the value of "history" over something called "black studies." Ultimately, it was the contribution that the latter could make to the former that excited James. Black studies per se held no intrinsic interest for him.

Given an uncertain bank balance, the absence of a network similar to the ones that sustained him during the 1930s and 1940s, and his declining health, it is perhaps not surprising that James mostly produced short pieces in this period.[67] It seemed increasingly unlikely, for example, that he would ever finish the projected book on Shakespeare. One of the last books to appear during his lifetime was *Nkrumah and the Ghana Revolution*, much of which had been composed in 1958–1960 and was finally published in 1977. Portions of the manuscript turned up in different publications in the 1960s, and, as he revealed in a letter to Martin Glaberman, his initial expectations for the book were quite high. "I am usually an exceptionally good judge of my own work," he wrote, "leaning towards underestimation instead of overestimation of the work. About the book: it is, I have not the slightest doubt, the best book that has appeared on Africa."[68]

Consciously highlighting the question of political leadership, as he had done in *The Black Jacobins* and elsewhere, James's book on Ghana devotes considerable attention to the changing nature of Nkrumah's relationship to the popular constituency for national independence and self-emancipation. As leader of the Convention People's Party, Nkrumah became the head of the new West African state, Ghana. For the first few years he was a genuinely popular figure, but he used his personal charisma to consolidate his control over the state. Under his centralizing administration, the bureaucracy gained considerable leverage over the national economy, and Nkrumah eventually turned from folk hero into dictator. In 1966, the one remaining countervailing power center within the state, the armed forces, initiated a coup while Nkrumah was touring European capitals. "The most astonishing aspect," writes the British historian Trevor Jones, "was not that it [the coup] took place at all, but that the ruling party and its integral wings collapsed so completely within the course of a few hours . . ."[69] The Western press reported that Nkrumah's abrupt fall from power was a consequence of two factors: economic mismanagement and the government's failure to implement its social program. In a subsequent, comparative analysis, Immanuel Wallerstein argued that postcolonial one-party regimes typically undergo a process whereby once the initial period of revolutionary momentum has passed, party cadres abandon the anticolonial party in favor of state employment. In the case of Ghana, this had the effect of cutting the regime off from outside criticism.[70]

In *Nkrumah and the Ghana Revolution*, James emphasizes neither economic mismanagement nor the dynamics of one-party rule in his analysis of Nkrumah's fall from power. Instead, his examination of the process leading from independence to military coup highlights certain flaws in the CPP's leader's personality—Nkrumah's vanity and paranoia, his failure to delegate responsibility or to draw on the energies of his numerous supporters throughout the country. While much of the historical narrative that the book provides is informative—its detailed account of the emergence of the Convention People's Party and the struggle for "positive action" is particularly engaging—his overall analysis could have benefitted from the type of comparative framework that Wallerstein employs.

In Part II of *Nkrumah and the Ghana Revolution*, the author discusses his own dealings with Nkrumah, and this is by far the more interesting half of the text. What becomes clear is that James felt that he had to think carefully about how, where, and when to criticize the regime. In 1960, for example, he gave a speech in the capital city of Ghana, Accra, warning of the need for being "doubly and trebly an honest man" because "these fellows are seeking to bribe you and corrupt you all the time, because that is the only way they can control or affect the economic life of the country."[71] The phrase "these fellows" referred, of course, to agents of foreign capital and outside state powers. The implied criticism, easily deciphered, was that these people were finding it easy to make friends and allies in the new Ghana. But in this speech the primary responsibility for Ghana's problems was external; James did not believe that Nkrumah was to blame if multinationals and the superpowers sought to promote their own interests in Africa.

Even by 1962, with Nkrumah facing heated criticism for human rights violations from domestic politicians and sympathetic observers abroad, James bent over backwards to avoid being seen as attacking a friend. "I am thankful and happy to know that Africa has produced so distinguished a master of the general strategy and details of the politics of humanity in the inhuman world in which we live," he gushed privately in a letter to the Ghanese leader.[72] His willingness to forgive Nkrumah has to be placed in a broader context where a whole generation of intellectuals lent their support to experiments of one kind or another despite signs that many of the new independent states were being run along dictatorial lines.[73] After the situation in Ghana deteriorated further, and Nkrumah had failed to respond to private letters, James finally published a critical account of Nkrumah's leadership in an article in the *Trinidad Evening News* in 1964. Noting that Nkrumah had been the target of two assassination attempts, he said that "something was wrong with his regime which demanded serious attention, otherwise people don't shoot."[74] James never heard from Nkrumah again.

Retreating from the peasant-centered analysis advanced in *The Gathering Forces*, James's analysis in *Nkrumah and the Ghana Revolution* placed less emphasis on the peasantry as a revolutionary force and stressed the need to transform the international system as a whole. Returning to the analysis of permanent revolution that he had advanced in *World Revolution* and elsewhere, he maintained that "[w]ithout economic, technological and educational help and encouragement from the advanced areas of Western civilization, Africa will go up and go down in flames, and heaven only knows when that conflagration will be halted."[75] In the 1960 speech given at Accra, he had argued:

> We should be careful in dealing with these matters to call things by their correct names, and classic socialism, and it is always good to begin with the classic definition, demands a very highly developed technological and industrial society. It demands people who for some years have been familiar with the latest developments of modern science and technology. It demands a population which is in its majority industrial workers . . . [76]

At the same time, more could have been done with the available human and technological resources. James suggested that Nkrumah's greatest flaw was in some respects similar to Toussaint's—that of failing to trust his supporters, to tap into their democratic spirit.[77]

To focus on James's partial critique of Nkrumah's political practice once he gained power, however, is to overlook the inflated claims he had initially made concerning Nkrumah's importance as a world historic individual. "I want to say here," he told the audience in Accra,

> and I want to say it most emphatically that when the time comes and the history of international socialism and the revolution to overthrow capitalism is written at the head of course will be names like Marx, there will be names like Engels, there will be the name of Lenin. But a place will have to be found for Kwame Nkrumah . . . (drowned by applause and shouts) . . . I say today, the center of the world revolutionary struggle is here in Accra, Ghana. (Loud applause)[78]

A certain amount of oratorical excess would have been natural on such an occasion. But the speech gives one the sense of how much James had invested in a certain image of Nkrumah's role on the historical stage. A reviewer for the *Times Literary Supplement* rightly complained that James had demolished the "sentimental imperialist myth of African political development" only to replace it with a sentimental Pan-African myth about Nkrumah as Lenin, Gandhi, and Toussaint L'Ouverture all rolled into one.[79]

By 1977, when *Nkrumah and the Ghana Revolution* finally appeared, the third wave of Pan-Africanism had subsided. Ghana continued to decline under military rule, Nyerere's African socialist experiment was quickly losing steam, and in general less attention was being paid to Pan-African ideals of black unity and cooperation across the diaspora. Black nationalism was on the retreat in the United States and Britain, with warring sects standing in for mass movements. Of course, vestiges of Pan-African ideology could still be found on campuses in both the advanced industrial and "underdeveloped" nations. However, as was the case with the international New Left, the crest of the wave had broken—ravaged by in-fighting, political misleadership, sheer physical exhaustion, state repression, and by the inevitable backlash that can threaten any movement for autonomy and equality.

In the Caribbean, the choices seemed largely limited to PNM-style neocolonialism or Cuban statism. Clearly, a militant Pan-Africanism would be incompatible with the former and suspicious of the latter. The main exceptions to these stark options were the reformist program advanced by Michael Manley's People's National Party after

its electoral triumphs in Jamaica in 1972 and 1976, and the participatory radicalism practiced by the New Jewel Movement in Grenada
from 1979 to 1983. Despite the brouhaha surrounding the collapse
of federation in the early 1960s, James enjoyed amicable relations
with Manley's father, Norman Manley, and was broadly supportive of
the program of social welfare and state-led development that the
younger Manley's regime embarked on during the mid-1970s. James
was also sympathetic to the fact that the People's National Party had
long been allied with "poets, painters, fiction writers, and cultural
intellectuals . . ."[80] Under Michael Manley's flamboyant leadership,
Jamaica briefly became an international symbol of Third World
resistance, not only for its music and culture but also for its redis-
tributive economics and for Manley's friendly overtures to the Cuban
government. However, the regime was beset by tremendous economic and political pressures, particularly during its second term,
and when the People's National Party regained power in the late
1980s Manley assured Western powers that he was firmly proenter-
prise and was no longer interested in joining forces with the Cubans
or other radical governments.

For four short years, Grenada's New Jewel Movement (NJM) led
a People's Revolutionary Government that attempted to lead the
Grenadian economy in a participatory and state socialist direction.
The NJM had come to power in March 1979 in the aftermath of a
mass popular uprising directed against a neocolonial government
headed by Eric Gairy. It had been formed in 1973 as a result of the
merger of two organizations, the Joint Endeavour for Welfare, Education and Liberation and the Movement for Assemblies of the People.
The latter was led by Maurice Bishop, an articulate and popular figure
who had known James in London in the 1960s and whose politics
reflected the combined influence of Black Power, Castroite, and Jamesian views. As the NJM moved closer to obtaining power, it embraced
a more orthodox Marxism-Leninism. Bishop told an interviewer in
1977 that the cadres of the New Jewel Movement had begun to identify with the Cuban model (which he described as "scientific socialism") by the mid-1970s.[81] Once in power, however, and with Castro's
blessing, Prime Minister Bishop's People's Revolutionary Government embraced the mixed economy and implemented a series of
imaginative reforms in the areas of education, health, industrial relations, and agriculture.[82] Tragically, in the fall of 1983 Bishop and five
of his colleagues were interned and later executed during a palace

coup led by Deputy Prime Minister Bernard Coard and other NJM *apparatchiks*. This coup d'etat provoked a U.S. invasion which led to the installation of a regime that marched in step with U.S. interests as these were defined by the Reagan administration.

In comparison to Jamaica or Grenada, postcolonial politics in Trinidad and Tobago seemed frozen under the hegemony of the People's National Movement. The parliamentary opposition, which continued to be rooted in ethnic politics, was typically noisy but rarely effective. The only major threat to Williams's rule came in 1970, when a succession of protests on behalf of Black Power led to talk of the possibility of a Left-inspired military uprising. Several of the protests were led by the Oilfield Workers Trade Union and by a student-based organization, the National Joint Action Committee. Out of sheer frustration, a few radicals resorted to arson to protest against the PNM's complicity in imperialism and capitalism—and as a result, some two hundred banks and government buildings (as well as the residence of the U.S. Vice Consul) went up in smoke in a single year (1970).[83] Williams was able to restore order in this period by arresting Black Power leaders, by appealing to middle-class, Indo-Caribbean, and business interests, and by making limited concessions to popular demands.[84] His rule was also backed by the presence of a U.S. naval task force in Trinidad's territorial waters.

Broadly speaking, James maintained a respectful and sometimes friendly stance vis-a-vis a variety of leftists in the region, including Manley and, before his untimely death, Maurice Bishop. Some of his contacts dated back to his work in the PNM and the federation movement. He had also come to know a number of academics and others through a West Indian study group that Richard Small and Norman Girvan had formed in 1962. The group met at James's home on Staverton Road in northwest London on Friday nights, which gave the Jameses the opportunity to discuss ideas and books with a promising circle of younger radicals. Participants in these Friday night sessions included future Harvard sociologist Orlando Patterson and the Guyanese scholar Walter Rodney.[85]

Through these connections, James enjoyed contact with a variety of groups that had sprung up in the late 1960s and early 1970s and that were influenced by the New Left and Black Power movements. These groups included the Trinidad-based New Beginnings Movement, the People's Democratic Movement of St. Vincent, and the Antigua-Caribbean Liberation Movement led by Tim Hector. As

Paget Henry has shown, at least one tendency within the latter became influenced by the worker-centric, prospontaneity program advanced in such texts as *Facing Reality*.[86] Throughout this period James was also in intermittent contact with a number of Jamaican intellectuals, some of whom were close to Manley's government.

As far as Cuba was concerned, James's attitude was usually enigmatic but occasionally uncritical. As we have seen, the first response of the Correspondence group was to encourage American workers to emulate the Cuban revolutionaries, and James and his coauthors had claimed in *The Gathering Forces* that Cuba was making great strides in realizing a socialist economy. However, James rarely had any sort of detailed comment to make about Castroism or its role in the Caribbean, except to say that it reflected something larger than simply "Stalinism" or "Communism." His description of the Cuban Revolution as "peculiarly West Indian, the product of a peculiar origin and a peculiar history," which appeared in the 1963 afterword to the second edition of *The Black Jacobins*, may be regarded as more or less representative of his overall approach.[87] James spent some time in Cuba in 1967 and 1968, participating in an international conference of "revolutionary intellectuals" convened by Cuban academics.[88] His main contribution to the proceedings was to interject from the convention's floor that the category of "intellectual" was historically obsolete and should be "abolished as a force."[89] As the Jamaican writer Andrew Salkey paints the scene, James's calculatingly provocative suggestion went over like a lead balloon. "Salon dead still. Consternation. Bewildered, silent delegates everywhere," he writes.[90]

Salkey's vivid depiction of this Havana sojourn emphasizes the older man's sense of detachment even as he finds him in "an excellent humour, wry and timely."[91] As he carries around art books and carefully nurses his health, James picks a rather idiotic fight with his group's hosts, who insist that it is indeed appropriate for Fidel to keep "telling the people, over and over again, that the democratic freedom of the vacillating Cubans will not be taken away from them."[92] Another event goes far more smoothly: the celebration of James's sixty-seventh birthday. In attendance were the poet Aime Cesaire, Daniel Guerin, the antipsychiatrist David Cooper, the Haitian writer Rene Depestre, Robert Hill, John La Rose, and approximately thirty others. Salkey describes the tribute as a "spontaneous" and "moving" affair at which James gave a short speech that was "provocative, salty and in the tradition of the man of letters."[93]

On some occasions he could be almost rapturous in praising the Cuban model. An essay on "The Birth of a Nation," written toward the end of the 1970s, ended on the following note: "We could have introduced another West Indian poet who, with pen and pencil, plunged into the depths of the Caribbean's harsh reality and superstition to paint the picture of the people as they are and as they feel. But we prefer the poet who begins: goodbye Mr. Wood, goodbye Mr. Taft, goodbye Mr. Nixon and ends with 'Good Morning, Fidel!'"[94]

Sporadic comments aside, the Caribbean leader that he was closest to was Walter Rodney, cofounder of the Working People's Alliance (WPA) of Guyana and noted scholar. As we have seen, Rodney had become drawn into James's West Indian circle in London in the mid-1960s and had consulted with the elder radical when he was studying at the School of Oriental and African Studies at the University of London. From the outset of their relationship, James was terribly impressed by the young man's theoretical abilities and political dedication. Rodney and James were very much in the same tradition, sharing in common a radically democratic, anti-Stalinist, and cross-ethnic conception of socialism. Rodney had returned to Guyana in 1974—the WPA was formed the following year—and became a leading opponent of the "cooperative socialist" (and later "Marxist-Leninist") government of Prime Minister Forbes Linden Burnham and the People's National Congress. Burnham's regime had become steadily more repressive in the 1970s, turning to political violence to achieve its ends. According to one political scientist, Rodney became a target of this wave of violence because he had "the gift of leadership."[95] By the late 1970s, Rodney was sleeping in a different house every night to avoid assassination. He was killed by a car bomb in June 1980.

Rodney's death reverberated across the Pan-African world. Three generations of Caribbean, West African, and North American leftists had come to appreciate his quiet, forceful style, and there was a great deal of distress concerning the circumstances of his murder, which was never properly investigated. His passing solicited a moving tribute from James at a meeting organized by *Race Today* at London's venerable Conway Hall: "We face, in the Caribbean, over the next ten or twenty years, a tremendous difficulty in developing the country, to make the government and the people really recognize what they are, feel what they are and do the immense work that we can do. And I know no single person in his age more suitable to carry on that work as Walter Rodney would have been."[96] James made it clear that Rodney would be missed. But in an essay published in 1982, he was quite harsh in his appraisal of Rodney's political work in Guyana. He faulted Rodney, and the WPA leadership as a whole, for failing to fully comprehend the regime's authoritarian nature and for not being prepared for a military-style confrontation:

> He recognized that Burnham meant mischief and that he was prepared to use all power, the armed power of the state, to destroy the opposition. Rodney knew that and he tried to organize against it. And he organized wrong. A key problem in the face of overwhelming state power is how to arm oneself against it. In fact, the arms for a revolution are there: the police and the army have them. What you have to do is to win over a section of the army, and you have arms. And you also take away arms from the government.[97]

James went on to chastise Rodney for staying in Guyana when conditions were so dangerous. He cited the example of Lenin living in exile and working from outside Russia to build a Bolshevik party.[98] Rodney represented the best of the international New Left. To James, it seemed tragically clear that even the best was not good enough.

The speeches and articles that James prepared on the subject of Walter Rodney were among his last public activities. For reasons of health, he withdrew from public speaking in early 1984, "although he continued to see many people in his home."[99] Visitors who arrived at the one-room flat on Railton Road in Brixton had various reasons for wanting to meet the legendary author and radical. While a few guests were journalists hoping for interviews, others were young leftists or friends of friends eager for advice about how to take back the political initiative from the newly resurgent right. In the early 1980s, when fears of nuclear war led to a revival of the Campaign for Nuclear Disarmament, many people wanted to talk about the bomb and the tactics appropriate to the age of exterminism. Feminist and environmental concerns would also come up in conversation. Some visits were of a more personal nature, involving people who knew James from earlier periods who wanted to find out how he was faring. The Brixton connection was important; the symbolic epicenter of Britain's Afro-Caribbean community, it was also the site of multiracial street pro-

tests and antigovernment riots in 1981 and 1985. The sense of reso-
nance with contemporary events was enhanced by the fact that
James's own small apartment was located above the offices of the
journal *Race Today*, which was edited by his comrade (and distant
relation) Darcus Howe. Friends of the journal, such as the poet and
musician Linton Kwesi Johnson, would regularly look in on him,
staying to talk or to simply watch television.

During this period he came to rely on the dedicated service and
friendship of Anna Grimshaw. The six years that she spent as his personal assistant were a tremendous boon to James in what was a lonely
and difficult period. Trained as an anthropologist at Cambridge University, Grimshaw appreciated not only his radical politics but his distinctive outlook. At the same time, she may not have fully shared his
infatuation with popular culture. It is for this reason that her recollection about the role of television in his final years is particularly
acute:

> The television was always on in James's room, but he didn't always
> watch it. He was very interested in watching old films, because he
> was fascinated by how actors moved around. He watched a film as
> he watched a cricket match, and was less interested in the story
> than in the particular characters people created on screen. He was
> also interested in soap operas, and watched American, Australian
> and British soap operas. He had seen the importance of soap operas
> as a modern art form, that they gave a chance for a new relationship
> to be constructed between audience and artist, between life and art.
> But he saw quite clearly that the modern soap opera was a distorted
> form, that it in fact was not an expression of creative form but was
> quite the reverse . . . he would never watch talking heads programs.
> He would say "I'm not listening to intellectuals talk at the end of the
> twentieth century," and would switch immediately back to some
> dire soap opera.[100]

As the 1980s wore on, James gradually slipped into physical infir-
mity. He told one friend at the beginning of the decade that "my physical shape is not as good as my physical form: I have trouble with the
legs and cannot walk very fast but my flow of speech is as strong as
ever, as I demonstrated on Radio and Television interviews, to the
astonishment of the surrounding population."[101]

It was natural that he would rely more and more on visitors and the media for his sense of what was going on in the world. Grimshaw reports that his "reading declined from about the mid-1980s; he had less and less energy or concentration . . ."[102] He slept quite a lot, but while his productivity dwindled, he never actually retired in any meaningful sense. He kept up with world affairs and tried to stay informed about the opinions and habits of virtually everyone who strayed into his sitting room. In the first half of the decade he reviewed books and cricket matches for *Race Today*, wrote about women writers and politics in Eastern Europe, and sent off disputatious letters to English newspapers on such topics as Lenin's commitment to democracy, and politics in the 1930s. He also listened to classical music through a boom box, just as "in the twenties in Trinidad he had a turntable. He wanted to hear music, and that was the form in which it came to him."[103]

Setting aside his work on Walter Rodney, his last articles were marked by their forward-looking and frankly optimistic character. In one of his most widely circulated pieces, he honored the poetry and fiction of Toni Morrison, Alice Walker, and Ntozake Shange for their confidence, insight, and authority. These three authors, he believed, were especially important because they were writing about black women in America, a group that had previously "been held in the background" and was now being placed "right in the front of American literature."[104] This had the effect not only of transforming contemporary American literature, but of challenging established conceptions of black and women's politics. "So it seems," he noted, "that in the women's movement, as usual in the United States, Black people took part; and they have taken a part in it which . . . is important not only to Blacks, but to society as a whole."[105] His essay ended with a reminder to all authors to "write what you think—and maybe what you write about your day-to-day, everyday, commonplace, ordinary life will be some of the same problems that the people of the world are fighting out. You must be able to write what you have to say, and know that that is what matters . . ."[106] This was no doubt the kind of advice he offered in person when Walker, Shange, Maya Angelou, Amiri Baraka, and other writers who came to see him in the 1980s.

He was equally impressed by the emergence of Poland's *Solidarnosc* movement in 1980–1981, which he saw as comparable in terms of general historical importance to the Hungarian uprising of 1956. "I don't argue with people any more about Socialism and Marxism," he boldly told one interviewer. "I say: there is Solidarity, the working class and the farmers, united in making a new society. Now you tell *me* what else Socialism is."[107] As he had always insisted, Soviet-style regimes had a tendency to generate enormous levels of mass resistance which threatened to undermine Communism's entire edifice. And in its earlier incarnation at least, *Solidarnosc* offered an example of the largely spontaneous form of working-class self-organization that James saw as the precondition for a transition to a socialist society. He was struck by the way in which a global media system advertised Solidarity's genesis and evolution, which served to inspire similar efforts in parts of Eastern Europe and China. At a pro-*Solidarnosc* rally held in 1981 in New York City, he spoke not only of events in Europe, but of the possibility of a social movement emerging "from below" in the United States. The speech once again returned to quintessentially Jamesian themes:

> I have spent twenty-five years of my life here and one thing I learned is: this is no European country. It has an individuality of its own. I have been watching the political system especially since Roosevelt came and brought in the New Deal and transferred a lot of power to the Executive. There are two big meetings here every four years. The Democratic Party meets and the Republican Party meets. These are national mobilizations, they are national mobilizations appealing to everybody. But when the day comes when people feel that those national mobilizations are not doing what they want them to do, there will not be any longer a national mobilization but there will be a mobilization of the nation. That is something else.[108]

As we now know, the mobilization of the nations of Central and Eastern Europe resulted in the creation of post-Communist systems that have combined parliamentary institutions with capitalist structural reforms accompanied by rising levels of social inequality. James, I think, would have been troubled but not discouraged by these developments. He would have applauded the demise of Communism in Europe and the former Soviet Union and would have expected that many present-day trends could be reversed or diverted. It is certainly absurd to imagine him believing that something called "history" had come to an abrupt conclusion, in Central and Eastern Europe, in the United States, or indeed anywhere else.

As was fitting, C. L. R. received a variety of awards and tributes in the 1980s. In-depth television interviews were aired in Britain and the West Indies, and *Toussaint L'Ouverture* was revised and performed on the London stage in 1986 under the title *The Black Jacobins*. Its author was awarded an Honorary Doctor of Letters by the University of the West Indies in 1983, and in 1985 a public library in the Hackney section of London was named in his honor. *Talking History*, a one hour conversation with the historian Edward Thompson, filmed in 1981, was shown throughout Britain in 1983 as part of ceremonies sponsored by the Greater London Council for the International Year of Peace.

The book *Cricket*, edited by Anna Grimshaw and published in 1986, collected half a century's worth of writings. Having received glowing reviews in the British press, *Cricket* went on to become one of Allison and Busby's biggest sellers. The earliest article featured, 1932's "The Greatest of All Bowlers: An Impressionist Sketch of S. F. Barnes," had first appeared in the Manchester *Guardian*. "The Decline of English Cricket," taken from 1985's *Race Today Review*, is not only a great title but is one of the very last articles James ever wrote. With the heft and panache of a book designed for a coffee table, Grimshaw's *Cricket* shows off some of the author's best prose. It also reminds us that over the years James published articles solely pertaining to cricket in an exotic array of outlets—all the way from specialist journals (*Cricket*, *Cricket Quarterly*, *The Cricketer*), to newspapers (Glasgow *Herald*, Manchester *Guardian*, Port of Spain *Gazette*) to political journals (*The Keys*, *The Nation*, *Race Today*) and edited books.

Allison and Busby could also take credit for publishing three volumes of selected writings: *The Future in the Present* (1977), *Spheres of Existence* (1980), and *At the Rendezvous of Victory* (1984). All three titles helped bring James's name to the attention of a new generation of readers. This is particularly true of Britain, where quality dailies and labor movement publications garnished the series with rave reviews. As several reviewers noted, the volumes recovered a number of pieces that had long since gone out of print. These include "Triumph"; "The Revolutionary Answer to the Negro Problem in the USA"; "Dialectical Materialism and the Fate of Humanity"; and "Every Cook Can Govern." The series also features carefully selected extracts from several books, such as *World Revolution*, *Mariners, Ren-*

egades and Castaways, and *Facing Reality*. The series' major weakness is that the individual volumes lack thematic coherence.

For several months in 1980, James stayed in San Fernando as an honored guest of George Weekes and the Oilfield Workers Trade Union. It was his last stretch as a public figure in the West Indies. In the winter of 1981 the OWTU awarded James the Labour Star, the Union's highest award, at their forty-third annual conference. As Consuelo Lopez writes, Darcus Howe led James to the front of the hall, where "hundreds of union delegates rose to applaud their defiant warrior. Easing his frail limbs into a chair, James watched his audience settle down to hear his speech on 'the seizure of power' . . . 'When the time comes for you to seize the power,' he reminded his audience, 'you won't need anyone to tell you. You will take it.'"[109] His relationship with the union was rooted in a common political bond and on a recognition of mutual needs: James's need for a West Indian political base, and the union's need for untarnished heroes.

While James's fiery rhetoric may have incited the passions of the union's cadre, in many circles these sentiments only helped cement his status as a political pariah. The establishment's open disdain was the source of some irritation for James, who left Trinidad shortly after receiving the Labour Star to return to London. When an interviewer from Trinidad's *Sunday Express* showed up at his flat in London in 1982, James caustically noted that "My name is mud in Trinidad. I get more recognition and understanding in the USA, in Canada and in this country than I get in Trinidad."[110] Asked by another interviewer in 1986 if he felt homesick for the West Indies, he flatly stated, "No, I don't miss it." He went on to explain that "[p]eople are always telling me that the climate is not as good here. But the climate is outside. I am in here, in the warm . . . In any case my education, the books I was brought up on, the sports, were all British. I feel at home here."[111] But he often reminded visitors that his favorite meal was *Bacalou* (stewed salt fish and white rice), a West Indian dish.[112]

Several years after this last visit, James was awarded the Trinity Cross, Trinidad and Tobago's highest national honor, at a ceremony in London attended by the prime minister of Trinidad, A. N. R. Robinson. His comrade-in-arms, George Weekes, received the Trinity Cross in the same year, 1988. Having only recently been demonized, both were on their way to becoming mythologized—by a government that, ironically, was more market oriented than its predecessor, the PNM. For James at least, this level of recognition was becoming familiar in Britain. A few years before the Trinity Cross ceremony, for example, the *New Society*'s David Widgery told that magazine's readers in an aside: "To the best of my ability, I have attempted not to hero-worship this man who, if marxists believed in such things, would be the greatest living marxist. And failed."[113] In the same period, the *London Times* referred to the elder radical as a "black Plato," with the paper's correspondent writing that it "is not necessary to be persuaded by all James's prophecies and Marxist jargon to recognize a sage and a good man."[114]

With his withdrawal from everyday activity, some observers may have sensed that James was no longer dangerous or controversial—a safe Marxist. But he continued to offer a potent symbol of erudition and revolutionary determination. His portrait on the cover of the third volume of selected writings, *At the Rendezvous of Victory*, taken by Lord Snowdon, captured an austere gentleman sitting on a stiff brown chair, tightly clutching an old-fashioned brim hat. It is an arresting portrait: complex, stately, resolute, but slightly haunted, melancholic. Yet despite the evidence of the photograph, he remained committed to the politics of radical transformation and was hopeful about the future. Thus, while it would be easy, it would also be a profound mistake to find the setbacks of the 1970s and 1980s registered in his deep brown eyes. The essential truth is that he never, for a single moment, appeared to become discouraged or irresolute in any way. He found particular solace in the fact that younger generations of activists were rediscovering and making use of his books and ideas. And he remained the personification of optimism.

C. L. R. James died of a chest infection on May 31, 1989, after a short illness. He had lived to the ripe age of eighty-eight. His body was returned to Trinidad and was buried in a cemetery near Tunapuna. Respectful obituaries appeared in major newspapers across the globe. In the *New York Times*, Selma Weinstein James observed that:

> C. L. R. James was fundamentally a political person and his great contribution was to break away from the very narrow and white male concept of what Marxist politics was. He saw the world, literature, sports, politics and music as one totality, and saw political life as embodying all of those, which was very different from the politics he walked into in the middle to late 1930s, first in England and then in the United States.[115]

His old friend, the cricket writer John Arlott, writing in the *Manchester Guardian*, noted that James was "a fluent lecturer and broadcaster, his voice pleasantly modulated, the sentences flowing as smoothly and roundedly as if he were reading them from script, instead of spinning them from an untrammelled and ordered mind."[116] Other obituaries referred to his eclectic range of interests, his unswerving fealty to Marxism, and his contributions to the history and the historiography of the Caribbean.

In the West Indies, his passing merited banner headlines. A lengthy editorial in the *Trinidad Guardian* remarked that it was doubtful whether "any developing country has produced a man of such wide-ranging intellectualism and such fervent action, a writer-philosopher-revolutionary whose life, in the final analysis, will remain a celebration of the capacity of the human mind and intellect."[117] The economist Lloyd Best, who had been close to C. L. R. from the late 1950s onwards, told a reporter that he "will always remain the dean above us and the master. It is impossible to imagine even an approximation to a replacement."[118] The prime minister, A. N. R. Robinson, called James "one of our most outstanding literary figures,"[119] while opposition leader Patrick Manning said that the Caribbean owed "an inestimable debt to James for his pivotal role in establishing a literary and intellectual tradition in this part of the world."[120] Manning's statement effectively signaled that the PNM's hostility to its old comrade and adversary had come to an end. Hereafter James would be regarded as part of the West Indian pantheon.

Despite the revisionist consensus over James's eminence, there was a small controversy over whether his body would receive a state funeral when it was finally returned to the West Indies. James had left three instructions regarding his final arrangements: that he be buried in Trinidad; that the Oilfield Workers would be responsible for whatever ceremonies took place; and that any memorial be strictly secular in character. The third instruction was particularly provocative in that the concept of a secular burial is virtually unheard of in Trinidad. Yet it was the second condition that generated the most political heat, and it was only after a great deal of wrangling that the government dropped its plans for a state funeral and agreed that the arrangements would rest in the hands of Weekes's successor, Errol McLeod, and the OWTU. The union held a "Ceremony of Return" at the national airport on Monday, June 12, 1989, and a "Celebration of a Life" at the union's Palms Club. The latter, attended by over one thousand people, featured tributes by George Lamming, Martin Glaberman, Darcus Howe, the OWTU's David Abdullah, and several others, as well as calypso music by two of its best-known practitioners, David Rudder and The Mighty Sparrow. At different junctures, steel drum orchestras played Stravinsky's *Rite of Spring* and *The International*. A smaller crowd formed a burial procession at Tunapuna Cemetery later that same day, under heavy rain. James was buried with his Trinity Cross.

◆◆◆

I visited North Trace and Tunapuna in early December, 1992, just prior to completing an earlier draft of this manuscript. North Trace is a tiny hamlet nestled in an agricultural breadbasket. The village, which consists of a few streets converging on a main road, cannot be found on any of the maps sold in Port of Spain. At one intersection there is a 1960s-style schoolhouse for primary-age students; it is sited next to the visible remains of a far older schoolhouse where Robert James once worked as a principal. It is not a wealthy area. In neighboring villages I saw barefoot children carry water in buckets from community wells to individual homes. The visit to North Trace reinforced my sense that James was accustomed to travel and migration, to making friends in a new context and seeing how people lived in different places, at a very early age.

Tunapuna is a far larger town lying on the heavily urbanized northwest corridor between Arima and Port of Spain. It is a bustling, industrious community, more crowded than it was in 1901, but in certain respects recognizable from James's description in *Beyond a Boundary*. The playing fields he once described looking out on seem to have been partially paved over, with the remainder turned into a playground; and his childhood home on Ward Street is now a forlorn edifice overgrown with weeds and vine. Certainly there are features of the town's landscape that would have been familiar to the boy training for his exhibition: vegetable markets, narrow lanes and houses set on concrete blocks, birdsongs, stray dogs, and the lush green hills of the Northern Range that lend an impressive backdrop to the activities below. Only the urban sprawl, the steady drone of the traffic, and the stores selling video tapes and other new commodities would have seemed strange or unfamiliar. And even these things could have been anticipated, for it had long been a place where commercial interests thrived, where goods were sold and traded, and where the world's inventions soon found their way.

The town cemetery abuts the main road where the railway once ran. It is an English-style graveyard, containing a slightly haphazard mixture of family plots, outdoor bric-a-brac, and solitary gravestones. A section of the area is marked "Hindu," implying that the rest is for Christians. Among the bramble and markers are a variety of animals, some hidden and some tethered: dogs, heron, gophers, bees, butterflies, and cattle were all visible on a hot day at the end of the rainy season. Ida Elizabeth James is buried near the entrance to the graveyard; her weathered tombstone lists her as having lived from 1876–1944. Her eldest son is buried toward the back of the site, and the gravestone, fashioned in the shape of an open book, is curiously impressive. One of the book's open pages carries a simple inscription: Cyril Lionel Robert James TC [Trinity Cross]/ 1901–1989/ A Man of Letters. The other page contains an apt quote from *Beyond a Boundary*:

> Times would pass, old empires would fall and new ones take their place, the relations of countries and the relations of classes had to change, before I discovered that it is not the quality of goods and utility which matter, but movement; not where you are or what you have, but where you have come from, where you are going and the rate at which you are getting there.

It is a good and decent resting place; as suitable a place as any, I suppose, to mark the passage of time.

Gravesite
Tunapuna, Trinidad
photo: Kent Worcester, 1992

APPENDIX I
Abbreviations

BBC	British Broadcasting Corporation
CIO	Congress of Industrial Organizations (USA)
CP	Communist Party
CPP	Convention People's Party (Gold Coast/Ghana)
DLP	Democratic Labour Party (Trinidad)
IASB	International African Service Bureau (Britain)
ILP	Independent Labour Party (Britain)
NAACP	National Association for the Advancement of Colored People (USA)
NJM	New Jewel Movement (Grenada)
OECD	Organization for Economic Cooperation and Development
OFWU	Oilfield Workers Union (Trinidad)
PNM	People's National Movement (Trinidad)
QRC	Queen's Royal College (Trinidad)
SDS	Students for a Democratic Society (USA)
SP	Socialist Party (USA)
SWP	Socialist Workers Party (USA)
TWA	Trinidad Workingmen's Association
UAW	United Auto Workers Union (USA)
UNIA	United Negro Improvement Association
USSR	Union of Soviet Socialist Republics
UWI	University of the West Indies
WFP	Workers and Farmers Party (Trinidad)
WP	Workers Party (USA)
WPA	Working People's Association (Guyana)

APPENDIX II
Glossary of Names

Author's note: This glossary provides biographical information on over three dozen individuals with whom James associated during his life. Further information on several of the organizations and individuals referred to herein can be found in *Encyclopedia of the American Left*, edited by Mari Jo Buhle, Paul Buhle, and Dan Georgakas, second edition forthcoming.

Martin Abern (Abramowitz) (1898–1949), was a founder of the American Communist Party and was elected to the CP's Central Committee at the youthful age of 23. In 1928 he was expelled from the Communist Party along with James Cannon and Max Shachtman on the grounds of organizing a Trotskyite faction and went on to play a leadership role in the SWP and its predecessor organizations until the 1940 split. "For several years after the split he worked closely with the largest of the political minority factions in the WP . . . [the Johnson-Forest tendency] but he remained in the WP when the tendency re-entered the SWP in 1948." Stan Weir, "1956: The Fading Revolution," *Against the Current*, September/October 1992, p. 43.

Sir Grantley Adams (1898–1971) studied law and religion at Oxford University and went on to become leader of the Barbados Labour Party and a key advocate of the cause of West Indian federation. Served as Prime Minister and also as President-General of the Barbados Workers' Union. He received a knighthood in 1952. In an unpublished document ("An Analysis of the Political Situation in Barbados"), dated July 1958, James described Sir Grantley as "an outstanding figure, self-made, a man of ability, character, and presence, confident but modest . . . certainly the type of West Indian politician who would be an asset to the Federal Government."

Grace Lee Boggs (1915–) is a Chinese-American born in New England who received a B.A. from Barnard College and a Ph.D. from Bryn Mawr in philosophy in 1940. Along with James and Dunayevskaya she was one of the preeminent figures in the Johnson-Forest tendency and played an active role in its programmatic development. Paul Buhle tells us that "Lee had first been swept up in politics during the excitement around the aborted March on Washington movement led by A. Philip Randolph. She had contacted the Workers Party almost by accident, through a small milieu around the University of Chicago submerged by Communist Party influence . . . Study classes of Marx, in light of political developments made Lee (and her competence in German) an indispensable addition to the group [i.e., the Johnson-Forest tendency]." Paul Buhle, *C. L. R. James: The Artist as Revolutionary*. London: Verso, 1988, p. 84. With her husband James Boggs, Grace Lee Boggs went on to become an influential figure within the humanist wing of the American New Left. Their book *Revolution and Evolution in the 20th Century* (1974) was a hit for the New York publishing house Monthly Review Press.

James Boggs (1919–1993) was an Alabama-born African-American who worked on an assembly line at Chrysler for nearly three decades. Boggs's first book, *The American Revolution: Pages from a Negro Worker's Notebook* (1963), became an important text among Detroit's younger radicals and other participants in the civil rights movement and the early New Left. This book was followed by *Racism and the Class Struggle: Further Pages from a Black Worker's Notebook* (1970) and other works.

James Burnham (1905–1987) was a professor of philosophy at New York University who had become active in Trotskyist politics through his participation in A. J. Muste's American Workers' Party, an independent leftist organization that merged with the Trotskyists in 1934. Burnham became famous for his best-selling book *Managerial Revolution* (1941), which he wrote shortly after dropping out of the

Trotskyist movement. *Managerial Revolution* alludes to, but does not mention, the theory of "bureaucratic collectivism" which Shachtman, Joseph Carter, and others developed to describe the totalitarian character of the Soviet regime. Burnham announced that he was no longer a socialist at the first Workers Party convention. By the early 1950s he was a key influence on the conservative author William Buckley and a senior editor of *The National Review*.

James Patrick Cannon (1890–1974) was a gifted political organizer with deep roots in midwestern radical traditions. Having joined the Socialist Party in 1908 and the Industrial Workers of the World in 1911, Cannon played a leading role in the formation of the Communist Party of America in the months following the Bolshevik Revolution. As a key party official Cannon was a delegate at the 4th and 6th Congresses of the Communist International. At the 6th Congress he stumbled across a long excerpt from Trotsky's "A Criticism of the Draft Program of the Communist International," a document he smuggled out of the Soviet Union and used as the basis for forming a secret Trotskyist faction inside the Communist Party. He was expelled from the CP in 1928 and, along with Max Shachtman and Martin Abern, was the principle founder of the first Trotskyist organization in the United States, the Communist League of America, in 1929. His numerous books include: *The First Ten Years of American Communism* (1962); *Notebook of an Agitator* (1973); *The Struggle for a Proletarian Party* (1943).

Joseph Carter (Friedman) (1910–1970). A founding member of the Communist League of America, and a leading intellectual in the Shachtmanite Workers Party. Carter was first to develop the theory of "bureaucratic collectivism" in opposition to Trotsky's theory of the "degenerated workers' state." After dropping out of the Workers Party in the late 1940s, Carter refrained from organized political activity and worked in a lower Manhattan bookstore.

Cornelius Castoriadis (1922–) is a prominent French intellectual whose organization *Socialisme ou Barbarie* collaborated with the Johnson-Forest tendency in the late 1940s to early 1950s. Castoriadis, who sometimes wrote under the pseudonyms Pierre Chaulieu and Paul Cardan, was born in Constantinople and studied law, economics, and philosophy in Athens. Having first embraced Communism and then Trotskyism, Castoriadis founded *Socialisme ou Barbarie* in 1949 in association with Claude Lefort and a small number of other Paris-based activists and intellectuals. The hallmark of the group was its opposition to Stalinism and bureaucratic capitalism and its commitment to *autogestion*, the theory of workers' self-management. Although it was disbanded in 1966, the group's ideas shaped the post-Marxism of the international student Left of late 1960s. For many years, Castoriadis worked as a professional economist at the OECD; he has been a practicing psychoanalyst since 1974. Three volumes of selected writings have been translated and edited by David Ames Curtis and published by the University of Minnesota Press: *From the Critique of Bureaucracy to the Positive Content of Socialism* (1988); *From the Workers' Struggle Against Bureaucracy to Revolution in the Age of Modern Capitalism* (1988); and *Recommencing the Revolution: From Socialism to the Autonomous Society* (1993).

Learie Nicholas Constantine (1901–1971). One of the century's most prominent West Indians, Learie Constantine received the M.B.E. (Member of the British Empire) in 1945 and was made a Baron in 1969 for his contribution to culture and to the cause of racial enlightenment. Constantine lived in Britain for most of his life but returned to his hometown of Tunapuna, Trinidad, to serve as minister of Works and Transport in Eric Williams's first administration. He later held the position of High Commissioner for Trinidad and Tobago in Britain. His books include *Cricket and I* (1933); *Cricketers' Carnival* (1948); *Cricketer's Cricket* (1949); *Cricket Crackers* (1951); *Colour Bar* (1954); and *The Young Cricketer's Companion* (1964).

Raya Dunayevskaya (1910–1987) served as Trotsky's secretary in Mexico in 1937–1938 and was expert in the field of political economy, especially Soviet political economy. Born in Russia, Dunayevskaya (nee Rae Spiegel) made a unique contribution to the Johnson-Forest tendency. In 1955 she and her followers broke with the Correspondence group and formed News and Letters, a "Marxist-Humanist" organization. Her major works include: *Marxism and Freedom: From 1776 until Today* (1958); *Philosophy and Revolution:*

From Hegel to Sartre and from Marx to Mao (1973); and *Rosa Luxemburg, Women's Liberation and Marx's Philosophy of Revolution* (1981).

Amy Ashwood Garvey (1897–1969) was a Jamaican who was married to Marcus Garvey for three years, 1919–1922. Marcus Garvey subsequently married her girlfriend, Amy Jacques Garvey. Amy Ashwood Garvey was a founding member of the Universal Negro Improvement Association and an active Pan-Africanist until the time of her death. During the 1930s Garvey ran a restaurant in London which was a favorite gathering place for Pan-Africanists. She returned to Jamaica during World War II.

Marcus Garvey (1887–1940) was a charismatic orator of humble origins who generated an enormous following among lower-class blacks across the African diaspora in the 1910s and 1920s by calling for the development of Afrocentric institutions and for a mass exodus "back to Africa." He founded the Universal Negro Improvement Association in his native Jamaica in 1914 and moved to the United States in 1916 where he attracted both mass support and government harassment for his problack activities. Through UNIA's newspaper *Negro World*, which Garvey founded in 1918, the cause of black nationalism was measurably enhanced on several continents. By the early 1920s, the UNIA had over one thousand chapters in forty countries. In 1927 Garvey was deported to Jamaica by the U.S. authorities on charges of mail fraud. Despite the fact that he died in relative obscurity (in England), Marcus Garvey remains a potent symbol of black aspirations for autonomy and freedom throughout the world.

Martin Glaberman (1918–) played a leading role in a succession of Johnsonite organizations, including the Johnson-Forest tendency, Correspondence, and Facing Reality. Glaberman worked as an autoworker in Detroit for twenty years and subsequently taught at Wayne State University. He is the author of several pamphlets, including *Punching Out* (1952), *Union Committeemen and Wildcat Strikes* (1955), *Be His Payment High or Low: The American Working Class of the 1960s* (1966), and *Mao as Dialectician* (1971), as well as a valuable full-length historical study, *Wartime Strikes: The Struggle Against the No-Strike Pledge in the UAW during World War Two* (1980). An accomplished poet, Glaberman is the author of *The Grievance: Poems from the Shop-floor* (1980) and *The Factory Songs of Mr. Toad* (1994). His publishing company, Bewick Editions, founded to keep some of James's work in print, may be reached at P.O. Box 14140, Detroit, MI 48214.

Albert Marie "Bertie" Gomes (1911–1978), a West Indian-born Portuguese creole, was a ubiquitous presence in modern Trinidad's literary and political movements. Publisher of the *Beacon* (1931–1933), Gomes went on to become a leading member of the pre-Independence Legislative Council and Executive Council and served as Minister of Labour in the period prior to 1956. His autobiography, *Through a Maze of Colour*, was published in 1974.

Anna Grimshaw (1957–) is a Cambridge-trained anthropologist and writer who has edited a number of James's books and essays, including *Cricket* (1986), *The C. L. R. James Reader* (1992), *American Civilization* (1993, with Keith Hart), and *Special Delivery: The Letters of C. L. R. James to Constance Webb, 1939–1948* (1995). Grimshaw served as James's personal assistant from 1984 until his death. She is the author of *Servants of the Buddha: Winter in a Himalayan Convent* (1992), and served as an editor of the *Fontana Guide to Modern Thought* (1987).

Daniel Guerin (1904–1988) was a Parisian-based libertarian communist and author of many books, including *Fascism and Big Business* (1939), *Negroes on the March: A Frenchman's Report on the American Negro Struggle* (1956), and *Anarchism: From Theory to Practice* (1970). Guerin was active in a wide range of movements, including the anticolonial movement in North Africa and the student movement of May 1968. For many years he attempted to sponsor a "practical brand of anarchism" through the aegis of the Organization Communiste Libertaire. His short book *The West Indies and Their Future* (1961) drew on his decades-long correspondence with C. L. R. James. Paul Avrich's *Anarchist Voices: An Oral History of Anarchism in America* (1995) includes an interview with Guerin.

Wilson Harris (1921–) is a noted author and essayist whose work is representative of the modernist tradition. His fiction, such as *Palace of the Peacock* (1960) and *The Whole Armour and the Secret Ladder*

(1963), is denser and more philosophical in tone than either George Lamming's or C. L. R. James's. The Guyanese-born writer struck up a friendship with James in the early 1960s.

Irving Howe (1920–1993), born Irving Horenstein, was a prominent democratic socialist and literary critic active in the Workers Party and its successor organization, the Independent Socialist League, until he broke with Shachtman in 1952. Two years later he cofounded the independent quarterly, *Dissent*, and contributed to numerous magazines and journals, including *Commentary*, *The New International*, *The New Republic*, *Partisan Review*, and *Politics*. A prolific critic and reviewer, his major works include *The UAW and Walter Reuther* (1949, cowritten with B. J. Widick), *William Faulkner* (1952), *Politics and the Novel* (1957), *The World of Our Fathers* (1976), and an autobiography, *A Margin of Hope* (1982).

Selma Deitch James (nee Weinstein) (1930–) is a writer, organizer, and public speaker who first gained political experience through her involvement in the Johnson-Forest tendency and Correspondence. She married C. L. R. James in 1956; it was his third marriage, and her first. In the 1960s she became active in the New Left and in the international women's movement; in 1972 she played a central role in the creation of International Wages for Housework, a militant feminist organization with branches in Britain, Italy, and the United States. The demand for "Wages for Housework" was animated by a critique of women's unpaid domestic labor. Securing payment from the state for labor done in the household was seen as a way of providing women with a real measure of independence and freedom. Among the pamphlets Selma James generated for the Wages for Housework campaign are *Women, the Unions and Work: Or What is Not to be Done* (1974), and *The Power of Women and the Subversion of the Community* (1975, with Mariarosa Dalla Costa).

Johnstone (Jomo) Kenyatta (c.1891–1978) attended the London School of Economics during the 1930s. He was widely admired among Pan-Africanists for his polemical and oratory skills and became president of Kenya when the nation was granted independence in 1963. He remained the country's president for the rest of his life. His book *Kenya: Land of Conflict* (1945) was published by the International African Service Bureau.

George Lamming (1927–) has written several well-received novels in a naturalistic vein, including *In the Castle of My Skin* (1953), *Age of Innocence* (1958), and *Season of Adventure* (1963). His single work of nonfiction, *The Pleasures of Exile* (1960), contains a chapter-length essay on *The Black Jacobins*; the book is dedicated to C. L. R. James (along with his children and two others), "whose friendship will never be measured or forgiven." A major figure in modern Caribbean literature, Lamming was born and continues to reside in Barbados. Paul Buhle's interview with Lamming, "C. L. R. James: West Indian," appears in Paget Henry and Paul Buhle, eds. *C. L. R. James's Caribbean* (1992).

Stephen Maharaj (1916–1984) entered politics as Uriah Butler's deputy and went on to become a prominent member of the Democratic Labour Party before being squeezed out in the early 1960s. Along with George Weekes and C. L. R. he was a cofounder of the Workers and Farmers Party, on whose behalf he contested the seat of Princes Town. Known as a fierce debater, his political career suffered for several years as a result of his association with the WFP.

T. Ras Makonnen, was the Abyssinian alias of George Thomas Nathaniel Griffity, who was born in British Guiana (Guyana), and became active in the International African Service Bureau as well as other Pan-African organizations. His book *Pan-Africanism from Within* (1973) provides an invaluable account of the movement in the 1930s, 1940s, and 1950s.

Michael Manley (1924–), long-time leader of the Peoples National Party, served as prime minister of Jamaica from 1972–1980 and from 1989–1992. Vice President of the Socialist International; author of *A History of West Indies Cricket* (1988) and other works. Gained a reputation for political militancy during the late 1970s by promoting democratic socialist policies and by expressing admiration for the Cuban model. After staging a remarkable political comeback in the late 1980s, Manley's approach had moderated considerably.

Norman Manley (1893–1969) was a key figure in postwar Jamaican politics and Oxford-trained leader of the People's National Party who built up a strong personal following in Kingston, Jamaica's capital city. An advocate of West Indian federation who played a pivotal role in the events leading to the collapse of federation negotiations in the late 1950s and early 1960s. For many years, Norman Manley was embroiled in a bitter political struggle with Alexander Bustamante, the leader of the Jamaican Labour Party and an opponent of federation.

Ethel Mannin (1900–1984) was an English left-wing writer who was friendly with Emma Goldman, George Orwell, and other prominent radicals of the 1920s and 1930s. She authored over fifteen novels, as well as travel books, childrens books, and other works. Her memorable account of having a garrulous C. L. R. over for tea is contained in her novel *Comrade O Comrade, Or, Low-Down on the Left* (1949). In the 1930s she was active in the Independent Labour Party, and after visiting Russia in 1934 turned to anarchism and, a few years later, militant pacifism. She also participated in some of the activities of the International African Service Bureau.

Ernest Rice McKinney (1886–1984) served as Trade Union Secretary for the Workers Party in the 1940s. Raised in West Virginia, McKinney worked as a journalist and organizer of the unemployed and was a member of the Communist Party from 1920–1926. In the 1920s he also became a contributing editor of *The Messenger*, a newspaper published in Harlem by civil rights leader A. Philip Randolph. Under his party name, David Coolidge, McKinney formulated and defended the majority position on "the Negro question" in a Workers Party debate with C. L. R. in 1945. During the 1970s he became a critic of the "black studies" movement and taught labor history at Rutgers University.

Alfred Hubert Mendes (1897–?) attended Queen's Royal College and later participated in the country's literary circles. He wrote two published novels: *Pitch Lake* (1933) and *Black Fauns* (1935), and worked for many years as the general manager of the Port Services Department in Port of Spain.

V. S. Naipaul (1932–) may be said to constitute the foremost representative of a successor generation of West Indian literary intellectuals to James's and Albert Mendes's. Vidiadhar Surajprasad Naipaul is a prolific essayist, travel writer, and novelist who has enjoyed a prominent career from his earliest novels onwards. Raised as a Hindu, Naipaul is a West Indian of "East Indian descent" who attended Queen's Royal College on a scholarship in the 1940s. In recent decades he has become identified with neoconservative causes, placing him in sharp contrast to left-leaning figures such as James, Harris, and Lamming.

Kwame (Francis) Nkrumah (1909–1972) was born in the village of Nkroful, Gold Coast. James helped introduce Nkrumah to George Padmore, who was to play a central role in Nkrumah's political development. Nkrumah had returned to the Gold Coast in 1947, finding that popular opposition to the British colonial regime had grown during his absence. The next year, he founded the Convention People's Party, which called for "positive action" against the colonial authorities. By 1950, the regime found itself coping with political strikes and violence against foreign-owned property, and Nkrumah was imprisoned for his antigovernmental activities. The CPP went on to receive the bulk of African votes in trial elections held in 1951, and by 1956 the British allowed the Gold Coast to become the first African nation-state to gain independence in the postwar period. Nkrumah was to remain in power until 1966, when he was deposed by a military coup. A useful secondary source is David Rooney's *Kwame Nkrumah: The Political Kingdom in the Third World* (1988).

George Padmore (1902 or 1903–1959) was one of James's closest friends and political associates. Padmore was a childhood friend of James who went on to play a pivotal role in sustaining the Pan-African movement from the 1930s until the very end of his life. Born Malcolm Ivan Meredith Nurse in Trinidad, Padmore went to the United States in 1924 to study medicine at Fisk University. Within a few years he had joined the Communist Party, traveling to Moscow in 1930 to work as a full-time organizer for the Negro Department of the Communist Trade Union International. As a Communist he cultivated an enormous number of political contacts, most of which he retained after breaking with the Communist movement in the mid-

1930s over its strategy of the "Popular Front" against fascism. Padmore remained a socialist and worked with Kenyatta, James, and others in the International African Service Bureau. His companion, Dorothy Padmore, also played a prominent role in numerous Pan-African campaigns. Along with Kwame Nkumrah, Padmore served as political secretary of the Fifth Pan-African Congress, and later held a position as Nkrumah's "personal advisor" from 1957 until his death in the fall of 1959. His major works include *The Life and Struggles of Negro Toilers* (1931), *Pan-Africanism or Communism* (1956), and *The Gold Coast Revolution: The Struggle of an African People from Slavery to Freedom* (1963).

George P. Rawick (1929–1990) was a Brooklyn-born socialist who had been expelled from a Communist youth group in the late 1940s on the grounds of "Titoism" and subsequently became active in a number of anti-Stalinist organizations in the United States. Rawick also produced an influential social history of American slavery, *From Sundown to Sunup: The Making of the Black Community* (1972), which served as the introductory text to a nineteen-volume collection of oral histories (*The American Slave: A Composite Autobiography*) conducted in the 1930s with former slaves. A recent compendium is dedicated to his memory: *Within the Shell of the Old: Essays on Workers' Self-Organization*, eds. Don Fitz and David Roediger (Charles H. Kerr, 1990).

Walter Rodney (1942–1980) was a committed Pan-Africanist and prolific professional historian. His many works include *The Groundings With My Brothers* (1969); *A History of the Upper Guinea Coast, 1540–1800* (1970); *How Europe Underdeveloped Africa* (1972); and *A History of the Guyanese Working People, 1881–1905* (1981). Leader of the Working People's Alliance in Guyana until his assassination.

Meyer Schapiro (1904–) is a prominent art critic and retired Columbia professor whose books *Vincent van Gogh* (1950) and *Paul Cezanne* (1952), along with a handful of essays, decisively shaped the field of modern art criticism. Later works include *Words and Pictures. On the Literal and the Symbolic in the Illustration of a Text* (1973); *Romanesque Art* (1977); and *Late Antique, Early Christian and Medieval Art* (1979).

Born in Lithuania and raised in Brooklyn, Schapiro is a lifelong socialist whose work has ranged across traditional boundaries of art criticism. An irregular contributor to *Dissent*, *Partisan Review*, and other journals, Schapiro was on friendly terms with C. L. R. James and Constance Webb throughout the 1940s and campaigned to help James avoid deportation from the United States in the early 1950s.

Max Shachtman (1904–1972) served as an alternate to the Communist Party's Central Committee until his expulsion in 1928. As a leader of the American Trotskyist movement, he edited the *Militant* and the *New International*. Author of *The Moscow Frame-Up Trials* (1937), and *The Bureaucratic Revolution* (1962), Shachtman had a marked flair for public speaking, radical journalism, and factional politics. After breaking with James Cannon in 1939–1940 he led the Workers Party in an independent Marxist direction until 1958, when he and most of his supporters joined the Socialist Party. Toward the end of his life he became a critic of the McGovernite wing of the Democratic Party and a supporter of the Vietnam War. Peter Drucker has written a useful biography: *Max Shachtman's Political Thought: An American Marxism in the American Century* (Humanities Press, 1994).

Boris Souvarine (1885–1984), a founder of the French Communist Party, was born in Kiev and met Trotsky in Paris during World War I. Born Boris Liefschitz, he took the name "Souvarine" from the name of a character in Emile Zola's *Germinal*. Souvarine's books include *Stalin: A Critical Survey of Bolshevism* (1939), and *A Contre-courant: Ecrits, 1925–1939* (1985).

Leon Trotsky (1879–1940) was a leader of the Russian Revolution and one of the finest polemicists of the Marxist tradition. Trotsky became a socialist in 1898 and became widely known in the revolutionary movement for his lucid prose style and charismatic personality. Elected leader of the St. Petersburg Soviet in 1905, Trotsky joined the Bolshevik Party only in 1917, on the eve of the October Revolution. He served as first commissar of foreign affairs for the Soviet government, and headed the Soviet Red Army during the Civil War. Trotsky formed the Left Opposition in 1923 in opposition to the bureaucratization of the revolutionary state. Expelled from the Communist Party of the Soviet Union in 1927, he was exiled to Turkey in

1929 and was living in Mexico at the time of his assassination in August 1940.

I. T. A. Wallace-Johnson (1894–1965) served as general secretary of the International African Service Bureau. A native of Sierra Leone, he became active in West African trade unionism in the postwar period.

Constance Webb (1921–) first became active in the area of civil rights for African-Americans in the late 1930s. Born and raised in Los Angeles, Webb worked as a model and actress in New York City and Los Angeles off and on in the 1940s and 1950s. In 1946 she married C. L. R. James; their marriage was rendered legal in the eyes of the U.S. authorities in 1948. They had one child, C. L. R. James, Jr. Through their friendship and lengthy correspondence, Constance Webb played a critical role in James's intellectual and personal development. Webb is the author of *Richard Wright: A Biography* (1968).

George Weekes (1921–) served as president general of the Oilfield Workers Trade Union from 1962–1987 and is currently a member of the Trinidad and Tobago Senate. A longtime friend of James's, and a critic of Eric Williams, Weekes played a visible role in the short-lived Workers and Farmers Party as well as in the 1970 Black Power disturbances. A useful biography is Khafra Kambon's *For Bread, Justice and Freedom* (1988).

Dr. Eric Eustace Williams (1911–1981) led the national independence movement in Trinidad and served as prime minister from 1962 until his death. Williams attended Queen's Royal College from 1922–1931 and was at Oxford from 1932–1939. He later taught at Howard University (1939–1948) before serving for nearly ten years on the professional staff of the Anglo-American Caribbean Commission in the late 1940s and 1950s. Author of numerous books, including *The Negro in the Caribbean* (1942); *British Historians and the West Indies* (1966); *From Columbus to Castro: the History of the Caribbean, 1492–1969* (1970); and *Capitalism and Slavery* (1944), a justly famous account of the economic foundations of the abolition of slavery. James and Williams were friendly from the mid-1920s until their political split in late 1960; Williams had visited James in Paris when the latter was working on *The Black Jacobins*, and they met in New York when Williams was teaching at Howard. In 1959, James wrote that "Because of this common background, I talk to him more easily and with quicker mutual understanding than with anybody I know." Quoted in Walton Look Lai, "C. L. R. James and Trinidadian Nationalism," Paget Henry and Paul Buhle, eds. *C. L. R. James's Caribbean* (1992).

Richard Wright (1908–1960). The superb American novelist and essayist whose work helped to transform the representation of African-Americans in American literature. Born in Natchez, Mississippi, Wright joined the Communist Party in 1932 and created a major stir with his brilliant, controversial novel *Native Son* (1940). After breaking with the Party in the early 1940s, he fraternized with Constance Webb and C. L. R. James and introduced them to Ralph Ellison, Chester Himes, and other writers. Wright moved toward an existentialist position and emigrated to Paris in 1947, where he died at the youthful age of fifty-two.

APPENDIX III
Selected and Annotated Bibliography
of the Secondary Literature

Author's note: This appendix offers a selective overview of some of the more significant contributions to the secondary literature. In preparing this appendix I have sought to provide a fair-minded account of a wide variety of materials, many of which offer different approaches the one advanced here. In order to assist readers who have a special interest in a given subject area, I have created six general categories that may be used to distinguish different literatures: Biography and Interpretation, Caribbean, Literature and Culture, Marxism, Pan-Africanism, and Sports. For a nearly comprehensive listing of secondary literature produced prior to the mid-1980s, see C. L. R. James, *At the Rendezvous of Victory*, pp. 291–299.

BIOGRAPHY AND INTERPRETATION

Paul Buhle, *C. L. R. James: The Artist as Revolutionary*. London: Verso, 1988. Buhle's biography provides an informative and idiosyncratic sketch of James's political and literary activities. Drawing on a wide reading of James's work, as well as on interviews and a thorough grounding in left-wing thought, this book provides a welcome alternative to more polemical approaches. The first chapter, on James's youth, is particularly well crafted. Buhle fails to fully develop the provocative theme of "the artist as revolutionary," however.

Paul Buhle, ed. *C. L. R. James: Life and Work*. London: Allison and Busby, 1986. An eclectic but essential contribution that provides a sense not only of James's thought but also of his personality. Buhle has helped stimulate interest in James's work in the United States and Britain, and has encouraged several generations of James's political associates to record their thoughts and recollections on paper. Several of these appear in this book, including fascinating reminiscences by Dan Georgakas, Constance Webb, Stan Weir, Wilson Harris, and others. The book also features scholarly essays by Robert Hill, Walter Rodney, Richard Small, Sylvia Wynter, and others, as well as a poem by Jim Murray.

Selwyn R. Cudjoe and William E. Cain, eds. *C. L. R. James: His Intellectual Legacies.* Amherst: University of Massachusetts Press, forthcoming.

Grant Farred, ed. *Rethinking C. L. R. James.* Oxford: Blackwell, forthcoming.

Grant Farred, "'Victorian with the Rebel Seed': C. L. R. James, Postcolonial Intellectual," *Social Text,* no. 38 (Spring 1994). A sophisticated review essay of recent sources arguing that "the Caribbean registers as an always already presence in James's work . . ."

Anna Grimshaw, *The C. L. R. James Archive: A Reader's Guide.* New York: C. L. R. James Institute, 1991. A meticulously annotated "reader's guide" to twenty feet of archival material dating from 1949–1989. The archive, which is based in Britain, contains manuscripts, letters, notebooks, and other materials. Better than any other single document, this thick pamphlet demonstrates the sheer range of James's intellectual concerns. In particular, it affirms the centrality of James's interest in cricket, literature, and popular culture and the catholicism of his underlying conception of radical politics. A number of previously unpublished manuscripts and letters that are cataloged here are reprinted in Grimshaw's *The C. L. R. James Reader.* Grimshaw's own reading of James's life and work, particularly after 1950, is set out in her introduction to the *Reader,* "C. L. R. James: A Revolutionary Vision for the Twentieth Century."

Anna Grimshaw and Keith Hart, *C. L. R. James and "The Struggle for Happiness.* New York: C. L. R. James Institute, 1991. *The Strug-*

gle for Happiness was the title given to the 1950 manuscript *Notes on American Civilization* by James and Grimshaw in the 1980s. This pamphlet offers a detailed introduction to one of James's most significant works, boldly resituating *American Civilization* in terms of James's overall intellectual development. Grimshaw and Hart highlight those passages in the manuscript which attend to questions of literature, popular culture, and the originality of American culture and society.

The C. L. R. James Journal. A recent venture that has the support of a range of scholars who come at James from different perspectives. One issue features selected speeches by Michael Foot, Martin Glaberman, Cedric Robinson and others delivered at the 1991 Wellesley conference on "C. L. R. James: His Intellectual Legacies," a conference which attracted over 200 participants. The journal also reviews material related to Pan-Africanism and Third World radicalism. (*The C. L. R. James Journal* is published by the C. L. R. James Society, which may be contacted at P.O.Box 82–725, Wellesley, MA 02181.)

Consuelo Lopez, "C. L. R. James: The Rhetoric of a Defiant Warrior," unpublished dissertation, Indiana University, 1983. While marred by factual errors, Lopez's Ph.D. dissertation contains interesting insights concerning the centrality of public speaking for James's political development and public persona. The section on the 1965–1966 period is especially useful.

Anuradha Dingwaney Needham, "Inhabiting the Metropole: C. L. R. James and the Postcolonial Intellectual of the African Diaspora," *Diaspora*, Vol. 2, no. 3 (Winter 1993). An essay in the cultural-studies mode that asks "what are we to make of the oppositional voices and visions shaped by . . . 'the contradictions of domination, the dialectic of imperialism'" (quoting Cedric Robinson).

Bishnu Ragoonath, ed. *Tribute to a Scholar: Appreciating C. L. R. James.* Mona, Jamaica: Consortium Graduate School, University of the West Indies, 1990. A collection of review essays by recent graduates of the University of the West Indies' graduate social science program. Of particular note is Aldrie Henry's "On Cricket," which offers a firm critique of James's "Eurocentricity." Additional essays attempt to integrate James's efforts with those of George Padmore, Kwame Nkrumah, Walter Rodney, and others. The forward is by UWI professor Norman P. Girvan, who studied with James in London in the 1960s and who provides a moving recollection of James's 1959 lecture on "The Artist in the West Indies": "He spoke with knowledge, feeling, authority, fluency and poetry. The words seemed to flow like a great river from the mountain to the sea, sometimes changing direction and even speed, sometimes digressing, but never ceasing in its forward motion, never uncertain about where it was coming from, and always seemingly confident that it was headed towards some glorious rendezvous with history."

Fredric Warburg, *An Occupation for Gentlemen*. New York: Houghton Mifflin, 1959. A priceless memoir featuring several passages that help capture the essence of one of Warburg's favorite authors.

CARIBBEAN

Denis Benn, *The Growth and Development of Political Ideas in the Caribbean, 1774–1983*. Mona, Jamaica: Institute for Social and Economic Research, University of the West Indies, 1987. Benn's intellectual history emphasizes the role of nationalist and Marxist thinkers in the development of an indigenous political culture. Chapter 5, on "Marxism and Socio-political Change: C. L. R. James to Cheddi Jagan" provides a stolid overview of two contrasting figures.

Bridget Brereton, *A History of Modern Trinidad, 1783–1962*. Oxford: Heinemann, 1981. Brereton's concise and admirably lucid introduction to the subject draws on a full range of scholarly sources. The book provides a concise overview of Trinidad's uneven development as an isolated outpost of the Spanish, French, and British empires. Features 14 plates.

Selwyn Cudjoe. *Resistance and Caribbean Literature*. Columbus: Ohio University Press, 1980. A Marxist-Leninist study of the "artistic forms used to carry the ideological content of Caribbean literature forward" that contains a useful discussion of the circle around *Trinidad* and *The Beacon*. In a key concluding passage,

Cudjoe says that if "Caribbean ltierature is to play more than a decorative function in our society there is a need for its mass dissemination among the population, with a greater thrust of our writers towards 'socialist realism'—the position in which the masses take up the struggle. It is to this new consciousness from which, and to which, the writer must now speak."

Selwyn Cudjoe, ed. *Eric Williams Speaks: Essays on Colonialism and Independence*. Wellesley, MA: Calaloux, 1993. A major collection of addresses and documents drafted by Williams in the 1950s and early 1960s, i.e., the run-up to national independence. Also features several photographs, including one of C. L. R., Selma and C. L. R. James, Jr., playing cricket, as well as essays by George Lamming, C. L. R. James, Selwyn Cudjoe, and Erica Williams-Connell, Williams's daughter. In the introduction, Cudjoe claims that "Eric Williams's articulation of the colonial problematic and his understanding of the sociopolitical needs of the society during that period are yet to be surpassed by any contemporary politician or political organization."

Patrick Ignatius Gomes, "C. L. R. James's Marxian Paradigm on the Transformation of Caribbean Social Structure: A Comparative Critique." Unpublished Ph.D. dissertation, Fordham University, 1980. An ambitious, book-length manuscript that seeks to integrate James's "Marxian Paradigm" and sociological literatures on underdevelopment and neodependency. Features a discussion of postwar political developments in Trinidad and the Caribbean and probes their connection to broader processes of economic growth and deepening social inequality.

Alistair Hennessy, ed. *Intellectuals in the 20th Century Caribbean. Vol. I. Spectre of the New Class: the Commonwealth Caribbean*. London: Macmillan Caribbean, 1992. A valuable collection which addresses James's contribution to West Indian intellectual life. The opening chapter, by the book's editor, reviews the abundant scholarly literature on "intellectuals" and reflects upon the particular dilemmas experienced by Caribbean intellectuals. Subsequent essays explore the role of the University of the West Indies, the historiography of Eric Williams and Walter Rodney, the "aesthetics of Negritude" and other subjects. Alrick Cambridge's "C. L. R. James: Freedom through History" offers a sophisticated synopsis of James's *Notes on Dialectics*, while my "A Victorian with the Rebel Seed" outlines James's biographical trajectory. Other contributors include Rex Nettleford, Kenneth Surin (see below), and Paul Sutton. Issued concurrently with a companion volume on the Hispanic and Francophone Caribbeans.

Paget Henry and Paul Buhle, eds. *C. L. R. James's Caribbean*. Durham, NC: Duke University Press, 1992. This important collection seeks to affirm James's Caribbean roots. Essays by Selwyn Cudjoe, Sylvia Wynter, Neil Lazarus, Walton Look Lai, and others address various aspects of James's writings and political activities, including his background, economic theory, participation in Trinidadian and Antiguan nationalism, conception of *Modern Politics*, and relationship to theories of deconstruction. The book also features interviews with James and George Lamming as well as excerpts from letters to Constance Webb and from the 1932 manuscript *The Life of Captain Cipriani*.

John Gaffer La Guerre, *The Social and Political Thought of the Colonial Intelligentsia*. Mona, Jamaica: Institute of Social and Economic Research, University of the West Indies, 1982. A compact analysis of the development of an anticolonial intelligensia in the West Indies and the African diaspora. La Guerre traces positions articulated by three members of this strata—George Padmore, J. E. Casely-Hayford, and James—and situates them nicely in an evolving historical context. Sympathetic to Padmore's "pragmatic" approach to questions of politics and ideology. Critical of James's primary orientation around Marxist ideas and sects and his failure to identify with mass Pan-African organizations. The chapters on James concentrates on his transition from a "liberal" to a socialist, paying particular attention to his work in the Trotskyist movement. While praising *The Black Jacobins*, La Guerre argues that the book could have made a larger contribution had its author shed his Marxist ideological baggage.

Darrell E. Levi, "C. L. R. James: A Radical West Indian Vision of American Studies," *American Quarterly*, Vol. 43, no. 3 (September 1991). Draws on James's life and work to suggest some of the ways in which the field of American studies could and should refer to "the experience of all the hemispheric inhabitants." Discusses *The Black Jacobins*, *Mariners, Renegades and Castaways*, and *Beyond a Boundary* in light of contemporary scholarship.

Ivar Oxaal, *Black Intellectuals Come to Power: The Rise of Creole Nationalism in Trinidad and Tobago*. Cambridge, MA: Schenkman, 1968. An engagingly written account of the rise of Eric Williams's PNM and the politics of anticolonial movements in the West Indies. Oxaal, a Norwegian-American academic, lived in Trinidad between 1961 and 1962 and draws on a wealth of sociological and anthropological observation in order to provide a "thick description" of "The Rise of Creole Nationalism." The book refers in detail to James's activities in the 1958–1962 period and also offers information on the Correspondence group and on the development of James's independent Marxism. In the mid-1950s Oxaal was active in Oberlin College's Eugene V. Debs Club, which contained a number of Shachtmanites.

Selwyn Ryan, *Race and Nationalism in Trinidad and Tobago*. Toronto: University of Toronto Press, 1972. A superior study of the development of party politics in Trinidad and Tobago that pays special attention to the rise of the PNM and the impact of communal politics. Today, Ryan is Trinidad's leading pollster and political analyst.

Andrew Salkey, ed. *Caribbean Essays*. London: Evans Brothers, 1975. A star-studded collection featuring essays by Albert Gomes, George Lamming, Norman Manley, Orlando Patterson, Eric Williams, and several others. The well-chosen extract from James's *Beyond a Boundary* nicely underscores the volume's central concern with the antinomies and complexities of the West Indian character.

Andrew Salkey, *Havana Journal*. London: Penguin, 1971. Salkey spent several months in Cuba in the company of Robert Hill, John La Rose, and C. L. R. James in the winter and spring of 1967–1968. Along with several dozen others, they had been invited to attend a "Cultural Congress" and witness the revolution for themselves. *Havana Journal* engagingly describes their various adventures in postrevolutionary Cuba. Salkey's stance throughout is sympathetic but not uncritical. He is particularly excited by the notion of a West Indian encounter with a fraternal Cuba. Salkey's book also recounts several delightful anecdotes revolving around James and his attachment both to "a well-thumbed coffee-table *Michelangelo*" and to the tenets of "international Socialism and Revolution."

H. P. Singh, *The Indian Struggle for Justice and Equality Against Black Racism in Trinidad and Tobago*. Couva, Trinidad: Indian Review Press, 1993. A collection of pamphlets published between 1962 and 1965 that address the "destiny of the Indian presence in Trinidad" in the early period of independence. Singh, a longtime Trinidad Indian Hindu activist, was a major critic of the People's National Movement. Singh's writings have been resuscitated by a new generation of Indian activists working on behalf of justice for the Indian populations of Trinidad, Guyana, and Surinam. The book features a long introduction by Kamal Persad and Ashram Maharaj, in which they argue that "the dominant theme in the history from 1955–1956 is the establishment of black neocolonial domination of the state and society." The book reprints both Singh's 1965 polemic against C. L. R. James, *The Indian Enigma*, and James's essay on "West Indians of East Indian Descent," in their entirety.

LITERATURE AND CULTURE

F. M. Birbalsingh, "The Literary Achievement of C. L. R. James," *The Journal of Commonwealth Literature*, Vol. 19, no. 1 (1984). Reviews James's literary efforts and links them to his opposition to racial oppression and social injustice. Helpful source for secondary literature on early West Indian literary movements.

Hazel V. Carby, "Proletarian or Revolutionary Literature: C. L. R. James and the Politics of the Trinidadian Renaissance," *The South Atlantic Quarterly*, Vol. 87, no. 1 (1988). Literary and historical exploration of James's early fiction in the context of the emergence of a "Trinidadian Renaissance." Attempts to connect James's work to current debates over "world literature."

Anna Grimshaw, *Popular Democracy and the Creative Imagination: The Writings of C. L. R. James, 1950–1963*. New York: C. L. R. James Institute, 1991. Recasting James's legacy, Grimshaw foregrounds his midcentury writings in the areas of criticism, cultural studies, and American studies. Rigorous in her use of research materials, Grimshaw has added a new dimension to the field of James studies. This pamphlet recovers such neglected works as *American Civilization* (1950), "Popular Art and the Cultural Tradition" (1954), and *A Preface to Criticism* (1955), as well as the correspondence with Constance Webb.

Cynthia Hamilton, "A Way of Seeing: Culture as Political Expression in the Works of C. L. R. James," *Journal of Black Studies*, Vol. 22, no. 3 (March 1992). This article, by a former student and research assistant of C. L. R. James, examines James's literary works as the "first expression of the sensitive social observation that forms the basis for much of his political and historical analysis."

Scott McLemee, "James Studies, Cultural Studies and Missing Links," *The C. L. R. James Journal*, Vol. 2, no. 1 (1991). Reflections on James's relationship to the field of cultural studies and on the character of his literary output in the 1950s. Argues that the secondary literature is in a state of "primitive accumulation," and that James's work anticipates the emergence of the field of cultural studies.

Aldon Nielsen, "Reading James Reading," *Hambone*, no. 10 (Spring 1992). A short, elegant essay that dissects James's 1965 lecture on the novelist Wilson Harris from a literary and political point of view.

Kenneth Ramchard, *The West Indian Novel and its Background*. London: Faber and Faber, 1970. Knowledgeable discussion of development of the West Indian novel in the twentieth century. Attempts to demonstrate that "London is indisputably the West Indian literary capital," and offers a sympathetic account of James's early fiction.

Edward W. Said, *Culture and Imperialism*. New York: Knopf, 1993. A searching exploration of "the historical experience of empire" as it was justified and challenged by great works of fiction and interpretation in the nineteenth and twentieth centuries. The section on "The Voyage In and the Emergence of Opposition" contains several long passages on James and *The Black Jacobins*, and originally appeared in "Third World Intellectuals and Metropolitan Culture," *Raritan*, Vol. IX, no. 3 (1990). Said argues that the apparent peculiarities of James's perspective are grounded in a specific historical and geographical context and are unlikely to be reprised by contemporary Third World intellectuals.

Reinhard W. Sander, "The Thirties and Forties," in Bruce King, ed. *West Indian Literature*. London: Macmillan, 1979. An erudite survey of West Indian literature in a period of dramatic innovation. Reviews James's *Minty Alley*.

Alan Wald, *The New York Intellectuals: The Rise and Decline of the Anti-Stalinist Left from the 1930s to the 1980s*. Chapel Hill: University of North Carolina, 1987. A major work of intellectual history and historical recovery that offers a sweeping yet sharply focused survey of the New York Intellectuals and their relationship to left-wing and anti-Stalinist movements. Although the New York Intellectuals have attracted considerable scholarly attention over the past decade, Wald is the only writer to have seriously considered James's relationship to the world of *Partisan Review*, *Dissent*, and *The New International*.

MARXISM

Tony Bogues, *Marxism and Black Liberation*. Cleveland: Hera Press, 1981. Shrewd essays advancing a broadly Jamesian conception of the relationship of Marxism to black nationalism and Pan-Africanism. The pamphlet also reprints "The Revolutionary Answer to the Negro Problem in the USA."

Paul Buhle, *Marxism in the USA: From 1870 to the Present Day*. London: Verso, 1987. Traces the development of an indigenous Marxist current in the United States. Highlights the role of different European ethnic groups in the making of a Marxist tradition in the nineteenth and early twentieth centuries. Draws an interesting comparison between the work of James and W. E. B. DuBois.

Alex Callinicos, *Trotskyism*. Minneapolis: University of Minnesota Press, 1990. Callinicos's history of the intellectual and institutional development of Trotskyism prior to and especially after its founder's murder in 1940 is particularly attuned to events in Britain, France, and the United States. Callinicos provides a short but astute critique of James's main contributions to Marxism, specifically in the areas of state capitalism and black nationalism. Quietly dismissive of what I have termed James's post-Leninism.

Harry Cleaver, *Reading Capital Politically*. Austin: University of Texas Press, 1979. In offering a "political" reading of Marx's *Das Kapital*, Cleaver's book provides a synoptic history of the concept of state capitalism, referring explicitly to the work of James, Dunayevskaya, and Castoriadis.

Charles Denby, *Indignant Heart: A Black Worker's Journal*. Boston: South End Press, 1978. A two-part memoir which takes the reader from the segregated Deep South to the auto plants of Detroit, and from the civil rights movement to the Communist Party and the American Trotskyists. The author became editor of the newspaper *News and Letters*. The first part of the book, written in the early 1950s, is particularly moving and insightful.

Raya Dunayevskaya, *The Marxist-Humanist Theory of State-Capitalism*. Chicago: News and Letters, 1992. This volume makes available a number of important essays written by Dunayevskaya in the early 1940s that advanced the state-capitalist critique of the Soviet Union and that played a major role in the creation and consolidation of the Johnson-Forest tendency. The informative introduction, by *News and Letters* writer Peter Hudis, sets forth the chief tenets of the Marxist-Humanist program developed by Dunayevskaya and her cothinkers once they broke with Johnsonism in 1955. Hudis briefly sketches the group's differences with James and his followers.

Scott McLemee and Paul Le Blanc, eds. *C. L. R. James and Revolutionary Marxism: Selected Writings, 1939–1949*. Atlantic Highlands, NJ: Humanities Press, 1993. A valuable and timely collection of ten Marxist polemics that James published during his American sojourn that also features short essays by Charles

Van Gelderen, Martin Glaberman, John Bracey, and Paul Buhle. Le Blanc's introduction contains a useful overview of James's American years. The book also features an afterword by Scott McLemee that reaffirms the importance of the American years for James's development as a revolutionary theorist.

Tim Wolforth, *The Struggle for Marxism in the United States*. New York: Labor Publishers, 1971. Written while the author was a leading member of the Workers League, a Trotskyist sect, the book provides a surprisingly coherent account of the emergence of U.S. Trotskyism and the 1940 split inside the Socialist Workers Party which produced the Shachtmanite Workers Party. The references to James are sympathetic but the main focus is on the circle around James Cannon. The book's final chapter, on the 1960s, is marred by a sectarian and dogmatic tone.

PAN-AFRICANISM

Tony Martin, "C. L. R. James and the Race/Class Question," *Race*, Vol. XIV, no. 2 (1972). Martin evaluates James's work in terms of its valorization of "class" above "race," arguing that James "has always been a much more thorough-going Marxist than many, black or white."

Cedric J. Robinson, *Black Marxism: The Making of the Black Radical Tradition*. London: Zed Press, 1983. A panoramic study that explores the interpenetration of European working-class radicalism and Pan-African mobilization across the African diaspora. Introduces the notion of "racial capitalism" and resists class-centered analyses of capitalism. Substantial sections explore the "Black Marxism" of James, Richard Wright, and W. E. B. DuBois. Suggests that James's energies were misdirected or squandered as a result of his belief in the centrality of the working class and the transcendental quality of many aspects of European high culture. Critiques James's "Victorian residues" and suggests that James unconsciously absorbed elements of imperial ideology even as he encouraged others to break with colonialism.

Peter Fryer, *Staying Power: The History of Black People in Britain*. London: Pluto, 1984. Fryer's massive study makes several references to James's activities in Britain. Excellent on 1930s and more generally on lesser-known political and social movements of blacks resident in Britain prior to and during World War II.

Vincent Harding, *There is a River: The Black Struggle for Freedom in America*. New York: Harcourt Brace Jovanovich, 1981. A synoptic overview of African-American struggles influenced by the Jamesian fusion of culture and politics.

SPORT

Jervis Anderson, "Cricket and Beyond: The Career of C. L. R. James," *The American Scholar*, Summer 1985. Anderson, a Jamaican author, provides an engaging, anecdotal account of James's contribution to the game of cricket.

Sheila Patterson, "Cricket and Other Codes: or a Tribute to C. L. R. James," *New Community*, Vol. 11, no. 4 (Autumn 1973). Patterson revisits the territory of *Beyond a Boundary* and finds that the "cricket ethic" shaped not only James and his milieu but several generations of colonial subjects.

Kenneth Surin, "C. L. R. James's Materialist Aesthetic of Cricket," in Alistair Hennessy, ed. *Intellectuals in the 20th Century Caribbean*. London: Macmillan Caribbean, 1992. Surin is one of a handful of scholars to have taken a serious look at James's writings on sport. He highlights the "dialectical" aspects of James's appreciation of cricket, which brings into focus not only the social and historical context of sport but also the evolution of technique. Surin provocatively claims that James's integration of cricket and social history has a pronounced (if unacknowledged) Weberian aspect in that it situates the development of cricket in terms of "Max Weber's threefold schema of charismatic inauguration, traditionalization, and routinization." He goes on to argue that this schema is unable to comprehend the *capitalist* dynamic of contemporary cricket practice. Surin also touches on James's affinities with the British literary theorist Raymond Williams.

Helen Tiffin, "Cricket, Literature and the Politics of De-colonisation: the Case of C. L. R. James," in Richard Cashman and Michael McKernan, eds. *Sport: Money, Morality and the Media*. Kens-

ington: New South Wales University Press, 1981. Tiffin argues
that James's attachment to a British identity is sharpest in the
context of his writings on cricket, and that this attachment
harbored a defense of the British Empire. Considers *Beyond a
Boundary* in relation to the novel *Minty Alley*.

NOTES

INTRODUCTION

1. George Lamming, *The Pleasures of Exile*. London: Allison and Busby, 1984 [1960], p. 47.

2. Edward Said, *Culture and Imperialism*. New York: Knopf, 1993, p. 248.

CHAPTER 1. BEYOND A BOUNDARY

1. C. L. R. James, *Beyond a Boundary*. London: Stanley Paul, 1963, p. 17.

2. Letter from C. L. R. James to Constance Webb, July 1944. Titled "Autobiography of a Man by Him," this letter contains a wealth of information about James's earliest years. Along with two other letters it is reprinted in Paget Henry and Paul Buhle, eds. *C. L. R. James's Caribbean*. Durham, NC: Duke University Press, 1992, pp. 17–27. This passage appears on page 20.

3. Selwyn D. Ryan, *Race and Nationalism in Trinidad and Tobago*. Toronto: University of Toronto Press, 1972, p. 3.

4. Heather Cateau, interview with Cyril Austin, May 1993 (Port of Spain). Austin reports that James's father prided himself on the use of his middle name.

5. Letter from C. L. R. James to Constance Webb, September 13, 1944. Reprinted in Henry and Buhle, eds. *C. L. R. James' Caribbean*, p. 25.

6. Buhle, "The Making of a Literary Life: C. L. R. James Interviewed," in Henry and Buhle, eds. *C. L. R. James's Caribbean*, pp. 56–57.

7. Quoted in Guy Debord, *Comments on the Society of the Spectacle*. London: Verso, 1990, p. 92.

8. Letter from C. L. R. James to Constance Webb, July 1944. Reprinted in Henry and Buhle, eds. *C. L. R. James's Caribbean*, p. 19.

9. The influence of *Culture and Anarchy* may be registered at many different sites within the Jamesian corpus. Arnold's High Victorian polemic certainly affirmed James's broad conception of culture and his belief in the importance of education and knowledge as well as personal qualities such as rectitude and perserverance. For this reason, it is surely not an accident that *Culture and Anarchy* is loaded with formulations that can easily be transposed into Jamesian rhetoric. For example: "Culture says: 'Consider these people, then, their way of life, their habits, their manners, the very tones of their voice; look at them attentively; observe the literature they read, the things which give them pleasure, the words which come forth out of their mouths, the thoughts which make the furniture of their minds . . .'" Another example: "In all directions our habitual courses of action seem to be losing efficaciousness, credit, and control, both with others and even with ourselves; everywhere we see the beginnings of confusion, and we want a clue to some sound order and authority. This we can only get by going back upon the actual instincts and forces which rule our life, seeing them as they really are, connecting them with other instincts and forces, and enlarging our whole view and rule of life." Matthew Arnold, *Culture and Anarchy*. New Haven: Yale University Press, 1994 [1869], pp. 35–36 and p. 96.

10. Letter from C. L. R. James to Constance Webb, July 1944. Reprinted in Henry and Buhle, eds. *C. L. R. James's Caribbean*, p. 19.

11. "The report would come. It would say that I was not trying. My father would be very angry and I would be upset for days. I got that dream steadily after I had left school . . . But the moment I had written a book [*World Revolution*], a piece of work which was recognized everywhere as worthwhile, that dream disappeared and I have never had it since." The essay is entitled "My Experience with Women." A copy is in the author's private collection.

12. Letter from C. L. R. James to Constance Webb, July 1944. Reprinted in Henry and Buhle, eds. *C. L. R. James's Caribbean*, p. 21.

13. James, *Beyond a Boundary*, p. 14.

14. Jervis Anderson, "Cricket and Beyond: The Career of C. L. R. James," *American Scholar* (Summer 1985), p. 356.

15. James, *Beyond a Boundary*, p. 35.

16. As I learned during my visit to QRC in 1992, he was enrolled by his father under the name Lionel James, as an Anglican.

17. In his first year his scores were the following: English, 91; Geography, 83; English History, 83; Diction, 49 (out of 50); Arithmetic, 91; French, 75; Latin, 85. His grades in 1917 were lower: Essay, 35 (out of 50); Story, 36 (40); Precis Writing, 31 (50); Books, 44 (60); History, 74 (100); Latin—Unprepared, 53 (100); Latin—Sentences and Prose, 56 (100); French—Unprepared, 69 (80); French—Diction, 14 (20); French—Composition and Story, 62 (100); French—Oral, 21 (30); Arithmetic, 100 (100); Algebra, 97 (150); Geometry, 143 (150).

18. His marks in 1917 were still high enough to place him in the top one-third of his class, and despite his status as a dedicated underachiever, he was the "Proximate Accessit" for the school's General Knowledge Prize in 1918. See *Q.R.C. 100: Being a Record of Queen's Royal College, 1870–1970.* Port of Spain: Queen's Royal College, 1970, p. 285.

19. James, *Beyond a Boundary*, p. 32.

20. Prior to working at Queen's Royal College, he taught at Pamphylia High School, the Government Training College for Teachers (where his father had received his teaching certificate) and at the Trinidad New College. See Carlton Comma, ed. *Who's Who in Trinidad and Tobago 1972–1973.* Port of Spain, 1973.

21. See Buhle, "The Making of a Literary Life," in Henry and Buhle, eds. *C. L. R. James's Caribbean*, p. 58.

22. Whether James himself ever considered applying to Oxford or Cambridge remains unclear; he certainly never expressed any regret about not having attended university. In the end, he only left Port of Spain after two important preconditions were fulfilled: (a) he had an invitation and a place to stay (with the cricketer Learie Constantine) and (b) he had a proven track record as a writer and essayist. In one interview, he stated that "[e]verybody knew that if I had worked at it I would have won a scholarship and gone away to England." See Buhle, "The Making of a Literary Life," in Henry and Buhle, eds. *C. L. R. James's Caribbean*, p. 58.

23. James, *Beyond a Boundary*, p. 13.

24. Helen Tiffin, "Cricket, Literature and the Politics of De-Colonisation: The Case of C. L. R. James," in Richard Cashman and Michael McKernan, eds. *Sport: Money, Morality and the Media.* Kensington, Australia: New South Wales University Press, 1981, p. 189.

25. William Carr, "West Indian Writing," University Radio Service mimeo, Kingston, Jamaica, n.d.

26. V. S. Naipaul, "Sporting Life," *Encounter*, vol. XXI, no. 3 (September 1963), p. 74.

27. C. L. R. James, "Return of a Wanderer: Comparisons between 1938 and 1953" [1953], reprinted in James, *Cricket*, p. 71.

28. James, "On the Origins," p. 24.

29. James, *Beyond a Boundary*, p. 25.

30. James, *Beyond a Boundary*, p. 39.

31. Untitled (and undated) autobiographical notes, housed at the archives of the Oil Workers Trade Union (San Fernando).

32. John Gaffer La Guerre, *The Social and Political Thought of the Colonial Intelligentsia*. Kingston, Jamaica: Institute of Social and Economic Research, 1982, p. 84.

33. Tony Martin, "Revolutionary Upheaval in Trinidad, 1919," *Journal of Negro History*, vol. LXIII, no. 3 (July 1973), p. 313.

34. Brereton, *A History of Modern Trinidad*, p. 161.

35. Alan MacKenzie, interview with C. L. R. James, October 1975.

36. He was similarly less than preoccupied with the opposite sex. In "My Experience With Women," he remembered being "more concerned with reading, with cricket and other activities of the kind and I don't know that sex occupied a very important part of my life."

37. Margaret Busby, "C. L. R. James: A Biographical Introduction," in C. L. R. James, *At the Rendezvous of Victory: Selected Writings*. London: Allison and Busby, 1984, p. vii.

38. See *Q.R.C. 100*, pp. 288, 295, and 299.

39. James, *Beyond a Boundary*, p. 59.

40. At the age of 21, he directed an operetta, *Gypsy Rover* (and played a jester); at the age of 28, he directed Moliere's *Le Bourgeois Gentilhomme* for the Maverick Club.

41. James's local reputation was enhanced when "La Divina Pastora" was selected for *The Best British Short Stories of 1928 (with an Irish and Colonial Supplement)*, edited by Edward J. O'Brien. New York: Dodd, Mead & Co., 1928.

42. C. L. R. James, "Triumph" [1929], reprinted in C. L. R. James, *The Future in the Present: Selected Writings*. Westport, CT: Lawrence Hill and Company, 1977, pp. 12–13.

43. James, "Triumph," p. 20.

44. Albert Gomes, *The Beacon*, July 1931. Cited in La Guerre, *The Social and Political Thought of the Colonial Intelligentsia*, p. 84.

45. C. L. R. James, *The Beacon*, August 1931. Cited in La Guerre, *The Social and Political Thought of the Colonial Intelligentsia*, p. 84.

46. C. L. R. James, "The Problem of Knowledge," *The Beacon*, March 1931, p. 23.

47. C. L. R. James, "Michel Maxwell Philip: 1829–1886: Sometime Solicitor-General of Trinidad: An Impression," *The Beacon*, September 1931. See Selwyn Cudjoe, "The Audacity of It All: C. L. R. James's Trinidadian Background," in Henry and Buhle, eds. *C. L. R. James's Caribbean*, pp. 39–55.

48. Albert Gomes, *Through a Maze of Colour*. Port of Spain: Key Caribbean Publications, 1974, p. 23.

49. This phrase is taken from John Gaffar La Guerre, *The Politics of Communalism: The Agony of the Left in Trinidad and Tobago, 1930–1955*. St. Augustine, Trinidad: Pan-Caribbean Publications, 1982, p. 17.

50. Cited in Kenneth Ramchand, "Introduction," *Minty Alley* [1936]. London: New Beacon Books, 1971, p. 9.

51. Gomes, *Through a Maze of Colour*, p. 23.

52. *The Beacon*, vol. 1, no. 1, March 1931. He goes on to say: "So will not mention them. Married—nothing else of importance."

53. Macdonald Celestin Taylor, "C. L. R. James—A Most Talented and Remarkable Man," *Sunday Express*, April 25, 1982, p. 13. Taylor reports that a local businessman, J. T. Johnson, offered to make James "manager of the new musical department of the departmental store on Frederick Street" as a result of his expertise in the area of jazz and classical music.

54. In the autobiographical essay "My Experience with Women," James explained that "[t]here were not too many books in my life that meant too much to me at that time. That one did. And I felt at the time that I knew all there was to be known about sex. What I know was that it gave me an attitude to sex which was, the best word that I can use, is scientific. It was something that took place and people reacted to it in various ways and some were normal and some were, what you might call, abnormal."

55. James, *Beyond a Boundary*, p. 119. He told Paul Buhle that the novel would have been about "my school days, my father teaching me in the elementary school, then I go to QRC, then I became a teacher in secondary schools . . . So it might seem to be my personal life, but in reality it would have been different stages of the form of existence of black people in the Caribbean." See Buhle, "The Making of a Literary Life," in Henry and Buhle, eds. *C. L. R. James's Caribbean*, p. 60.

56. Came Chabrol, Nurse and C. R. Browne,
Men of great fame and tried renown,
Each to add lustre to his name
And win his country lasting fame,
          But—Pascall bowled.
Barbados brought a great array
Of Batsmen who could stay all day,
They had defence, could force the game,
Bowl fast or slow, 'twas all the same,
          But—Pascall bowled.
Bring Hendren, Hobbs and D. J. Knight,
Jackie Herne to bowl and J. C. White
And Brown of Harts to keep the wicket,
Let them all come, those kings of cricket.
And bring Australians if you care
Whate'er the team we have no fear.
Put Bardsley down in your selection,
To Armstrong we have no objection,
          Just let Pascall bowl.
And when to England back they reach
And tread the sands of Dover's beach,
And people crowd around to know
The reason for their wretched show,
A tear will shine in Hendren's eye,
Jack Hearne will heave a bitter sigh,
And Hobbs will shake his head and cry,
"Well, friends, we made a decent try,
Armstrong and Bardsley, Hearne and I,"
          But—Pascall bowled.

C. L. R. James, "Pascall Bowled," reprinted in Learie Constantine, *Cricket and I*. London: Philip Allen, 1933, p. 40.

57. Ian Munro and Richard Sander, *Kas-Kas: Interviews with Three Caribbean Writers*. Austin, TX: African and Afro-American Research Institute, University of Texas, 1972, p. 37.

58. James, *Minty Alley*, p. 38.

59. James, *Minty Alley*, p. 244.

60. James, *Minty Alley*, p. 139.

61. James, *Minty Alley*, p. 107.

62. Michael Gilkes, *The West Indian Novel*. Boston: Twayne Publishing Company, 1981, p. 35.

63. He subsidized his political activities by working as a broker, auctioneer, and general commission agent.

64. The Trinidadian Workingmen's Association was renamed the Trinidadian Labour Party in 1934. Under Cipriani's leadership, the Party recruited thousands of members in the early 1930s. Cipriani was to remain a member of the Legislative Council from 1925, the first year in which a percentage of seats on the Council were open to elected members, until his death in 1945, and he was elected mayor of Port of Spain on eight separate occasions.

65. Ryan, *Race and Nationalism in Trinidad and Tobago*, p. 35.

66. Ryan, *Race and Nationalism in Trinidad and Tobago*, p. 43.

67. See Franklin W. Knight, *The Caribbean: The Genesis of a Fragmented Nationalism*. New York: Oxford University Press, 1978, p. 179.

68. The historian F. A. Hoyos notes that the strikes in Trinidad were followed by "disturbances in Barbados and strikes in British Guiana, St. Lucia and Jamaica . . ." Hoyos goes on to report that during this period of social upheaval, "some 46 persons were killed, 429 injured and thousands imprisoned in the course of restoring order in the disturbed lands of the Caribbean." F. A. Hoyos, *Grantley Adams and the Social Revolution: The Story of the Movement that Changed the Pattern of West Indian Society*. London: Macmillan Caribbean, 1988.

69. As many of the paper's sports pieces either went unsigned or were signed "Our Special Correspondent," the textual evidence is suggestive but not definitive. One article, for example, compares cricket players of the nineteenth century to contemporary players in a way that is reminiscent of pieces published elsewhere under James's name. In 1987, James told Paul Buhle that he wrote "one or two things" for *The Labour Leader*. "I was regarded as a literature person . . . When they wanted a piece of writing they came to me and that was an understanding." See Buhle, "The Making of a Literary Life," in Henry and Buhle, eds. *C. L. R. James's Caribbean*, p. 60.

70. C. L. R. James, *The Life of Captain Cipriani* [1932], excerpted in Henry and Buhle, eds. *C. L. R. James's Caribbean*, pp. 269–270.

71. La Guerre, *The Social and Political Thought of the Colonial Intelligentsia*, p. 87. In terms of James's own development, however, P. I. Gomes rightly notes that "James had come by now to a recognition of the structural factors inherent to colonialism . . ." Patrick Gomes, "C. L. R. James' Marxist Paradigm on the Transformation of Caribbean Social Structure," unpublished dissertation, Fordham University, 1980, p. 212.

72. Robert Hill, "In England, 1932–1938," in Buhle, ed. *C. L. R. James: His Life and Work*, p. 64.

73. Albert Gomes, "Editorial Commentaries," *The Beacon*, September 1932.

74. Cited in La Guerre, *The Social and Political Thought of the Colonial Intelligentsia*, p. 87.

75. C. L. R. James, *The Case for West-Indian Self-Government* [1933]. New York: University Place Book Shop, 1967, p. 31.

76. James, *The Case for West-Indian Self-Government*, p. 7.

77. C. H. Archibald, "C. L. R. James—A Critical Study," *The Royalian*, vol. 1, no. 2, December 1932, p. 16.

78. Archibald, "C. L. R. James," p. 17.

79. Archibald, "C. L. R. James," p. 17.

80. Archibald, "C. L. R. James," p. 19.

81. Letter from C. L. R. James to Constance Webb, July 4, 1944.

82. James, *Beyond a Boundary*, p. 114.

83. Letter from C. L. R. James to Constance Webb, April 24, 1939, quoted in Selwyn Cudjoe, "A Comrade and a Lover," *Trinidad and Tobago Review*, November 1992, p. 23.

84. Quoted in Anna Grimshaw, *The C. L. R. James Archive: A Reader's Guide*. New York: C. L. R. James Institute, 1991, p. 53.

85. C. L. R. James, "Discovering Literature in the 1930s" [1969], reprinted in C. L. R. James, *Spheres of Existence: Selected Writings*. London: Allison and Busby, 1980, p. 239.

CHAPTER 2. MODERN POLITICS

1. In a series published in the *Port of Spain Gazette*, James offered his "First Impressions" of life in London. In one of these he set out to capture "the atmosphere of Bloomsbury," concluding that "[a]nyone who lives in this place for any length of time and remains dull need not worry himself. Nothing he will ever do will help him. He was born that way." C. L. R. James, "Bloomsbury: An Encounter with Edith Sitwell" [1932], Anna Grimshaw, ed. *The C. L. R. James Reader*. Oxford: Blackwell, 1992, p. 48.

2. Gerald Howat, *Learie Constantine*. London: George Allen and Unwin, 1975, p. 76.

3. Part of the forward reads: "I would like here to give my best thanks to my West Indian friend Mr. C. L. R. James, who has given me valuable assistance in the writing of this book." Learie Constantine, *Cricket and I.* London: Philip Allan, 1933, p. ix.

4. Constantine, *Cricket and I*, p. 27–28.

5. C. L. R. James, *Beyond a Boundary*. London: Stanley Paul, 1963, p. 124.

6. James, *Beyond a Boundary*, p. 124.

7. James, *Beyond a Boundary*, p. 120.

8. James, *Beyond a Boundary*, p. 121.

9. On Nelson, see Anna Grimshaw, "Notes on the Life and Work of C. L. R. James," in Paul Buhle, ed. *C. L. R. James: His Life and Work*. London: Allison and Busby, 1986, p. 11. Grimshaw reports that the town's weavers were on strike during the summer and early fall of 1932.

10. Nelson was one of the ILP's strongholds; in 1912 the party had over 800 members in Nelson, making it the second largest branch in the country. See Joseph White, *Tom Mann*. Manchester: Manchester University Press, 1991.

11. James, *Beyond a Boundary*, p. 127.

12. The dedication page of *The Black Jacobins* reads: "To My Good Friends Harry and Elizabeth Spencer of Nelson, Lancashire, England."

13. David Widgery, "A Meeting with Comrade James," in Paul Buhle, ed. *C. L. R. James: His Life and Work*. Chicago: Urgent Tasks, 1981, p. 116.

14. Author's interview with George Rawick, December 28, 1981 (St. Louis).

15. Ras Makonnen, *Pan-Africanism From Within* (as recorded and edited by Kenneth King). London: Oxford University Press, 1973, p. 117.

16. For example, a Friends of Ethiopia Committee was formed in 1935 in Port of Spain, "with links to similar organizations elsewhere in the Caribbean." Two years later, a Club L'Ouverture was set up to "promote the interests of blacks in Trinidad and to disseminate knowledge about, and pride in, Africa." See Bridget Brereton, *A History of Modern Trinidad, 1783–1962.* Oxford: Heinemann, 1981, p. 174.

17. C. L. R. James, "The *Black Scholar* Interview," *Black Scholar*, May 1970.

18. C. L. R. James, "Fighting for the Abyssinian Empire," *New Leader*, June 5, 1936.

19. "What is the International African Service Bureau?" advertisement appearing on inside back page, Eric Williams, *The Negro in the Caribbean*. Manchester: IASB, 1942.

20. *Fact* (London), no. 18 (1938), p. 95. In a later advertisement, the Bureau announced that it sought "to help enlighten British public opinion about conditions in the Colonies, Protectorates and Mandated territories in Africa, the West Indies and other parts of the Empire. In this way the Bureau hopes that the people of the United Kingdom, who are supposed to be the 'trustees' of the Colonial peoples, will be in a better position to administer their trust." Inside backpage advert, Williams, *The Negro in the Caribbean*.

21. See Consuelo Lopez, "C. L. R. James: The Rhetoric of a Defiant Warrior," unpublished dissertation, Indiana University, 1983, p. 14.

22. Padmore's biographer describes it as "a well-produced three penny magazine, nearly impossible to come by today." James Hooker, *Black Revolutionary: George Padmore's Path From Communism to Pan-Africanism*. New York: Praeger, 1970, p. 49.

23. Makonnen, p. 119. He continues: "Then, after stirring them up for an hour, one would end with, 'Now you know it is against the law to sell papers or to ask for aid, but all the things we have just been talking about, and much more, are right here in our paper *International African Opinion*.' So sometimes I would clear more than twenty pounds worth in a single meeting."

24. Quoted in Howat, *Learie Constantine*, p. 78. A useful source on Padmore, James the IASB, and the League of Coloured Peoples is Imanuel Geiss, *The Pan-African Movement: A History of Pan-Africanism in America, Europe and Africa*. New York: Africana Publishing, 1974, chapter seventeen.

25. Despite their political differences (Robeson was close to the Communist Party), Robeson made a lasting impression on James. He was a kind of living combination of Bondman and Haynes—popular but never vulgar. Robeson was a well-spoken individual, but he carried himself like a star, not like an aesthete or an intellectual. See C. L. R. James, "Paul Robeson: Black Star" [1970], reprinted in *Spheres of Existence*.

26. C. L. R. James, "Toussaint L'Ouverture," *Life and Letters Today*, vol. XIV, no. 1 (Spring 1936), p. 17.

27. Although the play received decent notices, the theater critic for the London *Sunday Times* found that "Mr. James' dialogue is informative rather than suggestive: it lacks suppleness," but also admitted that "having an interesting subject . . . [it] holds the stage at the Westminster Theater." Quoted in James, "Paul Robeson," p. 258. A revised version of the play,

adapted by Dexter Lyndersay and C. L. R. James, is reprinted under the title *The Black Jacobins* in Grimshaw, ed. *The C. L. R. James Reader*, pp. 67–111.

28. Although *The Black Jacobins* generally received strong notices, the *New Statesman*'s critic complained that "Because he is a Communist, he wants to show us the worst . . . The intelligent historian should at least aim at impartiality. The fanatic cannot." See Flora Grierson, "Man's Inhumanity to Man," *New Statesman*, October 8, 1938. The book was published in France after the war: see C. L. R. James, *Les Jacobins Noirs, Toussaint L'Ouverture et la Revolution de Saint-Domingue*. Paris: Librairie Gallimard, 1949 (translated by Pierre Naville).

29. James, *The Black Jacobins*, p. 70.

30. Interview by Alan MacKenzie with C. L. R. James, October 1975 (London).

31. James, *The Black Jacobins*, pp. 375–377.

32. James, *The Black Jacobins*, p. 402. Unless otherwise noted, all emphases are in the original, as they are here. The appendix, entitled "From Toussaint L'Ouverture to Fidel Castro," is reprinted in Grimshaw, ed. *The C. L. R. James Reader*, pp. 296–314.

33. Note that James writes "West Indian" rather than "Caribbean." This may have reflected his own sense of identity, which was decisively shaped by British colonialism, Trinidadian mores and practices, and English and French high culture. In this context, it is perhaps significant that he spoke English and French, but never learned Spanish or Haitian Creole.

34. Cedric J. Robinson, *Black Marxism: The Making of the Black Radical Tradition*. London: Zed Press, 1983, p. 384. Kenyatta's *Kenya: Land of Conflict* was published by the IASB.

35. James, *The Black Jacobins*, p. 131.

36. James, *The Black Jacobins*, p. 287.

37. See Edward W. Said, "Third World Intellectuals and Metropolitan Culture," *Raritan*, vol. IX, no. 3 (Winter 1990), p. 44.

38. James, *The Black Jacobins*, p. 120.

39. See Leon Trotsky, *The Permanent Revolution* [1928], reprinted in *The Permanent Revolution and Results and Prospects*. New York: Pathfinder, 1969. See also Alex Callinicos, "Trotsky's Theory of Permanent Revolution and its Relevance to the Third World Today," *International Socialism*, no. 16 (Spring 1982); and Robin Blackburn, *The Overthrow of Colonial Slavery*. London: Verso, 1988.

40. On this point see Robert Hill, "In England, 1932–1938," in Buhle, ed. *C. L. R. James: His Life and Work*, p. 79.

41. On Williams's career as a historian, see Paul Sutton, "The Historian as Politician: Eric Williams and Walter Rodney," in Alistair Hennessy, ed. *Intellectuals in the Twentieth-Century Caribbean,* vol. 1: *Spectre of the New Class: the Commonwealth Caribbean.* London: Macmillan Caribbean, 1992; and Selwyn Cudjoe, "Eric E. Williams and the Politics of Language," in *Eric E. Williams Speaks: Essays on Colonialism and Independence* (Selwyn Cudjoe, ed.). Wellesley, MA: Calaloux, 1993.

42. C. L. R. James, *A History of Pan-African Revolt.* Chicago: Charles H. Kerr, 1995 [1939], pp. 99, 105, and 115. This edition features an informative introduction by the historian Robin D. G. Kelley.

43. Harry Wicks, who was active in Trotskyist politics, later testified that the Marxist Group "won over people of a very impressive calibre," including "C. L. R. James, a West Indian, brilliant speaker . . . [with] tremendous energy . . ." Cited in Duncan Hallas, "Revolutionaries and the Labour Party," *International Socialism*, no. 16 (Spring 1982), p. 17. See also *C. L. R. James and British Trotskyism: An Interview.* London: Socialist Platform, 1987. James and Wicks became friends in the 1930s, and Wicks's assistance is acknowledged in the introduction to James's 1937 book *World Revolution.*

44. "By the spring of 1935, at the latest, Trotsky had become convinced that the ILP leadership and its international allies were hopeless as a revolutionary prospect. In truth, the ILP leaders, who had managed to avoid joining the CP even in 1920, were never such. The fact was now obvious and Trotsky recognized it. A good many of his followers who were inside the ILP were unwilling to accept this obvious conclusion and to split, with their gains, from that party." Duncan Hallas, "Revolutionaries and the Labour Party," p. 17.

45. C. L. R. James, "Is This Worth a War? The League's Scheme to Rob Abyssinia of its Independence" [October 4, 1935], reprinted in C. L. R. James, *At the Rendezvous of Victory: Selected Writings.* London: Allison and Busby, 1984, p. 16.

46. C. L. R. James, *New Leader*, April 17, 1936.

47. At Neath Town Hall, James addressed over 150 Welsh rank-and-file trade unionists on "The War Danger." An ILP member reported that "Despite the cold, the audience were absorbed in C. L. R.'s address and everyone stayed right through to the end. There were only a couple of CPers present and whatever remaining shreds of influence they may have had in

Neath melted under C. L. R.'s withering fire." Document on file at Houghton Library, Harvard University, bMS Russ. 13.1 14819.

48. Duncan Hallas, "Revolutionaries and the Labour Party," p. 18.

49. Letter from C. L. R. James to Leon Trotsky, dated June 24, 1936, Houghton Library, bMS Russ 13.1 2068. In a 1938 conversation with the writer James T. Farrell, however, James acknowledged that the Trotskyists were sometimes overly preoccupied with "bookkeeping the theoretical errors of the Stalinists, showing that Stalin does not understand Spain and on and on ad infinitum." Letter from James T. Farrell to Meyer Schapiro, May 28, 1938, contained in the Schapiro archives at the Rare Book Collection at Columbia University's Butler Library.

50. "Lunacy or Logic? Two Views of One Book," *Controversy*, vol. 1, no. 6 (May 1937), p. 36.

51. Sam Bornstein and Al Richardson, *Against the Stream: A History of the Trotskyist Movement in Britain, 1924–1938*. London: Socialist Platform, 1986, p. 264.

52. C. L. R. James, *World Revolution: The Rise and Fall of the Communist International*. Atlantic Highlands, NJ: Humanities Press, 1993[1937], p. xxvi.

53. James, *World Revolution*, p. 16.

54. James, *World Revolution*, p. 19.

55. James, *World Revolution*, p. 37.

56. Warburg, *An Occupation for Gentlemen*, p. 211.

57. Fredric Warburg, *An Occupation for Gentlemen*. London: Hutchinson, 1959, p. 214. The title comes from an exchange Warburg had at a cocktail party in London, where a rather patrician fellow told him that publishing sounded very enjoyable, but was it an occupation for gentlemen?

58. Leon Trotsky, "On the History of the Left Opposition," Houghton Library, bMS Russ 13 T4559.

59. Boris Souvarine, *Stalin: A Critical Survey of Bolshevism*. New York: Longmans, Green & Co., 1939.

60. Souvarine, *Stalin*, p. 65.

61. Souvarine, *Stalin*, p. 676.

62. Will Reisner, ed. *Documents of the Fourth International*. New York: Pathfinder Press, 1973, p. 302.

63. Cited in Bornstein and Richardson, *Against the Stream*, p. 263. The Marxist Group eventually disintegrated after the expulsion, with its members finding their way into the Labour Party or other Trotskyist groupings.

64. Warburg, *An Occupation for Gentlemen*, p. 214.

65. Ethel Mannin, *Comrade O Comrade, Or Low-Down on the Left.* London: Jarrolds, 1949, pp. 134–135.

66. Reynolds says that one of James's two companions was Learie Constantine, "who was not very interested in politics at that time . . . it would, I suspect, have been more interesting to have detached Leary [sic] Constantine and talked to him; but whereas I could at least understand Trotskyist dialectics I could imagine no suitable opening move for a man known only as a cricketer." Reginald Reynolds, *My Life and Crimes.* London: Jarrolds, 1956, p. 117.

67. Warburg, *An Occupation for Gentlemen*, p. 215. Elsewhere in this book Warburg said that "James himself was one of the most delightful and easy-going personalities I have known, colorful in more sense than one. A dark-skinned West Indian negro from Trinidad, he stood six foot three inches in his socks and was noticeably good-looking. His memory was extraordinary. He could quote, not only passages from the Marxist classics but long extracts from Shakespeare, in a soft lilting English which was a delight to hear."

68. Quoted in Anna Grimshaw, *The C. L. R. James Archive: A Reader's Guide.* New York: C. L. R. James Institute, 1991, p. 59.

69. Leon Trotsky, "More on Our Work," Houghton Library bMS Russ 13 14557.

70. Letter from C. L. R. James to Constance Webb, 1942.

CHAPTER 3. EDUCATION, PROPAGANDA, AGITATION

1. I have written extensively on this period. See *C. L. R. James and the American Century: 1938–1953*, CISCLA, InterAmerican University of Puerto Rico, 1984; "C. L. R. James and the American Century," in Selwyn Cudjoe and William Cain, eds. *C. L. R. James: His Intellectual Legacies.* Amherst: University of Massachusetts Press, 1995; "C. L. R. James, Marxism and America," *Research and Society*, no. 4 (1991); and "C. L. R. James and the Gospel of American Modernity," *Socialism and Democracy*, vol. 8, nos. 2–3 (1992).

2. Scott McLemee, "American Civilization and World Revolution: C. L. R. James in the United States, 1938–1953 and Beyond," in Scott McLemee and Paul Le Blanc, eds. *C. L. R. James and Revolutionary Marxism: Selected*

Writings, 1939–1949. Atlantic Highlands, NJ: Humanities Press, 1993, p. 217.

3. At the same time, as McLemee has noted, "deep continuities" connect "James's British years with his American sojourn. That nexus is revolution." McLemee, "American Civilization and World Revolution," pp. 217–218.

4. Anna Grimshaw and Keith Hart, *C. L. R. James and "The Struggle for Happiness."* New York: C. L. R. James Institute, 1991, p. 37.

5. C. L. R. James, *Mariners, Renegades and Castaways: Herman Melville and the World We Live In*. New York: C. L. R. James, 1953, p. 193.

6. Letter from C. L. R. James to Grace Lee and Selma Weinstein, December 14, 1953. Cited in Anna Grimshaw, *The C. L. R. James Archive: A Readers' Guide*. New York: C. L. R. James Institute, 1991, p. 89.

7. Quoted in "C. L. R. James," MARHO, ed. *Visions of History*. New York: Pantheon, 1983, p. 287.

8. Letter from C. L. R. James to Constance Webb, 1939.

9. Cited in Tony Bogues and Kim Gordon, *Black Nationalism and Socialism*. London: Flame, 1979, p. 9.

10. C. L. R. James, "On the Origins," *Radical America*, vol. 1, no. 4 (July–August 1968), p. 23.

11. Cited in Tony Bogues, *Marxism and Black Liberation*. Cleveland: Hera Press, 1980, p. 32.

12. Cited in Bogues, *Marxism and Black Liberation*, p. 32.

13. On the Socialist Workers Party in the 1930s and 1940s see Robert J. Alexander, *International Trotskyism, 1929–1985: A Documented Analysis of the Movement*. Durham: Duke University Press, 1991, pp. 761–833; James P. Cannon, *The History of American Trotskyism*. New York: Pathfinder Press, 1972 [1944]; and Alan M. Wald, *The New York Intellectuals: The Rise and Decline of the Anti-Stalinist Left from the 1930s to the 1980s*. Chapel Hill: The University of North Carolina Press, 1987.

14. Author's interview with Martin Glaberman, May 31, 1981.

15. Frank Lovell, in *James P. Cannon as We Knew Him*. New York: Pathfinder Press, 1976, p. 138. Phyllis and Julius Jacobson recall "a very striking figure," with "a most magnetic handsomeness." They described James's 1938 lecture as a "spellbinding experience." Author's interview with Julius and Phyllis Jacobson (New York), November 22, 1992.

16. "British Empire Speech," *Socialist Appeal*, December 10, 1938.

17. Constance Webb, "C. L. R. James: The Speaker and His Charisma," in Paul Buhle, ed. *C. L. R. James: His Life and Work*. London: Allison and Busby, 1986, p. 169.

18. Letter from C. L. R. James to Constance Webb, 1939.

19. *Leon Trotsky on Black Nationalism and Self-Determination*. New York: Pathfinder Press, 1978, pp. 61–62.

20. He undertook some of this work himself in the late 1940s; see the two parts of *Stalinism and Negro History* [1949], reprinted in McLemee and Le Blanc, eds., *C. L. R. James and Revolutionary Marxism*, pp. 188–208.

21. C. L. R. James, "Preliminary Notes," Houghton Library bMS Russ 13.1 16953, p. 2.

22. James, "Preliminary Notes," pp. 10–11.

23. *Leon Trotsky on Black Nationalism and Self-Determination*, p. 55.

24. *Leon Trotsky on Black Nationalism and Self-Determination*, p. 50.

25. In the 1960s and 1970s, Breitman edited several volumes of Malcolm X's speeches for Pathfinder Press that sold (and continue to sell) in enormous quantities. A useful overview of the party's position is contained in Evelyn Sell, "How the Concept of the Dual Nature of the African American Struggle Developed," *Bulletin In Defense of Marxism*, vol. 10, no. 10, December 1992, pp. 5–13.

26. C. L. R. James, "Trotsky's Place in History" [1940], reprinted in McLemee and Le Blanc, *C. L. R. James and Revolutionary Marxism*, p. 129.

27. C. L. R. James, *Notes on Dialectics: Hegel, Marx, Lenin*. Westport, CT: Lawrence Hill and Company, 1980, p. 137.

28. C. L. R. James, "After Ten Years" [1946] reprinted in C. L. R. James, *Spheres of Existence: Selected Writings*. Westport, CT: Lawrence Hill and Company, 1980, p. 68.

29. J. R. Johnson, "Labor and the Second World War," *Socialist Appeal*, November 21, 1939. Several of James's anti-war articles are reprinted in Fred Stanton, ed. *Fighting Racism in World War II*. New York: Monad, 1980.

30. In a letter to Constance Webb dated 9/4/39, he wrote: "But to-date the majority [led by James Cannon] says of the minority 'Irresponsible, jittery and unprincipled, subject to social-patriotic pressure'. The minority says of the majority 'Stalinist, bureaucratic and unable to lead the party'. A split on

such issues would show the utmost irresponsibility on both sides." He changed his mind, I think, because the faction around Shachtman was younger, more dynamic, and genuinely interested in ideas, and because a split was inevitable. But he remained critical of the leadership of both factions; in "The Roots of the Party Crisis," which circulated inside the SWP in late 1939, he complained that the "upper crust of the leadership, both Majority and Minority, is rotten with those intellectual vices once described by Lenin—"lackadaisicalness, carelessness, slovenliness, untidiness, nervous haste, the inclination to substitute discussion for action, talk for work" (p. 14).

31. Constance Ashton Myers, *The Prophet's Army: Trotskyists in America: 1928–1941*. Westport, CT: Greenwood Press, 1977, p. 107. Cannon consequently sent an epistle to SWP branches in California: "I hear that Johnson, the disorganizer, is going to lead a discussion of the Los Angeles comrades on the organization question. This imprudence can only be based on the assumption that any kind of quackery can prosper in Southern California. But I know another California—the California of a group of resolute Trotskyists . . ." James P. Cannon, *Struggle for a Proletarian Party*. New York: Pathfinder Press, 1972, p. 193.

32. As evidenced by the large crop of memoirs and studies that have appeared in recent years, there is considerable interest in the activities and writings of the New York Intellectuals. See, *inter alia*, Alexander Bloom, *Prodigal Sons: The New York Intellectuals and Their World*. New York: Oxford University Press, 1986; Terry A. Cooney, *The Rise of the New York Intellectuals: Partisan Review and its Circle, 1934–1945*. Madison: University of Wisconsin Press, 1986; Irving Howe, *A Margin of Hope: An Intellectual Autobiography*. New York: Harcourt, Brace and Jovanovich, 1982; Richard H. Pells, *The Liberal Mind in a Conservative Age: American Intellectuals in the 1940s and 1950s*. New York: Harper and Row, 1985; and Alan Wald, *The New York Intellectuals: The Rise and Decline of the Anti-Stalinist Left from the 1930s to the 1980s*. Chapel Hill: The University of North Carolina Press, 1987.

33. Cannon, *Struggle for a Proletarian Party*, p. 6.

34. The definitive account of the internal life of the Workers Party, and the impact of proletarianization on party members, is Harvey Swados's novel *Standing Fast*, published by Ballantine (1970).

35. Dwight MacDonald, *Memoirs of a Revolutionist*. New York: Farrar, Straus and Cubahy, 1957, p. 278.

36. C. L. R. James, "Fraternity," *Workers Party Internal Bulletin*, November 12, 1940, p. 2.

37. Delmore Schwartz makes reference in his diary to meeting James at

a party at Dwight MacDonald's in 1939; see Elizabeth Pollet, ed. *Portrait of Delmore: Journals and Notes of Delmore Schwartz 1939–1959*. New York: Farrar Straus Giroux, 1986, p. 7. Scott McLemee deserves credit for digging up this and other, similarly intriguing, sources.

38. Conrad Lynn, *There is a Fountain*. Westport, CT: Lawrence Hill and Company, 1979, p. 81.

39. The first stanza of the poem reads: "If we must die—let it not be like hogs/Hunted and penned in an inglorious spot,/While round us bark the mad and hungry dogs,/Making their mock at our accursed lot."

40. Native Son, *"My Friends": A Fireside Chat on the War*. New York: Workers Party, 1940, p. 3.

41. Native Son, *"My Friends,"* pp. 6–7.

42. Native Son, *"My Friends,"* p. 10.

43. Native Son, *"My Friends,"* p. 12.

44. "The Workers Party stands for . . . The right to vote and be voted for everywhere throughout the country. The right to hold office, any office from the lowest to the highest . . . The right to be free from insult, degradation and proscription . . . The right to work at any job for which the Negro is qualified [sic] and to be paid the same wages received by other workers." Native Son, *"My Friends,"* p. 12.

45. Letter from C. L. R. James to Constance Webb, August 26, 1943.

46. Letter from C. L. R. James to Constance Webb, 1942.

47. Selwyn Cudjoe, "The Love Letters of C. L. R. James," *Trinidad and Tobago Review*, October 1992, p. 19.

48. J. R. Johnson, "Negro Masses and the Struggle for World Socialism," *Labor Action*, April 28, 1941, p. 7.

49. C. L. R. James, 1977 preface to "Down With Starvation Wages in South-East Missouri" [1941], reprinted in C. L. R. James, *The Future in the Present: Selected Writings*. Westport, CT: Lawrence Hill and Company, 1977, p. 89.

50. The cover of the unsigned pamphlet reads: "Down With Starvation Wages in South-East Missouri. 30 Cents an Hour. White and Colored Together." The back cover lists the strikers' demands, and the inside front cover reads "Black and White UNITE AND FIGHT!"

51. James, "Down with Starvation Wages in South-East Missouri," p. 94.

52. James, "Down With Starvation Wages in South-East Missouri," pp. 92–93.

53. It is unclear how much time James actually spent among sharecroppers in southeast Missouri, as opposed to meeting with their leaders in St. Louis. Albert Glotzer (whose party name was Albert Gates) stated in an unpublished letter sent to the *New York Times* (9/5/85) that "James never organized or taught tenant farmers. I was secretary of the Workers Party when it sent James 'into the field' to assist in the work of its St. Louis branch. He was specifically instructed to stay out of southeast Missouri, where the tenant farmers union was located. James's British-West Indian accent would put him in jeopardy in this area of terror against union activity." Buhle says James "volunteered to go to southeastern Missouri," but also reports that "he spent most of his time in St. Louis with only occasional forays into the countryside . . ." By way of contrast, Consuelo Lopez asserts that James spent several months in Lilbourn's South Delmo housing project. Certainly James's many articles for *Labor Action* would suggest that he spent more time in the area than Glotzer would allow. See Paul Buhle, *C. L. R. James: The Artist as Revolutionary*. London: Verso, 1988, p. 83; and Consuelo Lopez, "C. L. R. James: The Rhetoric of a Defiant Warrior," unpublished dissertation, Indiana University, 1983, pp. 75–94.

54. James, "The Revolutionary Answer to the Negro Problem in the USA" [1948], reprinted in Anna Grimshaw, ed. *The C. L. R. James Reader*. Oxford: Blackwell, 1992, pp. 182–189.

55. With George Padmore, T. R. Makonnen, Wallace Johnson, Jomo Kenyatta, and Peter Abrahams, James served as an advisory editor to the IASB's wartime pamphlet series, which published at least 5 titles, including Kenyatta's *Kenya: Land of Conflict* (1945) and Eric Williams' *The Negro in the Caribbean* (1942).

56. J. R. Johnson, "One Tenth the Nation," *Labor Action*, April 23, 1945.

57. J. R. Johnson, "Marcus Garvey," *Labor Action*, June 24, 1940.

58. James, "On the Origins," p. 24.

59. Cf. Maurice Isserman, *Which Side Were You On? The American Communist Party During the Second World War*. Middletown, CT: Wesleyan University Press, 1982; Mark Naison, *Communists in Harlem During the Depression*. Urbana: University of Illinois Press, 1983; Michael E. Brown, Randy Martin, Frank Rosengarten, and George Snedeker, eds. *New Studies in the Politics and Culture of U.S. Communism*. New York: Monthly Review Press, 1992.

60. C. L. R. James, "Stalinism and Negro History" [1949], reprinted in McLemee and Le Blanc, eds., *C. L. R. James and Revolutionary Marxism*, p. 188.

61. James, "Stalinism and Negro History," p. 204.

62. J. R. Johnson, "Native Son and Revolution" [1940], reprinted in McLemee and Le Blanc, eds., *C. L. R. James and Revolutionary Marxism*, p. 91.

63. See Michel Fabre, *The Unfinished Quest of Richard Wright*. New York: Morrow, 1973, p. 268.

64. Richard Wright wrote the introduction to Horace Cayton's and St. Clair Drake's seminal study, *Black Metropolis: A Study of Negro Life in a Northern City*. New York: Harcourt, Brace and Company, 1945, which examined the interplay of race and politics in Chicago.

65. See Fabre, *The Unfinished Quest of Richard Wright*, p. 268.

66. Constance Webb, untitled pamphlet, self-published, n.d. [1944]. I located a copy of this pamphlet in the Rare Book Collection at Columbia University's Butler Library, where it had been deposited by Meyer Schapiro. Only one hundred copies of the pamphlet were ever issued. While the cover lacks any markings of any kind, the inside cover reads: "Strictly private circulation. Each copy is numbered and is not to be sold or exchanged."

67. Webb, untitled pamphlet, p. 138.

68. "Wright's failure is his failure to see the individual, black and white, as representative of great social forces in motion. In all his work there is no mention of organized labor. The exclusion is not an oversight; he has never seen or been involved in the labor movement." Constance Webb, untitled pamphlet, p. 149. Five years later, she reiterated these charges: "When he lived in Chicago in 1932, the labor movement, as it is known today, reaching into every section of society, did not exist. His jobs were solitary, unconnected with large groups of workers. He worked as a house-servant, a dishwasher, errand boy, a postal clerk, a janitor, so that any tendency toward individual thinking was reinforced by his type of work . . . Wright's strength and his weakness are products of the period in which he came to maturity." Constance Webb, "What Next for Richard Wright?" *Phylon: The Atlanta University Review of Race and Culture*, 1949 (no. 2), p. 164.

69. See Constance Webb, *Richard Wright: A Biography*. New York: G.P. Putnam's Sons, 1968, p. 220. Her book was the first full-scale biography of Wright, and it received mixed reviews. Michel Fabre, in his book *The Unfinished Quest of Richard Wright*, is quite critical of Webb's effort, as is another biographer, Margaret Walker, who claims that Webb "failed to be suffi-

ciently objective and was frequently inaccurate, revealing her ignorance of simple dates, places, and records of literary works." See Margaret Walker, *Demonic Genius: A Portrait of the Man, A Critical Look of His Work*. New York: Warner Books, 1988, p. 2. Walker quotes from a *Newsweek* review by Saul Maloff that called *Richard Wright: A Biography* "chaotically organized, and absurdly inconclusive . . ." However, the back cover of Webb's book features a plug from the writer Gwendolyn Brooks, who calls it "remarkably inclusive . . . Publication of it is a very large event."

70. Webb, *Richard Wright*, p. 218.

71. Webb, *Richard Wright*, p. 220.

72. See Arnold Rampersad's notes to Richard Wright, *Early Works*. New York: Library of America, 1991, p. 896. Horace Cayton says that he and Richard Wright planned to collaborate on an anthology "to which we would invite a number of Negro students and intellectuals to contribute. We held one meeting in Wright's Brooklyn apartment, and among those whom I remember being there was Ralph Ellison and C. L. R. Jones [sic], a West Indian Negro who was an anti-Communist Marxist. This project, for some reason that I cannot now recall, fell through." Horace Cayton, *Long Old Road*. New York: Trident Press, 1965, pp. 249–250.

73. Webb describes a champagne party that the Wrights hosted in their first-class stateroom on the S.S. United States before it set sail for Paris. Constance, C. L. R., Ralph Ellison, Bernard Wolfe, and Mrs. Daniel Guerin were all in attendance. See Webb, *Richard Wright*, p. 263.

74. Author's interview with Julius and Phyllis Jacobson, November 22, 1992.

75. David Coolidge, "Negroes and the Revolution," *New International*, January 1945, pp. 9 and 13.

76. J. R. Johnson, "Resolution of the Minority," *New International*, January 1945, pp. 14 and 16.

77. Author's interview with Martin Glaberman, May 31, 1981.

78. James, "The Revolutionary Answer to the Negro Problem in the USA," p. 120.

79. James, "The Revolutionary Answer to the Negro Problem in the USA," p. 124.

80. Tony Martin, "C. L. R. James and the Race/Class Question," *Race*, XIV, no. 2 (1972), p. 187.

81. Charles Denby, *Indignant Heart: A Black Workers Journal*. Boston: South End Press, 1978 [1952], p. 173.

CHAPTER 4. MARINERS, RENEGADES, AND CASTAWAYS

1. Especially the vibrancy of Manhattan, which makes his near total absence from the literature on the New York Intellectuals both baffling and vexing. Like other luminaries on the scene in the 1930s–1950s (several of whom he knew and debated), James drew inspiration from the energy and cultural diversity of the city's streets, movie theaters, cafes, and parks. Furthermore, when it came to the interpretation of the country's literary culture, James had more in common with an Alfred Kazin or an Edmund Wilson than with, say, critical theorists of the Frankfurt School. One can only assume that the historians, biographers, and memoir-writers of the New York Intellectuals have found James's radicalism somehow distasteful.

2. Scott McLemee, "American Civilization and World Revolution: C. L. R. James in the United States: 1938–1953 and Beyond," in Scott McLemee and Paul Le Blanc, eds. *C. L. R. James and Revolutionary Marxism: Selected Writings, 1939–1949*. Atlantic Highlands, NJ: Humanities Press, 1993, p. 216.

3. "I dominate the group, originator, speaker, writer, political tactician. And when all is said and done—personally, I keep them [Dunayevskaya and Lee] at a very great distance." Letter from C. L. R. James to Constance Webb, November 7, 1948.

4. C. L. R. James, *Beyond a Boundary*. London: Stanley Paul, 1963, p. 149. A rejection of the Trotskyist position on the Soviet Union entailed a thorough overhaul of Marxism. As James later wrote: "I understood from the very start that when we had broken with Trotsky on the defence of the S.U., we had broken with Trotskyism fundamentally. I understood that it was no question of agreement on everything and difference on one important issue. Being the person I was, I had to decide first that this question had to be worked out and secondly where it would be most convenient for me at any rate to work it out. I decided to stay in the U.S." Letter from C. L. R. James to Martin Glaberman, December 18, 1962.

5. Other WP cadre also poured invective on James's approach. Joseph Carter referred to his "sterile conception of Marxism," and called his writing "pompous," "difficult to follow," and "not only false but also stultifying." Another comrade, Paul Temple, said that "Johnson is pretty far gone in his fantasy" and asked "What planet is Johnson writing about and on?" Ernest Lund called James a "left sectarian" who was "neither classic nor consistent," and Ben Hall dubbed the Johnson-Forest tendency "sectarian dream-

ers." See Irving Howe, "On Comrade Johnson's American Resolution—or Soviets In the Sky," *Workers Party Convention Bulletin*, no. 3, March 28, 1946; Joseph Carter, "Johnson's Mystification of Marxism: Or a Case of Unproductive Self-Expansion," *Workers Party Internal Bulletin*, October 1943; Paul Temple, "The Art of Muddling," *Workers Party Internal Bulletin*, December 1943; Ernest Lund, "Lenin's Attitude Toward Democracy in the Imperialist Epoch: His Polemic Against Johnson's Theoretical Forbears," *Workers Party Internal Bulletin*, January 1944; and Ben Hall, "Workers' Power," *Workers Party Internal Bulletin*, January 1944.

6. *The Coal Miners' General Strike of 1949–1950 and the Birth of Marxist-Humanism in the U.S.* Detroit: News and Letters, 1984, p. 7.

7. Paul Romano and Grace Lee, *The American Worker*. Detroit: Bewick, 1972 [1947], p. 2. Romano's essay is entitled "Life in the Factory"; Lee's is entitled "The Reconstruction of Society."

8. Romano and Lee, *The American Worker*, p. 47.

9. C. L. R. James, "Dialectical Materialism and the Fate of Humanity" [1947], reprinted in Anna Grimshaw, ed. *The C. L. R. James Reader*. Oxford: Blackwell, 1992, p. 181.

10. James, "Dialectical Materialism and the Fate of Humanity," p. 180.

11. James, "Dialectical Materialism and the Fate of Humanity," p. 170.

12. C. L. R. James, Raya Dunayevskaya, and Grace Lee, *The Invading Socialist Society*. Detroit: Bewick Editions, 1972 [1947], p. 14. The title's phrase is taken from Engels.

13. James, Dunayevskaya, and Lee, *The Invading Socialist Society*, p. 20.

14. *Essays by Karl Marx Selected from the Economic-Philosophic MSS.* New York: Johnson-Forest tendency, 1947. The group also issued an anti-Shachtmanite polemic, *The Balance Sheet: Trotskyism in the United States 1940–1947*, in the same year, and produced eleven internal bulletins.

15. Johnson-Forest's departure from the Socialist Workers Party was greeted with sarcastic asides from Shachtman's *Labor Action*, and a thoughtful essay on "Marxist Methods and Ideas and the Method and Ideas of Johnson-Forest" by George Novack and John G. Wright that appeared in the SWP's *Discussion Bulletin* (April 1951). A circle of approximately ten Johnson-Forest members decided to stay in the SWP, however. As Tim Wohlforth has written: "When Johnson split from the SWP in 1950 to build his own party, [auto worker Art] Fox and friends remained, holding to their view that the USSR was a state capitalist country. They were convinced, however, that the SWP was a revolutionary party with a proletarian leader-

ship that in time would come over to their views. They were deeply committed to a 'workerist' concept of party building, which, to their credit, they carried out in their own lives." Tim Wohlforth, *The Prophet's Children: Travels
on the American Left*. Atlantic Highlands, NJ: Humanities Press, 1993, p. 107.

16. A valuable selection of her writings on state capitalism is contained
in Raya Dunayevskaya, *The Marxist-Humanist Theory of State Capitalism:
Selected Writings*. Detroit: News and Letters, 1992. This volume features
such essays as "Is Russia a Part of the Collectivist Epoch of Society?" (1942),
"An Analysis of the Russian Economy" (1942), "The Nature of the Russian
Economy" (1946–1947), and "A New Revision of Marxian Economics,"
which originally appeared in *American Economic Review* (September 1944).
See also *Marxism and Freedom: From 1776 until Today*. New York: Columbia
University Press, 1988 [1958], chapter 13.

17. Cited in C. L. R. James, "After Ten Years" [1946], reprinted in
Spheres of Existence. Westport: CT: Lawrence Hill and Company, 1980, pp.
59–60.

18. Max Shachtman, "Is Russia a Workers' State?" *New International*,
December 1940.

19. Quoted in Albert Glotzer, *Trotsky: Memoir and Critique*. Buffalo:
Prometheus Books, 1989, p. 307.

20. Max Shachtman, *The Bureaucratic Revolution: The Rise of the Stalinist State*. New York: The Donald Press, 1962, p. 32.

21. J. R. Johnson, "Russia—a Fascist State," *New International* New
York, April 1941, p. 57. The notion that the USSR was a fascist state or that
it was moving in a fascist direction was not unheard of amongst anarchist
and other radical circles. Even the *New Republic*, which was generally supportive of the Popular Front, published a couple of articles that were compatible with some of James's ideas. See Vincent Sheean, "Brumaire: The
Soviet Union as a Fascist State," *New Republic*, November 8, 1939, reprinted
in Dorothy Wickenden, ed. *The New Republic Reader*. New York: Basic
Books, 1994, pp. 452–457.

22. James, Dunayevskaya, and Lee, *The Invading Socialist Society*, p. 3.

23. James, Dunayevskaya, and Lee, *The Invading Socialist Society*, p. 4.

24. Paul Berman has aptly noted that the Johnsonite analysis is that
socialism "has been progressing stage-by-stage for a hundred years, as a
shadow alternative under capitalism. Its growth isn't normally visible and
has nothing to do with left-wing parties or unions or the fate of radical politicians. Whether working people consciously think about the socialist alter-

native doesn't matter either, not in the short run. For capitalism creates the socialist alternative willy-nilly, and when capitalism grows and spreads, so does its socialist shadow . . ." Paul Berman, "Spirit of '67," *Village Voice Literary Supplement*, September 1983, p. 91.

25. On Trotsky's expectation that the coming war would generate revolutionary upheavals, see Baruch Knei-Paz, *The Social and Political Thought of Leon Trotsky*. New York: Oxford University Press, 1978, pp. 541–543.

26. C. L. R. James, "In the International Tradition: Tasks Ahead for American Labor" [1944], reprinted in McLemee and Le Blanc, eds., *C. L. R. James and Revolutionary Marxism*, p. 164.

27. J. R. Johnson, "Socialism and the National Question," *New International*, October 1943, p. 283.

28. Paul Buhle, "Introduction," C. L. R. James, *State Capitalism and World Revolution*. Chicago: Charles Kerr, 1986 [1950], pp. xviii-xix.

29. The letters to Constance Webb also disclosed a more melancholy side of James's personality. "In the last seven years," he wrote in one letter, "I believe I have been the loneliest man in the world; our ideas and plans and perspectives are so big, our work, and our concrete sphere is so small" (10/13/48).

30. See C. L. R. James, "Lenin and the Problem," reprinted in *Nkrumah and the Ghana Revolution*. Westport, CT: 1977, pp. 189–213, and in Grimshaw, ed. *The C. L. R. James Reader*, pp. 331–346.

31. J. R. Johnson, "Education, Propaganda, Agitation: Postwar America and Bolshevism." Workers Party internal document, 1943, p. 3.

32. Johnson, "Education, Propaganda, Agitation," p. 32.

33. Johnson, "Education, Propaganda, Agitation," p. 6.

34. Johnson, "Education, Propaganda, Agitation," p. 35.

35. The phrase was coined by Martin Glaberman in his introduction to C. L. R. James, *State Capitalism and World Revolution*. Detroit: Facing Reality, 1969, p. 2.

36. C. L. R. James, *Notes on Dialectics: Hegel, Marx, Lenin*. London: Allison and Busby, 1980.

37. James, *Notes on Dialectics*, p. 55.

38. James, *Notes on Dialectics*, p. 117.

39. C. L. R. James, *Party Politics in the West Indies*. San Juan, Trinidad: Inprint Caribbean Ltd., 1984 [1962], p. xix.

40. Cited in Anna Grimshaw, *Popular Democracy and the Creative Imagination: The Writings of C. L. R. James 1950–1963*. New York: C. L. R. James Institute, 1991, p. 5.

41. Letter from C. L. R. James to Constance Webb, December 14, 1944.

42. Letter from C. L. R. James to Constance Webb, August 2, 1948.

43. Letter from C. L. R. James to Constance Webb, August 1948.

44. Letter from C. L. R. James to Constance Webb, postmarked August 26, 1948.

45. James' translation was never published. A severely shortened version of Guerin's study was finally published—*sans* footnotes—under the title *Class Struggle in the First French Republic: Bourgeois and Bras Nus, 1793–1795*. London: Pluto Press, 1977, translated by Ian Patterson.

46. The Schomburg collection contains a letter from C. L. R. James to Lyman Paine, dated October 2, 1948, in which he confesses that "I am a gambler now."

47. Letter from C. L. R. James to Constance Webb, April 15, 1947.

48. Quoted in Anna Grimshaw, *The C. L. R. James Archive: A Reader's Guide*. New York: C. L. R. James Institute, 1991, p. 105. In the autobiographical document "My Experience with Women," James confessed that "I was lacking in the fact that I never completely committed my life and my way of living to her life and to her way of living, and when she asked me what I wanted, I hesitated and didn't work at it because it meant that to request of her what I wanted meant ultimately that my freedom and independence to live my own life as I wanted would also be committed to her. And the fact remains that I did not want anything in particular from her, due to my ignorance and stupidity" (p. 28).

49. Grimshaw, *Popular Democracy and the Creative Imagination*, pp. 5–6.

50. Quoted in Grimshaw, *Popular Democracy and the Creative Imagination*, p. 6.

51. Stan Weir, an activist in the Workers Party, fondly remembered "a late supper in the Village at Connie's Calypso Restaurant after seeing *The Glass Key* starring Alan Ladd. Our table companions had never heard cinema analysis used so effectively to relate the depths of alienation in our society, but I knew as I switched attention momentarily from them, to myself, and back to James, neither had I." See Stanley Weir, "Revolutionary Artist," in Buhle, ed. *C. L. R. James: His Life and Work*, p. 184. Connie's Calypso Restaurant was a popular dining establishment that welcomed interracial cou-

ples like C. L. R. and Constance. The novelist James Baldwin worked there as a waiter during the late 1940s.

52. See, *inter alia*, his speech to American progressives on the implications of Poland's *Solidarnosc* movement: "Poland" [1981], reprinted in *At the Rendezvous of Victory*; and "Three Black Women Writers: Toni Morrison, Alice Walker, Ntozake Shange," originally published in *Cultural Correspondence*, new series no. 2 (Winter 1983), and reprinted in Grimshaw, ed. *The C. L. R. James Reader*, pp. 411–417.

53. Grimshaw and Hart, *C. L. R. James and "The Struggle for Happiness,"* p. 27.

54. C. L. R. James, *American Civilization*, edited by Anna Grimshaw and Keith Hart (Oxford: Blackwell, 1993), p. 31.

55. James, *American Civilization*, pp. 98 and 102.

56. Grimshaw and Hart, *C. L. R. James and "The Struggle for Happiness,"* p. 3.

57. James, *American Civilization*, pp. 264 and 274. James was not uncritical of certain aspects of the national culture. As he wrote to Constance Webb in 1947: "The vigor, the energy, the organizing ability of these Americans astonish me. But the theoretical sloppiness is astonishing too."

58. James, *American Civilization*, p. 275.

59. James, *American Civilization*, p. 277.

60. James, *American Civilization*, p. 256.

61. James, *American Civilization*, p. 225.

62. James, *American Civilization*, p. 276.

63. James, *American Civilization*, p. 119.

64. James, *American Civilization*, p. 119.

65. James, *American Civilization*, p. 124.

66. James, *American Civilization*, p. 121.

67. James, *American Civilization*, p. 139.

68. James, *American Civilization*, p. 159.

69. G. W. F. Hegel, *Reason in History*. New York: Library of Liberal Arts, 1953 [1857], p. 43.

70. James, *American Civilization*, p. 166.

71. James, *American Civilization*, p. 194.

72. James gingerly approached the question of male homosexuality at the end of the chapter on "The Women." He noted that Americans "have a unique attitude to it. They hate it, they denounce it, they are on guard against it." The discussion ends on a cryptic note: "The writer believes that hidden here are avenues of investigation to new relationships among men and new relationships between men and women, both sexual and otherwise. And here for the time being, the matter will have to stay" (pp. 223–224).

73. James, *American Civilization*, p. 214.

74. James, *American Civilization*, p. 215.

75. With the aid of the NAACP, James attempted to make the strongest case possible for U.S. citizenship. He enlisted the help of Meyer Schapiro and other influential friends in mounting a defense committee.

The scholar Gerald Horne has charged James with a lack of "courage" in this period, on the grounds that he "grovelled" before the U.S. authorities in order to obtain citizenship papers. Horne cites a letter in which James assured NAACP leader Walter White that the "idea that I was a dangerous agitator abroad is entirely ridiculous," and in which he avowed that "I would get rid of every copy of *World Revolution* [a key document in the prosecution's case] that I could, because I no longer believe in it." Quoted in Gerald Horne, *Communist Front? The Civil Rights Congress, 1946–1956*. Rutherford, NJ: Fairleigh Dickinson University Press, 1988, pp. 63–64. Certainly James's self-presentation was disingenuous at times, as if the break with Trotskyism meant that his political views were now somehow compatible with mainstream American values. But the question of "courage" is a nonissue: James had more than demonstrated his courage by his political activities and in particular by his principled (if myopic) opposition to World War II.

76. C. L. R. James, *Mariners, Renegades and Castaways: Herman Melville and the World We Live In*. New York: C. L. R. James, 1953, p. 150.

77. James, *Mariners, Renegades and Castaways*, p. 200.

78. James, *Mariners, Renegades and Castaways*, p. 13.

79. James, *Mariners, Renegades and Castaways*, p. 136.

80. James, *Mariners, Renegades and Castaways*, p. 136.

81. James, *Mariners, Renegades and Castaways*, p. 105.

82. James, *Mariners, Renegades and Castaways*, p. 101.

83. Darrell E. Levi, "C. L. R. James: A Radical West Indian Vision of

American Studies." *American Quarterly*, vol. 43, no. 3 (September 1991), pp. 495–496.

84. O'Brien [Peter Mallory], "Johnsonism: A Political Appraisal." Detroit: News and Letters, April 1956. O'Brien goes on to claim that over 8,000 copies were "distributed free to Senators, Congressmen, Governors, Mayors, Judges, plus intellectuals, professors and scientists of prestige, etc. Postage alone on this big giveaway cost the organization over $1,000 . . . Whenever a person would send in money for one copy, he got eight or ten copies from the author . . ."

85. Letter from C. L. R. James to Martin Glaberman, Wayne State University archives, dated 12/3/62.

86. Letter from C. L. R. James to Martin Glaberman, Wayne State University archives, dated 12/62.

87. Paul Buhle, "Introduction," *Urgent Tasks* (Chicago), 1982, p. 2.

CHAPTER 5. FACING REALITY

1. They tied the knot in a small civil ceremony in September 1956 at the Hampstead Town Hall. It was witnessed by Dr. David Pitt, a civil rights activist and an old friend of the groom's.

2. George Lamming, *Natives of My Person*. Ann Arbor: University of Michigan Press, 1992 [1972], p. 166.

3. Lamming, *Natives of My Person*, p. 330.

4. On Padmore's political evolution, see James R. Hooker, *Black Revolutionary: George Padmore's Path from Communism to Pan-Africanism*. New York: Praeger, 1967.

5. See Martin Glaberman, "Letters," in Paul Buhle, ed. *C. L. R. James: Life and Work*. London: Allison and Busby, 1986, p. 154.

6. Kwame Nkrumah, *Ghana: The Autobiography of Kwame Nkrumah*. New York: International Publishers, 1971 [1956], p. 44.

7. James was later to attend a party in 1957 held in Padmore's honor on the eve of his trip to Ghana to become advisor to Nkrumah, and they also met up in Ghana later that year. See Hooker, *Black Revolutionary*, p. 132.

8. In an article written for the *Manchester Guardian*, on the "Return of a Wanderer: Comparisons between 1938 and 1953," James expressed a modest degree of pleasure at being back in England. He rather casually lets it slip that he "devoured" *Wisden* (the annual compendium of cricket statistics)

while living in the United States, and matter-of-factly concludes that "games and players are less remote, closer to ordinary humanity than in 1938," which presumably was a good thing. The article is reprinted in C. L. R. James, *Cricket* (ed. Anna Grimshaw). London: Allison and Busby, 1986, p. 71–73.

9. Lamming's fictionalized portrait of a single-minded political conspirator, Surgeon, closely matches this general profile. Surgeon, we learn, "allowed his dreams to hurry his speech." A "pioneer in the cause of colonies," he had "a hunger for completeness." Like James, Surgeon eschewed self-analysis: "Introspection was not a habit that Surgeon encouraged." See Lamming, *Natives of My Person*, pp. 112, 190, and 106.

10. A larger collection of documents by and about James, covering the U.S. years and the period since his death, is perhaps more accessible to scholars at the C. L. R. James Institute in New York. See Jim Murray, ed., *The C. L. R. James Research Guide*, forthcoming. Researchers interested in using this collection can write to the C. L. R. James Institute at 505 West End Avenue, Apartment 15C, New York, NY 10024. Also see Anna Grimshaw, *The C. L. R. James Archive: A Reader's Guide*. New York: C. L. R. James Institute, 1991.

11. Grimshaw, *The C. L. R. James Archive*, p. 62.

12. Letter from C. L. R. James to C. L. R. James Jr., February 19, 1957, available at the C. L. R. James Institute.

13. Ivar Oxaal, *Black Intellectuals Come to Power*. Cambridge, MA: Schenkman Books, 1968, p. 78.

14. This phrase is taken from Clifford Geertz, *The Interpretation of Cultures: Selected Essays*. New York: Basic Books, 1973.

15. Matthew Ward [Si Owen], *Indignant Heart: A Black Worker's Journal*. Detroit: Correspondence, 1952.

16. Martin Glaberman, *Punching Out*. Detroit: Bewick Editions, 1972 [1952], p. 28.

17. Lefort told one interviewer that Correspondence "had come to conclusions similar to ours concerning the USSR, bureaucracy, and the conditions for an autonomous struggle of the exploited. Their conception of workers' daily resistance in industry was particularly fruitful . . ." See "An Interview with Claude Lefort," *Telos*, no. 30 (Winter 1976–1977), p. 177.

18. Jean-Francois Lyotard, *Peregrinations: Law, Form, Event*. New York: Columbia University Press, 1988, p. 62. Lyotard joined *Socialisme ou Barbarie* in 1954 and was prominent in the breakaway *Pouvoir Ouvrier* group for several years. Formed in 1964, *Pouvoir Ouvrier* emerged out of a faction

inside *Socialisme ou Barbarie* that opposed Castoriadis's break with orthodox Marxism. Today, Lyotard is a world-famous philosopher and theorist of
postmodernism.

19. The first mimeographed *Correspondence* appeared on November
15, 1951 and led off with news of a miners' wildcat strike in West Virginia.
Even this early prototype features reviews of popular books and movies, as
well as international reports and a section on "philosophy and political
economy."

20. *The Correspondence Booklet*. Detroit: Correspondence, September
1954, p. 65.

21. Author's interview with Martin Glaberman, May 31, 1981.

22. *The Correspondence Booklet*, p. 1. This figure reflected the fact that
the group provided salaries to three full-time employees, including the
paper's editor.

23. Cited in letter from C. L. R. James to "Pound," 1954, Martin Glaberman papers, Walter Reuther Library, Wayne State University.

24. Letter from C. L. R. James to Martin Glaberman, July 1964, Wayne
State University.

25. Open letter from Freddy Paine to friends, March 1955, Wayne State
University.

26. Raya Dunayevskaya, "Political Organizer's Report," April 1955,
Raya Dunayevskaya papers, Walter Reuther Library, Wayne State University. Following the split, the News and Letters group circulated a document,
"Johnsonism: A Political Appraisal," which bombastically compared James
to Stalin. James believed, the author claimed, that "in some mystical manner,
he would be able to rally hundreds if not thousands . . . His rewriting of our
history stands on a par with that of Stalin." O'Brien, "Johnsonism: A Political
Appraisal," Detroit: News and Letters, April 1955.

27. The blurb on the back of one of her books captures the group's
devotion to Dunayevskaya and its impressive institutional memory: "Raya
Dunayevskaya is the founder of Marxist-Humanism in the United States. She
was the first to develop the theory of state capitalism, which marked her
break from Trotsky at the outset of World War II, and worked out the philosophy of Marxist-Humanism both as a global concept and as it is rooted in
the United States in labor, the Black dimension and women's liberation. The
documents over a forty-year period that embody her development of the
inseparability of philosophy and revolution as the dialectics of liberation are
preserved on microfilm in the Wayne State University Labor Archives under

the title: 'The Raya Dunayevskaya Collection—Marxist-Humanism in the United States, 1941 to today.'" See Raya Dunayevskaya, *Philosophy and Revolution: From Hegel to Sartre and from Marx to Mao*. Sussex: Harvester Press, 1982.

28. After considerable internal debate, the Shachtmanites decided to wind down the Workers Party in favor of a more modest organizational vehicle, the Independent Socialist League. Almost a decade later, the League's leadership approached the Socialist Party (SP) to propose that the two organizations merge their dwindling forces. The Socialists rejected this proposal but allowed Shachtmanites to join on an individual basis. Although some League members opposed fusing with the Socialist Party, Shachtman and Michael Harrington led a majority of League members into the SP.

29. The last issue of *Correspondence* under a Johnsonite rubric was dated February 1962. After that, an explicitly non-Marxist newspaper was produced by Grace Lee Boggs and James Boggs for a couple of years that attempted to reach the burgeoning civil rights movement. Their split is discussed below.

30. Dan Georgakas has described the relationship between the James household and the Correspondence group as "a bit schizoid": "they were extremely attentive to his views on all subjects, but did not wish to become one more cult wed to a leading personality in exile whose every whim could convulse the faithful. Consequently, while his letters from Britain were read and studied within the immediate circle, in public events his leadership was played down." Dan Georgakas, "Young Detroit Radicals, 1955–1965," in Paul Buhle, ed. *C. L. R. James: His Life and Work*. London: Allison and Busby, 1986, p. 183.

31. Martin Glaberman, *Union Committeemen and Wildcat Strikes*. Detroit: Bewick Editions, 1971 [1955], p. 23.

32. "On the day of the performance, the play was performed and, as far as we can gather, the prizes were given by popular applause and the popular vote. You must remember that the dramatic companies used to rehearse for one year and the successful tragedians were looked upon as some of the greatest men in the state. Yet it was the public, the general public of fifteen or twenty thousand people, that came and decided who was the winner." C. L. R. James, "Every Cook Can Govern: A Study of Democracy in Ancient Greece" [1956], reprinted in *The Future in the Present*. Westport, CT: Lawrence Hill and company, 1977, p. 123.

33. See, for example, *Modern Politics* (1960).

34. A fourth letter, addressed to the literary critic Frank Kermode, is

also reprinted, even though it was written in the early 1980s. Although its inclusion nicely highlights the underlying continuities in James's mature cultural-political perspective, it potentially undermines the reader's appreciation for the specific conjuncture which conditioned the author's rediscovery of criticism as a form of political practice.

35. Letter to Jay Leyda, March 7, 1953, reprinted in Grimshaw, ed. *The C. L. R. James Reader*, p. 231.

36. Grimshaw, ed. *The C. L. R. James Reader*, p. 232.

37. Letter to Meyer Schapiro, March 9, 1953, reprinted in Grimshaw, ed. *The C. L. R. James Reader*, p. 237.

38. Grimshaw, ed. *The C. L. R. James Reader*, p. 239.

39. Grimshaw, ed. *The C. L. R. James Reader*, p. 240.

40. Grimshaw, ed. *The C. L. R. James Reader*, p. 240.

41. Grimshaw, ed. *The C. L. R. James Reader*, p. 240.

42. Letter to Frank Kermode, September 15, 1982, reprinted in Grimshaw, ed. *The C. L. R. James Reader*, p. 242. James and Redgrave became friends in the late 1960s. In her autobiography she says that "James gave me and several others lessons on *Das Kapital,* and because of James, though not on his advice, I went up to Collets bookshop and bought Lenin's *The State and Revolution*"(p. 184). Their friendship subsided once she decided to join the Socialist Labour League, which James recommended she not do. See *Vanessa Redgrave: An Autobiography.* New York: Random House, 1994, pp. 183–185.

43. Letter to Bell, June 1953, reprinted in Grimshaw, ed. *The C. L. R. James Reader*, p. 221.

44. Grimshaw, ed. *The C. L. R. James Reader*, p. 223.

45. C. L. R. James, "Popular Art and the Cultural Tradition" [1954], reprinted in *Third Text*, no. 10 (Spring 1990), p. 3.

46. James, "Popular Art and the Cultural Tradition," p. 3.

47. James, "Popular Art and the Cultural Tradition," p. 6.

48. James, "Popular Art and the Cultural Tradition," p. 8. He writes on the next page: "Since Aristotle and Plato and the decline of the Greek city-state, criticism of necessity no longer has the mass popular audience as the center of its conceptions. It is the modern film which has restored this possibility."

49. He argues that the overall quality of films declined during the Depression as the national audience fragmented and as those involved in the

production of movies were subjected to various forms of commercial and political censorship. As in *American Civilization*, his main point had to do with the turn towards violence that filmmakers embarked upon as economic relations soured. James, "Popular Art and the Cultural Tradition," p. 10.

50. James, "Popular Art and the Cultural Tradition," p. 4.

51. James, "Popular Art and the Cultural Tradition," p. 10.

52. C. L. R. James, *A Preface to Criticism* (mimeo), p. 4. The complete document is available to researchers at the C. L. R. James Institute. A key excerpt is featured in Anna Grimshaw, ed. *The C. L. R. James Reader*. Oxford: Blackwell, 1992, pp. 255–260.

53. James, *A Preface to Criticism*, p. 2.

54. James, *A Preface to Criticism*, p. 12.

55. James, *A Preface to Criticism*, p. 73.

56. James, *A Preface to Criticism*, p. 93.

57. Open Letter from C. L. R. James to U.S. comrades, March 15, 1956, Wayne State University.

58. Ferenc Feher and Agnes Heller, "The Hungarian Revolution," *Radical America*, vol. 16, no. 3 (1983), p. 118.

59. Lewis Coser and Irving Howe, "Revolution in Eastern Europe," *Dissent*, no. 3 (November 1956), p. 3.

60. Letter from C. L. R. James to "Neff" [Lyman Paine], November 1956, Wayne State University archives.

61. The original typescript of Castoriadis's chapter as well as other documents concerning his role in the production of *Facing Reality* are presumed missing as a result of the fact that Castoriadis had to store his correspondence at a friend's house after De Gaulle came to power in 1958 and initiated a police crackdown against subversives. (It was at this point that Castoriadis changed his pen name from Pierre Chaulieu to Paul Cardan.) I would like to thank David Ames Curtis for his prompt response to my queries concerning the James-Castoriadis connection.

62. C. L. R. James, Grace Lee, and Pierre Chaulieu, *Facing Reality*. Detroit: Bewick Editions, 1974 [1958], p. 91.

63. Quoted in James, Lee, and Chaulieu, *Facing Reality*, pp. 77–78.

64. James, Lee, and Chaulieu, *Facing Reality*, p. 81.

65. James, Lee, and Chaulieu, *Facing Reality*, p. 82.

66. See Paul Berman, "Facing Reality," in Buhle, ed. *C. L. R. James: His Life and Work.*

67. Dunayevskaya, *For the Record*, p. 5.

68. Cornelius Castoriadis, "For a New Orientation" [1962], reprinted in *Recommencing the Revolution: From Socialism to the Autonomous Society.* Minneapolis: University of Minnesota Press, 1993, p. 13.

69. Dunayevskaya, *For the Record*, p. 5.

70. James and Grace Lee Boggs and Freddy and Lyman Paine, *Conversations in Maine: Exploring Our Nation's Future.* Boston: South End Press, 1978, p. 287.

71. Facing Reality produced a monthly newsletter, *Speak Out*, during the 1960s. The group's pamphlets included *Negro Americans Take the Lead* (1964), and Glaberman's *Mao as Dialectician* (1971). Circulating James' writings was a key function of the organization, which issued his *Marxism and the Intellectuals* in 1963 and *Lenin, Trotsky, and the Vanguard Party* in 1964. The group was officially disbanded in 1970.

72. See Dan Georgakas and Marvin Surkin, *Detroit: I Do Mind Dying.* New York: St. Martin's Press, 1973.

73. Letter from C. L. R. James to Martin Glaberman, December 3, 1962, Wayne State University.

74. Irving Howe, *A Margin of Hope: An Intellectual Autobiography.* New York: Harcourt, Brace and Jovanovich, 1982, p. 31.

CHAPTER 6. PARTIES AND POLITICS IN THE WEST INDIES

1. Nex Rettleford, quoted in Jervis Anderson, "Onward and Upward with the Arts: Derek Walcott's Odyssey," *The New Yorker*, December 21, 1992, p. 79.

2. "The populations in the British West Indies have no native civilization at all. People dance Bongo and Shango and all this is very artistic and very good. But these have no serious effects upon their general attitude to the world. These populations are essentially Westernized and they have been Westernized for centuries." C. L. R. James, *Party Politics in the West Indies.* San Juan, Trinidad: Inprint Caribbean Ltd., 1984 [1962], p. 81.

3. See Selwyn D. Ryan, *Race and Nationalism in Trinidad and Tobago.* Toronto: University of Toronto Press, 1972, pp. 120–127.

4. Cary Fraser, *Ambivalent Anticolonialism: The United States and the*

Genesis of West Indian Independence, 1940–1964 (Greenwood Press, 1994), p. 139.

5. Quoted in Ryan, *Race and Nationalism in Trinidad and Tobago*, p. 275.

6. At one point Williams announced that the "only university at which I shall lecture in the future is the University of Woodford Square, and its several branches throughout the length and breadth of Trinidad and Tobago." Quoted in Jeremy Taylor, *Masquerade*. London: Macmillan Caribbean, 1986, p. 36.

7. George Lamming, *The Pleasures of Exile*. London: Allison and Busby, 1984 [1960], p. 211.

8. The Red House, an imposing, neo-Renaissance edifice located on the western side of Woodford Square, is the historic seat of the Government of Trinidad and Tobago and housed the PNM government after Independence. The building was rebuilt in 1906 after having been destroyed three years earlier by rioters.

9. Basil Wilson, "The Caribbean Revolution," in Paul Buhle, ed. *C. L. R. James: His Life and Work*. London: Allison and Busby, 1986, p. 121.

10. Ivar Oxaal, *Black Intellectuals Come to Power*. Cambridge, MA: Schenkman Publishers, 1968, p. 3.

11. Halfway through *Natives of My Person*, the James-like character Surgeon announces: "I put the past behind me that very moment I gave the Commandant my word." See George Lamming, *Natives of My Person*. Ann Arbor: University of Michigan Press, 1992 [1972], p. 147.

12. Later, there would be profound skepticism, as leftist nationalists chastised James for his identification with Western values, and for his failure to construct an alternative to the PNM. Criticisms of this kind were raised at the conference "C. L. R. James: His Intellectual Legacies" held at Wellesley College in 1991. I refer to these issues in my chapter on "The Question of the Canon: C. L. R. James and *Modern Politics*," in Paget Henry and Paul Buhle, eds. *C. L. R. James' Caribbean*. Durham: Duke University Press, 1992.

13. Quoted in Oxaal, *Black Intellectuals Come to Power*, p. 120.

14. Quoted in Fraser, *Ambivalent Anti-Colonialism*, p. 156. Fraser goes to report: "Despite the lack of evidence, the consul general saw James as a threatening figure within the PNM. The fact that Williams was close to James, whose party-building activities and views increased his influence, was also a source of concern."

15. Eric Williams, "Perspectives for Our Party" (1958), reprinted in *Eric E. Williams Speaks: Essays on Colonialism and Independence*, edited by Selwyn R. Cudjoe. Wellesley, MA: Calaloux Publications, 1993, p. 209.

16. Williams, "Perspectives for Our Party," p. 217.

17. Walter Annamunthodo's loyalty was to C. L. R. rather than the People's National Movement. He later claimed that "I could not have broken with James, not on penalty of death." See Louis B. Homer, "We Shall See What We Shall See," *Trinidad and Tobago Review*, October 1992, p. 36. James wrote an introduction to Annamunthodo's pamphlet *Sugar Dissected*, which he privately published in 1966, and which James described as "a little masterpiece" in contrast to the "babel of tongues, which to a large degree constitutes politics in Trinidad and Tobago . . ." (Author's private collection.)

18. Quoted in Ryan, *Race and Nationalism in Trinidad and Tobago*, p. 214.

19. *The Nation*, December 20, 1958.

20. C. L. R. James, "Our Upper Classes," *The Nation*, February 28, 1959.

21. This was the title of James's 1960 pamphlet that attempted to reassure the country's Indian population of the PNM's benign intentions.

22. A more nuanced view was offered by Winston Mahabir in his autobiography. Mahabir, an Indian Christian and a physician, was a member of the PNM's cabinet prior to Independence. In his book he writes: "It would be a gross distortion to lay blame for the recrudescence of racial antagonisms at the door of Eric Williams and the PNM. It would be equally unrealistic to exculpate Eric Williams entirely. As the leading politician in Trinidad since 1956, he had an unrivalled opportunity to exercise a positive influence upon the betterment of race relations. Yet my impression was that, although he had a firm intellectual grasp of the need for co-operation between the races, he never made any serious attempt to bridge the emotional gap that lay between him and the Indians." Dr. Winston Mahabir, *In and Out of Politics*. Port of Spain: Inprint Caribbean, 1978, p. 207.

23. See H. P. Singh, *The Indian Enigma, a Review of Mr. C. L. R. James' "West Indians of 'East Indian' Descent," or a Study in Coolietude*. San Juan: Vedic Enterprises Ltd., 1965, p. 21 and 14. This pamphlet, along with a number of other polemics aimed at Eric Williams and the PNM, has been reprinted in H. P. Singh, *The Indian Struggle for Justice and Equality Against Black Racism in Trinidad and Tobago*, edited by Kamal Persad and Ashram B. Majaraj. Couva, Trinidad: Indian Review Press, 1993.

24. Quoted in Jervis Anderson, "Cricket and Beyond," *American Scholar*, Summer 1985, p. 358.

25. Anderson, "Cricket and Beyond," p. 359. Also see James, *Beyond a Boundary*, chapter eighteen.

26. Quoted in Earl Gooding, *West Indies at the Crossroads*. London: Penguin, 1989, p. 90.

27. C. L. R. James, "Lecture on Federation" [1958], reprinted in C. L. R. James, *At the Rendezvous of Victory: Selected Writings*. London: Allison and Busby, 1986, p. 90.

28. C. L. R. James, "Federation—What Now?" [1959], reprinted in James, *At the Rendezvous of Victory*, p. 122.

29. James, "Federation—What Now?" p. 122.

30. Paget Henry, "C. L. R. James and the Caribbean Economic Tradition," in Henry and Buhle, eds. *C. L. R. James' Caribbean*, p. 160–161.

31. Quoted in Ryan, *Race and Nationalism in Trinidad and Tobago*, p. 293.

32. A detailed account of the divergent role of Jamaica, Trinidad, and Barbados in the federation project is contained in F. A. Hoyos, *Grantley Adams and the Social Revolution: The Story of the Movement that Changed the Pattern of West Indian Society*. London: Macmillan Caribbean, 1988, pp. 203–230. Cary Fraser's book provides another useful overview of the rise and fall of the federalist project. Daniel Guerin also addressed the topic of federation in his political survey of the West Indies. In the book's very last paragraph he asks "But why deceive ourselves? The West Indian Confederation has slight chance of being born within the framework of the present capitalist and colonial society: sixteen years ago, in 1945, the Caribbean Labour Congress forcefully affirmed 'that there is no hope for the West Indies unless they become a Socialist Commonwealth.'" Daniel Guerin, *The West Indies and Their Future*. London: Dennis Dobson, 1961, p. 174.

33. Gooding, *West Indies at the Crossroads*, p. 106.

34. Hoyos, *Grantley Adams and the Social Revolution*, p. 208.

35. Oxaal, *Black Intellectuals Come to Power*, p. 133.

36. Oxaal, *Black Intellectuals Come to Power*, p. 134.

37. Ryan, *Race and Nationalism in Trinidad and Tobago*, p. 231. For an overview of U.S. policy and the decolonization process, see Cary Fraser, "Understanding American Policy Towards the Decolonization of European Empires, 1945–1964," *Diplomacy & Statecraft*, vol. 3, no. 1 (March 1992), pp. 105–125.

38. During the Chaguaramas affair James had written that the Americans demonstrated "incredible thick-headedness and bovine obstinacy. A sense of power and the arrogance of dominion seems to shut off the functioning of certain parts of the brain." C. L. R. James, *The Nation*, August 7, 1959. He adopted a different rhetoric in articles such as "Dr. Eric Williams— PNM Political Leader: A Convention Appraisal," published in March 1960.

39. Letter reprinted in James, *Party Politics in the West Indies*, p. 73.

40. Quoted in James, *Party Politics in the West Indies*, p. 96.

41. *The Nation*, October 7, 1960.

42. Quoted in Eric Williams, *Inward Hunger: The Education of a Prime Minister*. London: Andre Deutsch, 1969, p. 268.

43. James, *Party Politics in the West Indies*, p. 70.

44. James, *Party Politics in the West Indies*, p. 51.

45. James, *Party Politics in the West Indies*, p. 51.

46. The country's real Gross Domestic Product had increased 8.5% on an annual basis from 1951–1961; eighty thousand barrels of oil were being produced *per day* by 1960. Figures taken from *Islands of the Commonwealth Caribbean: A Regional Study*. Washington, D.C.: U.S. Government Printing Office, 1989.

47. Williams remained fully capable of shifting leftwards if the circumstances warranted. Having embraced the West, and having engineered the expulsion of the party's leading radical, Williams gave a speech in March 1961, *Massa Day Done*, which brilliantly affirmed his anti-imperialist credentials. "There was no civilized society on earth so entirely destitute of learned leisure, literary and scientific intercourse and liberal recreation," he explained, as that of the West Indian plantation economy. "Massa Day Done connotes a political awakening and a social revolution." The speech was widely circulated by the PNM; these quotations are taken from Andrew Salkey, *Caribbean Essays*. London: Evans Brothers, 1973, p. 125 and 119.

48. C. L. R. James, "The West Indian Middle Classes," reprinted in C. L. R. James, *Spheres of Existence: Selected Writings*. Westport, CT: Lawrence Hill and Company, 1980, p. 139.

49. James, "The West Indian Middle Classes," p. 134.

50. James, "The West Indian Middle Classes," p. 135.

51. C. L. R. James, "The Artist in the Caribbean" [1959], reprinted in C. L. R. James, *The Future in the Present: Selected Writings*. Westport, CT:

Lawrence Hill and Company, 1977, p. 185. In this speech, James calls attention to the absence of a national tradition in the West Indies that is capable of generating or sustaining great artistic achievement. He goes on to argue that "[t]hese conditions can be changed . . . the threads of a tradition can be discovered among us and made into a whole . . . But to do that, we must have the consciousness that the nation which we are hoping to build, as much as it needs the pooling of resources and industrialization and a higher productivity of labor, needs also the supreme artist" (pp. 189–190).

52. James, "The Artist in the Caribbean," p. 185. By "shallow roots" he had in mind the absence of a national tradition in the West Indies. "For us and for people like us there is no continuous flow such as for instance the Bachs into Haydn into Mozart into Beethoven . . . There is no Donne in our ancestry for us to rediscover and stimulate the invention of new forms and new symbols" (pp. 184–185).

53. James, "The Artist in the Caribbean," p. 185.

54. James, *Party Politics in the West Indies*, p. 159. The section on The Mighty Sparrow is reprinted in James, *The Future in the Present*, pp. 191–201. James reports that he "used to go and hear him record . . ." (p. 191).

55. Writing in *The Nation*, James described Carnival as "the extraordinary spectacle of entertainment, sport, free competition, and the practice of the arts to one degree or another, being carried on by a populace; in fact, by all sections of the population, without any inculcation from above, without any educational instruction, without any encouragement or stimulus by philosophically minded person or persons who are interested in the arts as such." C. L. R. James, "Carnival" [1959], Anna Grimshaw, ed. *The C. L. R. James Reader*. Oxford: Blackwell, 1992, p. 286.

56. Sparrow's "Jean and Dinah," which attacks the U.S. position on Chaguaramas, boasts: "It's the glamour boys again/We are going to rule Port of Spain/No more Yankees to spoil the fete." Why are the Yanks such spoilers? Sparrow described the barroom behavior of the American soldiers: "But leave them alone, don't get in a rage/When a Yankee drunk he don't study age/For whether she is 24, 25 or 80/I am sure it would not interest a drunken Yankee/For when you drink Barbaro Nectar it doesn't matter how old she is/As long as the Yankee get what is his." James adds: "Sparrow is uninhibited about what he sees. He doesn't get in a rage. But he views the world with a large detachment. His irony and wit are the evidence." James, *Party Politics in the West Indies*, pp. 160–161.

57. James, *Party Politics in the West Indies*, p. 160.

58. James, *Party Politics in the West Indies*, p. xx.

59. James, *Party Politics in the West Indies*, p. 143.

60. James, *Party Politics in the West Indies*, p. 111.

61. James, *Party Politics in the West Indies*, p. 172.

62. "[F]or many years, the printed volumes lay in a warehouse in Port of Spain under guard. Ultimately, Williams relented to the extent of letting a New York book dealer buy the lot and take it out of the country." Martin Glaberman, "Introduction," C. L. R. James, *Modern Politics*. Detroit: Bewick Editions, 1973, p. i.

63. James, *Modern Politics*, p. 119.

64. James, *Modern Politics*, p. 3.

65. James, *Modern Politics*, p. 97.

66. James, *Modern Politics*, p. 5.

67. James, *Modern Politics*, p. 4. Emphasis in the original.

68. James, *Modern Politics*, p. 61.

69. James, *Modern Politics*, p. 154. Recapitulating one of the themes of *American Civilization*, James argues that the potential for "great strides" coexists with the threat of social collapse and nuclear war. James calls this his "main theme": "the consciousness of total breakdown—return to barbarism, the possibility of suicidal self-destruction . . ." (p. 69). This breakdown is rooted, finally, in capitalism's rapacious, destructive nature: "it is capital that rules, and it is capital that dictates the manners and morals of those who submit themselves to it" (p. 74).

70. Buhle, *C. L. R. James: The Artist as Revolutionary*, p. 166.

71. Patrick Gomes, "C. L. R. James' Marxian Paradigm on the Transformation of Caribbean Social Structure," unpublished dissertation thesis, Fordham University, 1980, p. 229.

72. James, "Books to Read," *Modern Politics*, p. 167.

73. James, *Modern Politics*, p. 90.

74. "He has remained rail-thin ever since. A tendency towards palsy now also became almost overwhelming, making the very act of eating (or, as a lecturer, holding his notes) difficult." See Paul Buhle, *C. L. R. James: The Artist as Revolutionary*. London: Verso, 1988, p. 128. Anna Grimshaw, who spoke to James at length about this period of his life, emphasizes the role in which financial worries and the lack of a close network of comrades slowly drained his energies. See Anna Grimshaw, Jim Murray, and Kent Worcester,

C. L. R. James in the 1980s: A Conversation with Anna Grimshaw. New York: C. L. R. James Institute, 1991.

75. No such apology was given by James when he lectured in May 1964 to the West Indian Students Union in London on the topic of "Tradition and the West Indian Novel." The text of this lecture was published by the Students Union as a pamphlet (subsidized by his old friend Learie Constantine), and reprinted in Wilson Harris, *Tradition, the Writer and Society.* London: New Beacon, 1967.

76. C. L. R. James, "A National Purpose for Caribbean Peoples" [1964], reprinted in James, *At the Rendezvous of Victory,* p. 143.

77. The terms of the house arrest restricted him to Barataria, where his sister Olive lived, and to her house between 6 P.M. and 6 A.M.

78. Oxaal, *Black Intellectuals Come to Power,* p. 182.

79. A section of the report, which specifically concerned James and his friend Walter Annamunthodo, intoned that "From evidence before us it appears that Mr. James is a native of Trinidad and an author of some report, well known in England and America." The report concluded that although James was a confirmed Marxist and an enemy of constitutional government, there was no evidence that he had ever engaged in dangerous or counterstate forms of activity. *Report of the Commission of Enquiry into Subversive Activities in Trinidad and Tobago.* Port of Spain: Government of Trinidad and Tobago, 1965, p. 9.

80. An editorial in *The Nation* published on July 15, 1966, warned that a "specter is haunting the trade union movement . . . The specter is the political ideology of MARXISM dressed up in the white robes of purity." Quoted in Khafra Kambon, *For Bread, Justice and Freedom.* London: New Beacon, 1988, p. 167.

81. Cited in Consuelo Lopez, "C. L. R. James: The Rhetoric of a Defiant Warrior," unpublished dissertation, Indiana University, 1983, p. 1.

82. See Anna Grimshaw, *The C. L. R. James Archive: A Reader's Guide.* New York: C. L. R. James Institute, 1991, pp. 24.

83. See Grimshaw, *The C. L. R. James Archive,* pp. 23–25. The party made a special effort to reach out to rural farmers and workers. In one WFP pamphlet, J. M. Dube called for the "break-up of the large land holdings" to distribute farm land to rural people. "There is ample, sound, scientific evidence for the measure, if only one is prepared to read what has been discovered on peasant experimental farms," he concluded somewhat cryptically. See J. M. Dube, *Settling the Farmers.* Port of Spain: Workers and Farmers Party, 1965, p. 7.

84. Cited in Oxaal, *Black Intellectuals Come to Power*, p. 182.

85. Williams urged an audience of PNM supporters in San Fernando to "Go out and finish up with the Marxist ideology which goes to Havana, Cuba . . . Castro has no business setting up any revolutionary organisation in order to interfere with and disrupt the normal development of Trinidad and Tobago." See Eric Williams, *Inward Hunger*, p. 335.

86. See Lopez, "C. L. R. James: The Rhetoric of a Defiant Warrior," p. 138.

87. Walton Look Lai, "C. L. R. James and Trinidad Nationalism," in Henry and Buhle, eds. *C. L. R. James' Caribbean*, pp. 199.

88. Look Lai, "C. L. R. James and Trinidadian Nationalism," p. 199.

89. Ivar Oxaal, *Race and Revolutionary Consciousness*. Cambridge, MA: Schenckman Books, 1971, p. 11.

90. George Lamming and Paul Buhle, "C. L. R. James: West Indian," in Henry and Buhle, eds. *C. L. R. James' Caribbean*, p. 31.

91. On the campaign, see Lopez, "C. L. R. James: The Rhetoric of a Defiant Warrior," pp. 128–150.

92. Look Lai, "C. L. R. James and Trinidadian Nationalism," p. 200.

93. Ian Munro and Reinhard Sander, *Kas-Kas: Interviews with Three Caribbean Writers*. Austin, TX: African and Afro-American Research Institute, University of Texas, 1972, p. 38.

CHAPTER 7. AT THE RENDEZVOUS

1. V. S. Naipaul, *A Way in the World*. New York: Knopf, 1994, pp. 107 and 135.

2. Naipaul, *A Way in the World*, p. 116.

3. Naipaul, *A Way in the World*, pp. 127–128.

4. Naipaul, *A Way in the World*, pp. 130–131.

5. Naipaul, *A Way in the World*, pp. 111–112.

6. Naipaul, *A Way in the World*, pp. 134 and 133.

7. Naipaul, A Way in the World, pp. 160–161.

8. Naipaul, *A Way in the World*, p. 161.

9. Author's interview with George Rawick, December 28, 1980.

10. Author's interview with George Rawick, December 28, 1980. Another visitor, the Scottish historian James Young, met C. L. R. James in 1956 and described him as "a modest, open-minded, and innovative socialist thinker." See James D. Young, *Making Trouble: Autobiographical Explorations and Socialism.* Glasgow: Clydeside Press, 1987, p. 51.

11. In *Beyond a Boundary*, James reports that as a young man he subscribed "[n]ot only to *The Cricketer*, but the *Times Literary Supplement*, the *Times Educational Supplement*, the *Observer*, the *Sunday Times*, the *Criterion*, the *London Mercury*, the *Musical Review*, the *Gramophone*, the *Nouvelle Revue Francaise*, the *Mercure de France*, for some time the *Nation* and the *New Republic*, the editions of the *Evening Standard* when Arnold Bennett wrote in it, and the *Daily Telegraph* with Rebecca West. I read them, filed most of them, I read and even bought many of the books they discussed. I had a circle of friends (most of them white) with whom I exchanged ideas, books, records and manuscripts." C. L. R. James, *Beyond a Boundary*. London: Stanley Paul, 1963, p. 70.

12. It was also in this period that James's *A History of Negro Revolt* was reprinted by former activists in the Student Non-Violent Coordinating Committee under the title *A History of Pan-African Revolt* (1969), and that *The Black Jacobins*, having been republished by Vintage in 1963, circulated widely on campuses.

13. James, *Beyond a Boundary*, p. 150.

14. A portion of the manuscript was written while Selma and C. L. R. were living in a Spanish village in the late 1950s. The couple also spent time visiting Greece and southern France.

15. C. L. R. James, "Nationalist Strain," *New Statesman*, January 18, 1958.

16. James, "Nationalist Strain."

17. James, *Beyond a Boundary*, p. 13.

18. Neil Lazarus, "Cricket and National Culture in the Writings of C. L. R. James," in Paget Henry and Paul Buhle, eds. *C. L. R. James's Caribbean.* Durham: Duke University Press, 1992, p. 94.

19. James, *Beyond a Boundary*, p. 192.

20. James, *Beyond a Boundary*, p. 194.

21. James, *Beyond a Boundary*, p. 202.

22. James remained interested in the history of cricket. See C. L. R. James, *Cricket* (ed. Anna Grimshaw). London: Allison and Busby, 1986.

23. See Kenneth Surin, "C. L. R. James' Materialist Aesthetic of Cricket," in Alistair Hennessy, ed. *Intellectuals in the Twentieth-Century Caribbean*, vol. 1: *Spectre of the New Class: the Commonwealth Caribbean*. London: Macmillan Caribbean, 1992, pp. 131–162.

24. Quoted on the back cover of Paul Buhle, ed. *C. L. R. James: His Life and Work*. Chicago: Urgent Tasks, 1981.

25. For a more sympathetic analysis, see Sylvia Wynter's "In Quest of Matthew Bondsman," in Buhle, ed. *C. L. R. James: His Life and Work*. Wynter argues James's book offers a spirited attack on "bourgeois mythology in its aesthetic form and deconstructs a central aspect of the ruling *social imaginaire* . . . He is taking them [the fine arts] out of the box in which bourgeois critical canons, responding to a socio-ideological code rather than to a purely critical conceptual imperative, have confined them" (p. 63).

26. James, *Beyond a Boundary*, p. 151.

27. James, *Beyond a Boundary*, pp. 151 & 152.

28. James, *Beyond a Boundary*, p. 153.

29. James, *Beyond a Boundary*, p. 109.

30. Martin Walker, "Diary," *Manchester Guardian*, August 31, 1982.

31. V. S. Naipaul, "Sporting Life," *Encounter*, XXI, no. 3 (September 1963), p. 74.

32. Margaret Manning, "Cricket was all that Mattered," *Boston Globe*, June 3, 1984. She was reviewing the 1984 Pantheon Books edition.

33. In the third volume of selected political and social writings, Castoriadis's translator and editor summarizes his position: "that, beyond the workplace, political activity on the part of the industrial proletariat in Western countries had disappeared; that privatization, consumerism, and the bureaucratization of all aspects of people's lives were becoming the rule; that youth and women would be in the forefront of those entering into action against these processes as they and others came to express a tendency toward autonomy in their invention of new forms of living; and that new revolutionary explosions would not replicate in reality the (already false) Marxist-Leninist model of 'economic contradictions' leading to demands for the dictatorship of a party advocating nationalization and planning, but rather would express unforeseeable attempts by all strata to reconstruct their lives in democratic, grass-roots fashion." See David Ames Curtis, "Foreword," Cornelius Castoriadis, *Recommencing the Revolution: From Socialism to the Autonomous Society*. Minneapolis: University of Minnesota Press, 1993, pp. viii-ix. While James would have accepted—and may have

anticipated—much of this analysis, he retained, as Castoriadis insisted, a "fidelity to traditional Marxism above all else . . ." See Cornelius Castoriadis, "For a New Orientation," in *Recommencing the Revolution*, p. 8.

34. See C. L. R. James, "Lenin and the Problem" [1960], reprinted in Anna Grimshaw, ed. *The C. L. R. James Reader*. Oxford: Blackwell, 1992, pp. 331–346. Also see Moche Lewin, *Lenin's Last Struggle*. New York: Monthly Review Press, 1968.

35. C. L. R. James, "Marxism 1963." London: mimeo, 1963. In the author's private collection.

36. James, "Marxism 1963."

37. See C. L. R. James, "Black Studies and the Contemporary Student" [1969] in James, *At the Rendezvous of Victory*, pp. 195–196.

38. C. L. R. James, "Existentialism and Marxism." London: mimeo, 1966. In the author's private collection.

39. James, "Existentialism and Marxism."

40. C. L. R. James, with Martin Glaberman, William Gorman and George Rawick, *The Gathering Forces*. Detroit: Facing Reality mimeo, 1967. This quotation is taken from an extract from *The Gathering Forces* that appears under the title "Peasants and Workers" in C. L. R. James, *Spheres of Existence: Selected Writings*. Westport, CT: Lawrence Hill and Company, 1980, p. 192.

41. Author's interview with George Rawick, December 28, 1980.

42. James et al., "Peasants and Workers," p. 211.

43. James et al., "Peasants and Workers," p. 211.

44. James et al., *The Gathering Forces*, p. 26.

45. James et al., *The Gathering Forces*, p. 49.

46. The British writer David Widgery criticized James for being "insufficiently consistent in applying his own criteria for socialist self-emancipation to Nkrumah, Castro, and other revolutionary nationalists." See David Widgery, "A Meeting with Comrade James" [1980], in Buhle, ed. *C. L. R. James: His Life and Work*, p. 115.

47. James et al., *The Gathering Forces*, p. 67.

48. C. L. R. James, "World Revolution: 1968," *Speak Out*, no. 20/21 (June 1968), p. 1.

49. James, "World Revolution: 1968," p. 3.

50. C. L. R. James, "Notes on France," *Speak Out*, vol. 2, no. 2 (February 1969), p. 4.

51. James, "World Revolution: 1968," p. 2.

52. "Black Academy Presents Awards," *New York Times*, September 21, 1970.

53. "Black Intellectuals Divided over Ideological Direction," *New York Times*, April 28, 1975.

54. *Black Scholar*, September 1970.

55. He made the same point in letters to Stokely Carmichael (Kwame Toure), the "Black Power" advocate and one-time leader of the Student Nonviolent Coordinating Committee.

56. "C. L. R. James," *Black World*, March 1974, p. 22.

57. C. L. R. James, "Towards the Seventh: The Pan-African Congress— Past, Present and Future," reprinted in Michael Manley, *Not for Sale*. San Francisco: Editorial Consultants, Inc., n.d., pp. 40–41, and in *At the Rendezvous of Victory*. This speech was delivered at the First Congress of All-African Writers in Dakar, Senegal, on January 8, 1976.

58. Consuelo López, "C. L. R. James: The Rhetoric of a Defiant Warrior," unpublished dissertation, Indiana University, 1983, p. 188.

59. C. L. R. James, "Black Studies and the Contemporary Student" [1969], reprinted in James, *At the Rendezvous of Victory*, p. 186.

60. James, "Black Studies and the Contemporary Student," p. 189.

61. James, "Black Studies and the Contemporary Student," p. 190. Or, as he remarked at the conclusion of his talk: "Life presents you with some strange difficulties, and, at times, you have to run with the hare and hunt with the hounds" (p. 201).

62. James, "Black Studies and the Contemporary Student," p. 194.

63. James, "Black Studies and the Contemporary Student," p. 193.

64. James, "Black Studies and the Contemporary Student," p. 195.

65. James, "Black Studies and the Contemporary Student," p. 195.

66. But it was consistent with the friendly references he made to Abraham Lincoln as he set forth a research agenda for the black studies movement. James evinced a tremendous fondness for the American president, emphasizing Lincoln's evolution as a politician, and showing how the commander in chief had arrived at a "new conception of what black people were"

in the context of their performance in the Civil War. "The democratic creed had had worthy expounders before him," James admitted, but he went on to claim that "[n]one ever had so dramatic a stage, so comprehensive an audience." See "Abraham Lincoln: The 150th Anniversary of his Birth" [1959] and "Black Studies and the Contemporary Student," both in Grimshaw, ed. *The C. L. R. James Reader*, pp. 281–285, 390–404.

67. Two exceptions are "The Atlantic Slave Trade and Slavery: Some Interpretations of their Significance in the Development of the United States and the Western World," *Amistad I*, John A. Williams and Charles F. Harris, eds. New York: Vintage Books, 1970; and "The West Indian Intellectual," the introductory essay to a new edition of J. J. Thomas's *Froudacity*. London: New Beacon, 1969 [1889]. The former was co-written by William Gorman.

68. Letter from C. L. R. James to Martin Glaberman, dated March 2, 1965.

69. Cited in Manning Marable, "C. L. R. James and Nkrumah." Dayton, OH: Dayton Black Research Associates, mimeo, n.d., p.3.

70. Immanuel Wallerstein, "The Decline of the Party in Single-Party African States," in Joseph LaPalombara and Martin Weiner, *Political Parties and Political Development*. Princeton: Princeton University Press, 1972.

71. C. L. R. James, *Nkrumah and the Ghana Revolution*. Westport: CT: Lawrence Hill and Company, 1977, p. 176.

72. Quoted in James, *Nkrumah and the Ghana Revolution*, p. 180.

73. According to Paul Buhle, James spoke highly of the Zambian leader Kenneth Kaunda. See Buhle, *C. L. R. James*, p. 141.

74. Quoted in James, *Nkrumah and the Ghana Revolution*, p. 182.

75. James, *Nkrumah and the Ghana Revolution*, p. 19.

76. James, *Nkrumah and the Ghana Revolution*, p. 171.

77. "Africa (and other countries as well, but Africa in particular) will go crashing from precipice to precipice unless the plans for economic development are part of a deep philosophical concept of what the mass of the African people need. This is where Nkrumah failed." James, *Nkrumah and the Ghana Revolution*, p. 188.

78. James, *Nkrumah and the Ghana Revolution*, p. 164.

79. Isobel Appiah, *Times Literary Supplement*, December 2, 1977. The book's last chapter is taken from the second edition to *A History of Pan-African Revolt* (1969), where the author goes over the top in celebrating Nyer-

ere's theory of *Ujamaa* (African socialism): "It is sufficient to say that socialist thought has seen nothing like this since the death of Lenin in 1924, and
its depth, range and the repercussions which flow from it, go far beyond the
Africa which gave it birth . . ." (p. 223).

80. Jervis Anderson, "Onward and Upward with the Arts: Derek Walcott's Odyssey," *The New Yorker*, December 21, 1992, p. 74.

81. *Maurice Bishop Speaks: The Grenada Revolution and its Overthrow,
1979–1983.* New York: Pathfinder, 1983, p. 22.

82. On the Bishop government's reforms, see, *inter alia*, Steve Clark,
"Introduction," *Maurice Bishop Speaks*, pp. xxii–xxv.

83. See C. L. R. James, "The Caribbean Confrontation Begins," *Race
Today*, September 1970; and Oxaal, *Race and Revolutionary Consciousness*.

84. Reflecting on the state of Trinidadian politics in 1979, James
described a depoliticalization of the Afro-Caribbean population. He found
that few people held out any hope that change could arrive through political
means, either from within or from without the electoral system. See C. L. R.
James, "Whither Trinidad and Tobago," *Race Today*, November–December
1979.

85. Rodney later described how he and several others met with C. L. R.
and Selma "over a period of two to three years on a fairly regular basis."
James's contribution, he remembered, was "a certain sense of historical
analysis . . . The group might do some reading and try to understand what a
text says. But James gave it that added dimension which nobody else in the
group could easily acquire in being able to say: this is what Lenin was about;
this is what Trotsky was doing; he had just come from this conference or this
debate, or this was his specific programmatic objective when he was writing,
and so on." See *Walter Rodney Speaks: The Making of an African Intellectual.*
Trenton: Africa World Press, 1990, pp. 28–29.

86. See Paget Henry, "C. L. R. James and the Antiguan Left," in Henry
and Buhle, eds. *C. L. R. James's Caribbean*, pp. 225–262.

87. C. L. R. James, "From Toussaint L'Ouverture to Fidel Castro"
[1963], reprinted in Grimshaw, ed. *The C. L. R. James Reader*, p. 296.

88. Author's interview with Robin Blackburn, June 6, 1992 (Ann
Arbor).

89. The gist of his presentation was that the phase of the West Indian
leadership of struggles in underdeveloped countries was over and that "it is
in the application of this capacity to the life of the Americas that the West
Indian intellectual will find the necessary element for the development of

culture . . ." While he calls the Cuban Revolution the "climax" of a particular tradition in the West Indies, he goes on to say that the West Indian masses should have been "formally represented" at the convention, in order to help "prepare the way for the abolition of the intellectuals as an embodiment of culture."

90. Andrew Salkey, *Havana Journal*. London: Penguin, 1971, p. 110. Robin Blackburn of *New Left Review* remembered a somewhat more receptive audience. Author's interview with Robin Blackburn, June 6, 1992.

91. Salkey, *Havana Journal*, p. 61.

92. The words are James's. Salkey, *Havana Journal*, p. 58.

93. Salkey, *Havana Journal*, p. 91.

94. C. L. R. James, "The Birth of a Nation," in Susan Craig, ed. *Contemporary Caribbean: A Sociological Reader*, vol. 1. Port of Spain: Susan Craig, 1981, p. 35.

95. Pierre-Michel Fontaine, "Walter Rodney: Revolutionary and Scholar in the Guyanese Political Cauldron," in Edward A. Alpers and Pierre-Michel Fontaine, eds. *Walter Rodney, Revolutionary and Scholar: A Tribute*. Los Angeles: Center for Afro-American Studies and African Studies Center, 1982, p. 29.

96. C. L. R. James, "C. L. R. James on Walter Rodney," *Race Today*, November 1980.

97. C. L. R. James, "Walter Rodney and the Question of Power," *Walter Rodney, Revolutionary and Scholar*, p. 138.

98. James, "Walter Rodney and the Question of Power," pp. 139–140.

99. See Anna Grimshaw, Jim Murray, and Kent Worcester, *C. L. R. James in the 1980s: A Conversation with Anna Grimshaw*. New York: C. L. R. James Institute, 1991, p. 2.

100. See Grimshaw, Murray, and Worcester, *C. L. R. James in the 1980s*, p. 10. Another interesting anecdote emerged when I asked Anna and Jim about whether James had a sense of eternity. Jim first noted that when James received invitations from churches to speak he would reply that "spirituality wasn't of interest to him." Anna then pointed out that he "wasn't a strict rationalist, either . . . the artist in him was very interested in those areas which artists excavate." She described the time when a "very respectable gentleman from Jamaica showed up, in his fifties or older, a very proper, old-fashioned sort of gentleman, and he sat down and told this story to us of how he believed his house had been bewitched. He lived in Cambridge, and he

told this tale of his neighbors and how they had bewitched him and his wife. It went on for about an hour. C. L. R. was there nodding, asking questions, taking it as a serious account. The story was resolved successfully, as the neighbors moved and the bewitching ceased. Afterwards, James said to me, 'What did you think of that?' I said, 'It's an interesting story.' He said, 'Well, I found it absolutely fascinating. These things can happen you know.'"

101. Letter from C. L. R. James to Lord Fenner Brockway, July 22, 1980. Unmarked document housed at the archives of the Oil Workers Trade Union.

102. Grimshaw, Murray, and Worcester, *C. L. R. James in the 1980s*, p. 2.

103. Grimshaw, Murray, and Worcester, *C. L. R. James in the 1980s*, p. 11.

104. C. L. R. James, "Three Black Women Writers: Toni Morrison, Alice Walker, Ntozake Shange" [1981], reprinted in Grimshaw, ed. *The C. L. R. James Reader*, p. 411.

105. James, "Three Black Women Writers," p. 411.

106. James, "Three Black Women Writers," p. 417.

107. "C.C. Interviews James on Poland," *Cultural Correspondence*, new series #2 (Winter 1983), p. 20.

108. C. L. R. James, "Poland" [1981], reprinted in *At the Rendezvous of Victory*, p. 272.

109. Lopez, "C. L. R. James: The Rhetoric of a Defiant Warrior," pp. 151–152.

110. Hugh Lynch, "My Name is Mud in Trinidad," Sunday *Express*, March 21, 1982, p. 14.

111. Clive Davis, "In Praise of Cricket and Revolution," *Trinidad Guardian*, February 27, 1986, pp. 11–12.

112. See Salkey, *Havana Journal*, p. 107.

113. Widgery, "A Meeting With Comrade James," in Buhle, ed. *C. L. R. James: His Life and Work*, p. 115.

114. Phillip Howard, "C. L. R. James on the Necessity to Attack," *London Times*, July 2, 1980. In the same year, James told a reporter from another newspaper that he would like to finally settle in "my liking place, Florence." David Leitch, "C. L. R. Still Battling for Marx," *Sunday Telegraph*, September 25, 1980.

115. C. Gerald Fraser, "C. L. R. James, Historian, Critic and Pan-Africanist, is Dead at 88," *New York Times*, June 2, 1989.

116. John Arlott, "Behind the Marxist Crease," *Manchester Guardian*, June 2, 1989.

117. "James, the Promethean," unsigned lead editorial, *Trinidad Guardian*, June 2, 1989.

118. "Best: He Will Always Remain the Master," *Daily Express*, June 1, 1989, p. 1.

119. "PM: Outstanding Literary Figure," *Daily Express*, June 1, 1989, p. 1.

120. *Daily Express*, June 5, 1989.

Index

■

Austin, Cyril, 5, 245n
A Way in the World, 173–175, 287n

Back to Africa, 59
Balance Sheet: Trotskyism in the United
    States 1940–1947, The, 267n
Baldwin, James, xv
Baraka, Amiri, 205
Barnes, S. F., 207
Beacon, The, 15, 16–17, 21, 26, 248n,
    249n, 252n
Bell, Daniel, 133, 277n
Bellow, Saul, 66
Bennett, Arnold, 7, 17
Berger, John, 119
Berman, Paul, 268–269n, 279n
Best, Lloyd, 210
Best British Stort Stories of 1928, 248n
Beyond a Boundary, 14, 25, 115, 144,
    145, 173, 177, 212, 245n, 246n,
    247n, 248n, 249n, 252n, 253n, 266n,
    282n, 288n, 289n; cricket, xii, 10, 14;
    race, 12; Trotskyism, 86; Tunapuna,
    211; West Indies, 28, 122, 178–182;
    writers influence, 4
"Birth of a Nation," 201
Bishop, Maurice, 199, 200
Black Boy: A Record of Childhood and
    Youth, 75–76
Blackburn, Robin, 293n, 294n
Black Intellectuals Come to Power, 274n,
    280n, 282n, 286n, 287n
Black Jacobins: Toussaint L'Ouverture and
    the San Domingo Revolution, The, xii,
    35–36, 39–40, 49, 103, 183, 187,
    206–207, 253n, 255n, 288n; African
    independence, 36; British empire, 59;
    internationalism, 37; politics, 195;
    revolution, 39; West Indies, 201
Black Marxism: The Making of the Black
    Radical Tradition, 255n
Black Metropolis: A Study of Negro Life in
    a Northern City, 264n
Black Nationalism and Socialism, 259n
Black Revolutionary: George Padmore's
    Path From Communism to Pan-Afri-
    canism, 254n, 273n

blacks, xi, 32, 33, 36, 40, 117, 205; Abys-
    sinia, 31; American, 73–74, 108; cap-
    italism, 191; integration, 78; middle
    class, 14; nationalism, xiii, xv, 58, 193,
    198; politics, 47, 114; Power, 177,
    193, 199, 200; race, 12, 16–17, 62; rac-
    ism, 24, 57–60, 79, 100–101; strug-
    gles, 83; studies, 177, 191, 194–195
Black Scholar, 189, 253n, 291n
"Black Studies and the Contemporary
    Student," 191
Black World, 291n
Bloom, Alexander, 261n
Boggs, James, 129, 142; Grace Lee Boggs,
    279n
Bogues, Tony, 259n
Bolsheviks, 45, 87, 92, 98, 114, 203;
    break with Mensheviks, 46; princi-
    ples, 95–96, 184
Bondman, Matthew, 9, 11, 21, 179
"Books and Writers," 17
Bornstein, Sam, 257n, 258n
Boston Globe, 182, 289n
Braithwaite, Fitz, 32
Breitman, George, 62
Brereton, Bridget, 248n, 253n
British Colonial Office, 151, 156, 161
Brockway, Lord Fenner, 295n
Bronte sisters, 7
Brooks, Gwendolyn, 265n
Brown, H. Rap, 190, 193
Buhle, Paul, 95, 113, 168, 245n, 247n,
    249n, 251n, 263n, 269n, 270n, 273n,
    285n, 287n, 292n
Bulletin in Defense of Marxism, 260n
Bureaucratic Revolution: The Rise of the
    Stalinist State, 268n
Burnham, Forbes Linden, 202–203
Burnham, James, 64, 66
Busby, Margaret, 14, 248n
Butler, Uriah, 22, 170, 173

Call, The, 189
Callinicos, Alex, 255n
Campaign for Nuclear Disarmament,
    203